Dimensions of Change

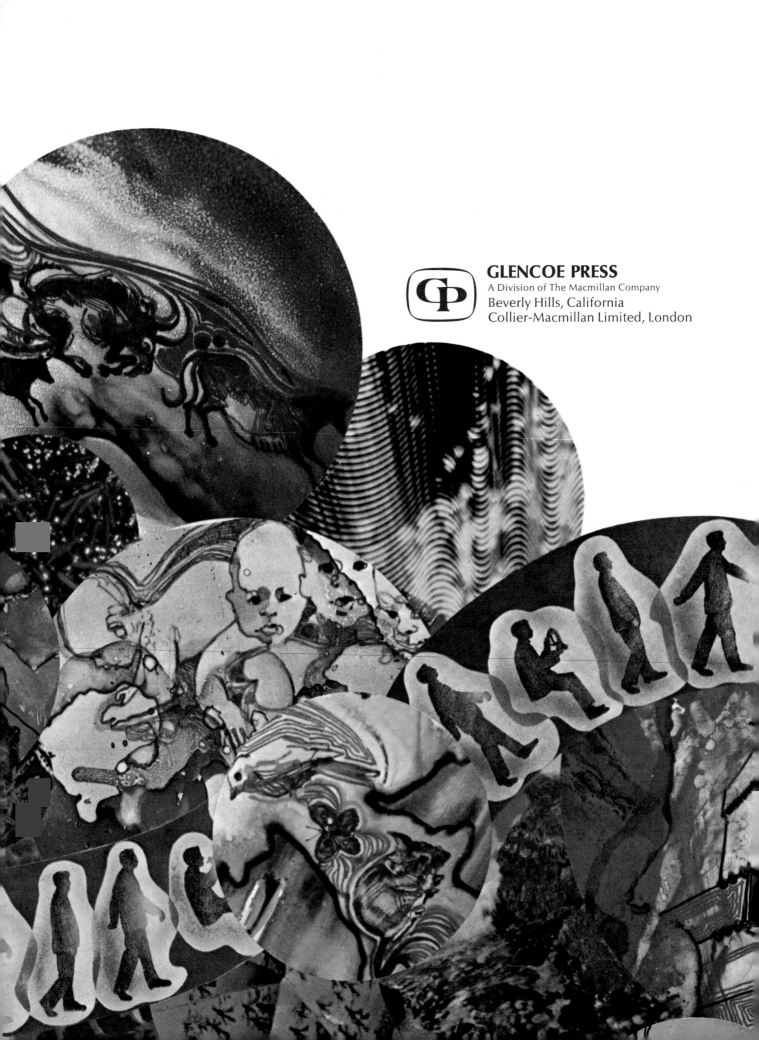

GLENCOE PRESS
A Division of The Macmillan Company
Beverly Hills, California
Collier-Macmillan Limited, London

Dimensions of Change

by **DON FABUN**
Publications Director
Kaiser Aluminum & Chemical Corporation

assisted by:
KATHY HYLAND
and **ROBERT CONOVER**
Art Director

GLENCOE PRESS
A Division of The Macmillan Company
8701 Wilshire Boulevard
Beverly Hills, California 90211
Collier-Macmillan Canada, Ltd., Toronto, Canada

Library of Congress catalog card number 73-173690

First printing, 1971

DIMENSIONS OF CHANGE is a combined edition of:

Ecology: The Man-made Planet Copyright © 1970, Kaiser Aluminum & Chemical Corporation

Shelter: The Cave Re-examined Copyright © 1970, Kaiser Aluminum & Chemical Corporation

Energy: Transactions in Time Copyright © 1970, Kaiser Aluminum & Chemical Corporation

Food: An Energy Exchange System Copyright © 1970, Kaiser Aluminum & Chemical Corporation

Mobility: From There to Here Copyright © 1971, Kaiser Aluminum & Chemical Corporation

Telecommunications: One World-mind Copyright © 1971, Kaiser Aluminum & Chemical Corporation

TABLE OF CONTENTS

FOOD: An Energy Exchange System

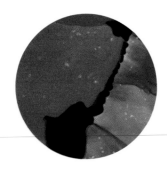

MOBILITY: From There to Here

TELECOMMUNICATIONS: One World — Mind

INTRODUCTION

When we first started up this path (and it's been a long and arduous one), we were looking for something. We didn't find it. The seemingly simple question was—are there technological solutions to some of the social, moral, political and philosophic problems of our time? Turned out it was not a simple question, and it may have been the wrong one to begin with. But, of course, we did not know that when we began. If human life is discovering the unknown, then to that extent, this trip was alive. Unknown to us; perhaps everyone else already knew. The six sections that have been fumbled together to make a sort of "book" are stages in an odyssey that, like the original one, was doomed from the start. Nevertheless, there were some interesting adventures along the way. Let us tell you about some of them.

Our first adventure was with ecology. Others had gone this way before, of course, and many have since. But the fact that a trail is well traveled does not necessarily mean it is a satisfactory one (think of any freeway you've been on); it just means it has a lot of traffic.

Glancing about we found, perhaps unsurprisingly, in the words of Gertrude Stein, there was "no there, there." The ecological sciences, with few exceptions, turned out not to be sciences at all; just clusters of unrelated information. The one thing that did appear to be true was that technological man is rapidly destroying his environment and that very little is being done to halt the process. The technology to stop the destruction exists; it is, with rare exceptions, not being used. Nor does it seem that it will be used much more in the next thirty years.

We shook our heads sadly, but perhaps more wisely, and trudged on to another area. Here we looked at human housing. There wasn't much to look at. Although the technology to build shelter for humans that would be livable, even comfortable, at low cost, apparently exists, it isn't being used in any way that helps very many people — not in this country, anyway.

Now pretty depressed, we ambled further down the path to take a glance at the generation, distribution and use of energy in technological societies today. Not much hope there, either. Still burning coal and oil, for reasons that can only be explained on the political level; not on the technological one.

Glad to move along from that dismal scene. We paused to look at the food industry on a worldwide basis. Same old story. The globe already produces all the food that the people on it now need. But two-thirds of the people on the planet are malnourished. The agricultural technology to increase food production, processing, storage and distribution *already* exists. But it is not being used.

We trod on and took a look at mobility, as now expressed by human transportation systems. This is such a mess that no sane man could believe it. Yet the movement of living organisms and material objects, when considered as "bits" moving sequentially along a channel, is a relatively simple communications problem and susceptible to the application of communications theory and general systems analysis. Both systems have been available for some years now, but the technological solutions are not used.

The last meadow we meandered into is what, for lack of a better word, we have chosen to call "telecommunications." Here the scene was much brighter; liquid crystals shimmered, man-made satellites smiled down at us, we had a few quite friendly conversations with humpback whales and bottlenosed dolphins, and tried to read the language of fish and birds and squirrels. For us, this was a delightful end to our journey; perhaps you will find it so, too.

And so, we came to the end of the trail.

But, assuming that human lives are supposed to have a "purpose," beyond reproducing the species, what, if anything, did we learn from this string of adventures?

The thing that seems to come out most clearly is that there are technological solutions to many of our contemporary human problems, but in no field that we stumbled into (possibly excepting communications) did we find them being used in any significant way, or any indication that they might be in the next three decades.

Why aren't currently available technologies being used? We suggest that the imposition of institutions — governmental, religious, educational, corporative — which were formed in agrarian and rural times, simply do not allow a technological society to function at anywhere near the efficiency that it could. And by efficiency we mean the least "heat loss" in any energy transaction. Through their vast bureaucratic waste, most existing institutions dissipate much of the human and ecologic benefits that could be enjoyed if the institutions adapted themselves to the post-industrial-age realities of the contemporary technological era.

This is not to say that technology, as usually defined, can solve *all* our problems. We don't believe it can. We feel that it might help to solve *some* of them.

There is no reason why electronically controlled machines could not produce all of the material things people need. There is no reason why agricultural science cannot produce all of the food people can eat. There is no reason for clusters of school buildings when the same educational function can be performed by electronics. There is no reason why political candidates should not be elected by the people (instead of as they are now) simply by dialing a telephone to vote, with a "voice-profiler" to identify them to prevent duplicate voting. There is no reason why every person should not have — as a birthright — a livable income, comfortable shelter, medical care and security in his old age. There is no reason to continue the kind of 19th Century transportation systems we have today. There is no reason to have cities, when the same communicative function can be achieved by electronic systems beamed to smaller communities. There is no reason why the courts and justice systems should be clogged with long-delayed trials, when they easily could be conducted through closed-circuit television.

There is no reason. No reason at all.

And we guess that's kind of the overall message of the pages that follow.

from *The Drawings of Heinrich Kley*, Borden Publishing Co., Alhambra, California

chapter 1.

ECOLOGY:
The Man-Made Planet

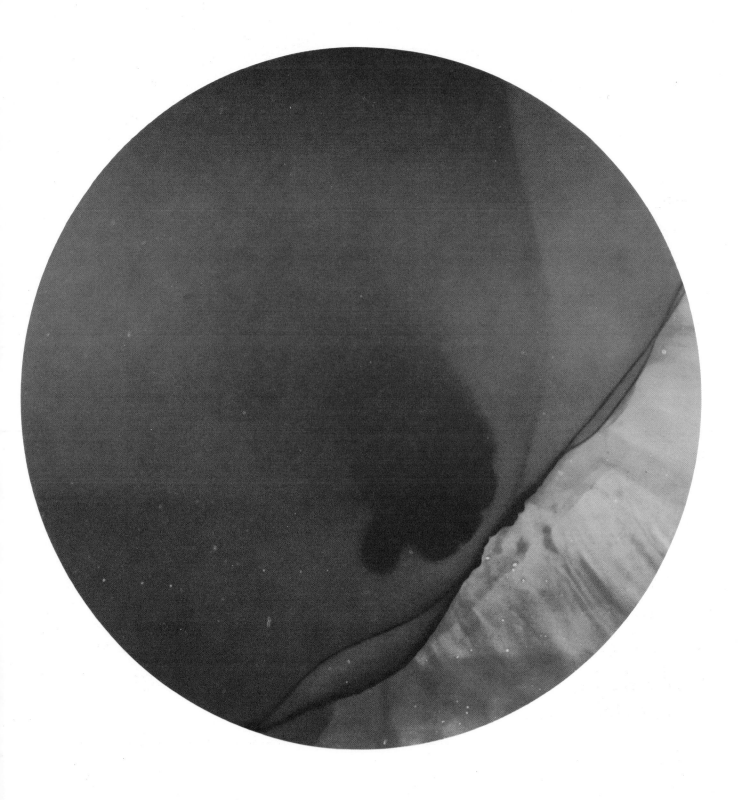

1.

Spaceship Earth

...I mete and dole unequal laws unto a savage race, that hoard, and sleep, and feed, and know not me. I cannot rest from travel ...I am a part of all that I have met; yet all experience is an arch wherethro' gleams that untraveled world whose margin fades forever and forever when I move... This gray spirit yearns in desire to follow knowledge like a sinking star, beyond the utmost bound of human thought ...The lights begin to twinkle from the rocks; the long day wanes: the slow moon climbs: the deep moans round with many voices. Come my friends, 'tis not too late to seek a newer world... ALFRED, LORD TENNYSON / "Ulysses" – 1842

Once upon a time there evolved upon this planet an organism that was ill-suited for survival. It could not run fast enough to escape its enemies; if caught, its teeth and claws were small protection. It was too big to hide under a leaf and too weak to burrow deeply into the ground. To survive, it took refuge in caves where a fire at the entrance kept predators at bay. If the fire ran out of fuel, this creature could hurl rocks and thus drive all but the most

by
things
possessed

determined enemies away. *Its security was measured by the amount of firewood it could accumulate and the number of rocks it could gather and store in the cave against the terrors of the night.*

Now, you see, this was a very important sort of thing. All other creatures grew bigger teeth, or learned to run faster. Alone among all the creatures on earth, the one we are describing turned to *things* for its survival. This was, in the end, to make all the difference.

After a while, this creature learned to cultivate some edible plants to supplement the food it could get by gathering and hunting. Growing food was, at best, uncertain and in any event depended on the seasons, which could not be controlled. The creature began to store its surplus foods. *His security against the vagaries of nature was measured by how much he could grow and how much he could store.*

His feeling for being at least partly in control of his destiny was based on the gathering of things. Well-being was measured quantitatively—the more the better. From the very beginning, he was motivated by fear—fear of pain, fear of death, fear that there wouldn't be enough.

In time, this creature's activities produced so much that it became more convenient to represent the accumulation of things by other things, smaller and easier to carry or to exchange. These symbols —although intrinsically of no value—assumed the same value as things. And men—or at least most men—became engaged in the acquisition and accumulation of the symbols of things. They did this even when they no longer had any need for them. The symbols were the surrogates for the rocks piled in the cave against the coming of the night.

Think of this system as being reinforced, over and over, through hundreds of generations and thousands of years, through social approval, ritualization and acculturation. That there was something basically wrong with this way of life may be exemplified by the fact that those who refused to subscribe to the accumulation and storage of things (Christ, Mohammed, Buddha) became the founders of the world's great religions.

Throughout all of this, nature was the "enemy." The purpose of the life of this strange creature we

Evolution has been compared to a labyrinth of blind alleys and there is nothing very strange or improbable in the assumption that man's native equipment, though superior to that of any other living species, nevertheless contains some built-in error or deficiency which predisposes him toward self-destruction.

Arthur Koestler/*The Ghost in the Machine*, 1967

In the obsessive-compulsive mechanism, the overriding purpose of the behavior is to attempt to achieve some security and certainty for the person who feels threatened and insecure in an uncertain world...I see the obsessional maneuver as an adaptive technique to protect the person from the exposure of any thoughts or feelings that will endanger his physical or psychological existence...

Leon Salsman, M.D./*The Obsessive Personality*, 1969

The point is that the engineers—all of those who take the engineering approach, build the bridge and get the people and the cars from one side of the river to the other and to hell with the side effects—are shaping the nation unchecked, molding the land and murdering thousands of its inhabitants, raping America while the rest of us look the other way. *Their's is a rape from which America can never, never recover.*

Gene Marine/*America the Raped*, 1969

I have yet to see any problem, however complicated,
which, when you looked at it the right way,
did not become still more complicated.

POUL ANDERSON

A hundred years ago a chemical theory was
uncovered that retains broad significance. It is
known as the "Law of the Minimum."

*Under ideal circumstances, a reaction will
continue until restrained by exhaustion of whatever
essential ingredient is present in least supply.*

What is our essential ingredient in least supply?
And how much of it do we possess?
We do not know.

S. P. R. Charter/*Man on Earth,* 1962

There is another design that is far better. It is the
design that nature has provided...It is pointless to
superimpose an abstract, man-made design on a
region as though the canvas were blank. It isn't.
Somebody has been there already. Thousands of
years of rain and wind and tides have laid down
a design. Here is our form and order. It is inherent
in the land itself—in the pattern of the soil,
the slopes, the woods—above all, in the patterns
of streams and rivers.

William H. Whyte/*The Last Landscape,* 1968

have described was to "conquer" nature, "tame" the wilderness, "make war" on pests and vermin, "control" the rivers. Life was a "battle" against the elements; only "the fittest" survived. Whole species of other life forms: plants, insects, reptiles, fish, amphibians, birds, and mammals were exterminated, most usually because they represented a "threat" against the accumulation of things; sometimes for "sport."

If an individual human being walked into a contemporary psychiatrist's office and exhibited the symptoms just described:

1. Pervasive fear, anxiety and persistent feelings of insecurity...

2. Obsession with the accumulation of things or the symbols of things...

3. Fear of losing any portion of what already has been accumulated, even though it served no life-supporting purpose...

4. Hostility against any living being that threatened to diminish the accumulation, because this meant the reduction of security...

5. Deep feelings of depression following each "success," because the "success" was not permanent; in a changing world it could be reversed into defeat. And so there followed a greater effort to achieve "real" success—a compulsive and destructive behavior pattern that reinforced itself because every success was, in reality, a failure...

If a person exhibiting such behavior were, as suggested, to enter a psychotherapist's office, his general problem would probably be diagnosed as a chronic form of depression, and he might be characterized as an "obsessive" personality, acting out compulsive patterns that, while intended by him to increase his security, actually serve only to reinforce his fear.

Had this activity entered the acute phase—expressed in the senseless killing of other living beings and the progressive destruction of his habitat, he probably would be considered "paranoid" and put away in an institution.

Unfortunately, since the chronic obsessive personality is so widespread throughout mankind, a person exhibiting these symptoms and this behavior would be considered "normal" and "sane."

(Continued on page 8)

Lest we be too critical of ourselves, let us remember that, for this poorly endowed creature, no other behavior would have insured its survival for tens of thousands of years. The rude stones in the cave finally proliferated into the tools of the industrial revolution; it became quite possible for man to produce everything material he needed, and even most of the things he could want (an important distinction). The ages of scarcity had died. But the old, compulsive reactions continued.

The cave was now so full of stones that there was no longer any room to live in it. Or almost none. The creature was imprisoned by itself.

Had this been an individual patient, and not a species, the psychotherapist might have suggested that the observed behavior was irrational. Therapy would probably proceed along the lines of leading the patient to accept his own condition—namely, that he was but a part of a whole, living entity; that he shared the planet with billions of other beings whose species history had still not been acted out. He could not know on what adventure they were embarked; he could only accompany the long trek as far as he could go. There was nothing to fear. The same life force this individual represented had lived in a thousand guises, again and again; in crystals, in limestone shells and scales, and feathers and fur.

He had—and has—only one responsibility. And that is to keep the system going. And this, unfortunately, is exactly what he is not doing. He is destroying the only habitat he has, and he cannot even plead "survival" as an excuse.

In somewhat the same sort of way that a geologist or paleontologist can reconstruct from the strata of stones or the bones in a tar pit another time and another set of survival systems, we will try now to put together a few of the bones of our recent past to see how we somehow managed to be stranded on this rapidly sinking island. If we know what went wrong, there may still be time to do something about it.

The contamination of the air, the water, and the land surface of the globe was brought about by

It has been suggested by Arthur Koestler that whenever a man lies down on an analyst's couch, he speaks from three minds; his own and that of a mammal and a reptile...

Illustration by Frank Ansley

the interaction of a number of factors, creating a resonance that reinforced its own waves, until now they threaten to engulf the technological civilizations entirely.

It is doubtful that very many thinking people, even among the early ecologists, foresaw how, when these technological processes began to interact, they would introduce a catastrophic effect on that system of processes that is sometimes called the "ecosphere." The ecosphere, as we understand it now, is a gossamer-thin web of living things that, through mutual support, constantly renew themselves. It is a system of energy exchanges. Death and birth are inextricably interwoven in this mesh. But it is a fragile sort of thing. Here's how the present situation came about.

1. *The introduction of agriculture.* This has had the long-term effect of over-simplifying the environment, erasing genetic alphabets, and making whole systems of life more vulnerable to change.

2. *The industrial revolution,* with its emphasis on thermal operations. The "extractive" industries destroyed large areas of surface through the dumping of "wastes"; the manufacturing industries led to the destruction of large forested areas, particularly in the Middle East, Southern Europe and the United States. When burning wood gave way to burning "fossil" fuels, such as coal and petroleum, there was added to the pollution of the atmosphere carbon and sulfur compounds that could not be easily assimilated by the environment.

3. *The invention of the gasoline combustion engine.* This not only pressed hard upon petroleum resources that might better be used as a source of protein, but added complex chemicals to the atmosphere which through interaction with solar radiation and with each other created smog in urban areas.

4. *The rapid growth in human population,* very largely due to the reduction of the death rate through the application of medical science and public health technologies. There is no indication that fertility rates have increased anywhere in any human society, but more people survive to become fertile, and the period of fertility lasts longer.

The growing population exerted pressures of a

Illustration by Frank Ansley

Man stands at the end of a long cycle of energy exchanges in which there is a calculable and irreversible loss of energy at each exchange. A grown adult irradiates heat equivalent to that of a 75-watt bulb. His total energy output, in 12 hours of hard physical work, is equivalent to only 1-kilowatt hour. He requires daily 2200 calories of food intake, 4½ pounds of water and 30 pounds of air, and he discards five pounds of waste. Considered as an energy converter, man is the least efficient link in his particular "food chain," and for this reason the most vulnerable to catastrophic ecologic change. Such a change can be caused by overloading the energy circuit. There are two new humans added to the globe's population *every second.*

new magnitude on the producers, leading to an acceleration of agriculture, particularly in "one-crop" farming, and to increased industrialization. These waves compounded; the more that was produced the more people survived, the higher the population growth rate, and the greater the destruction of the environment.

5. *The increased urbanization of the world's human populations.* With the spread of mechanized agriculture, or the impoverishment of the soil, more and more people "left the land," and trekked to the cities. The result is that the cities, like vast "predatory organisms," themselves producing nothing ecologically, press hard upon the agricultural areas. The urban areas are enormous consumers of chemical energy, and their chief product is waste material that cannot—or at least is not—being reintroduced into the ecologic system.

6. *The clustering of extractive and manufacturing processes.* These gathered around areas of inexpensive fuel or energy sources (coal, natural gas, petroleum, hydroelectric power); water (as a solvent, coolant, waste disposal system); low cost labor supplies (the relatively uneducated and poor people); and inexpensive transport (ocean frontages, lakes, rivers, canals, valley configurations with low gradients).

Extractive industries clustered around the sources of raw materials: concentrations of minerals, stands of forests, or in the center of grasslands, as in the grain belts of the middle west in the U.S. The result of clustering was to increase the number of pollutants in each ecologic area. Where the waste products of one or two producers presented no problem, the waste products of ten or twenty in the same area did. Pockets of pollution began to accumulate. (We define "pollution" as any input into a system that cannot be assimilated and recycled within the system.)

When all of these inputs, these economic "bones" are pieced together, they form a monster that no one foresaw, no one wanted, but which is now galloping through our environment. As the "I Ching" says, "No Blame." Whatever happened, every human being who felt he had to have more of everything, at less cost, was to blame. So—us all.

And it is precisely this point we have tried to make here. The destruction of the habitat, the rending of the web of life upon this planet, is the result of a species that is driven by fear, even though that fear may no longer be technologically justified.

Just so long as people want something "cheaper," they will put pressure upon the manufacturers, and the manufacturers will produce it "cheaper" all right; but at an enormous cost to the natural environment. With the spread of technology, with the increase in population, the "real" cost of what we produce is the destruction of the system that produced it. We know now, even if we didn't before, that if "waste" products are recycled into the system, they can be used and used again. "Waste" is a human judgment, and not a very good one at that. Natural systems know no waste, except the loss of heat in energy exchanges.

If the cost of reinserting "waste" back into the system is considered to be a "natural" cost of producing the product, then we really have no ecologic problem. Except for a small heat loss, nothing is taken from the system, and it constantly regenerates itself.

Having constructed this monster out of old bones lying around the place, let us consider whether we can distinguish between real problems and false ones. A real problem is one, as we define it, for which we do not now have a solution. An unreal problem, again by our definition, is one that we know how to solve, but don't.

The "population problem" is, by this definition, not a real one. It is not a "real" one in that we know how to solve it, and that, in any event whether we do much if anything at all, it will solve itself.

In some places, the population increase will stop simply because there is not enough food to support it; famine, malnutrition, war, and plagues will stop it.

Some technological controls can be applied. We already know what they are; contraception, sterilization, abortion, infanticide, geronticide, or simply the refusal of the "have" economies to supply food and medicines to the "have not" economies. In different cultures and to a different degree, probably all of these methods will be used.

(Continued on page 12)

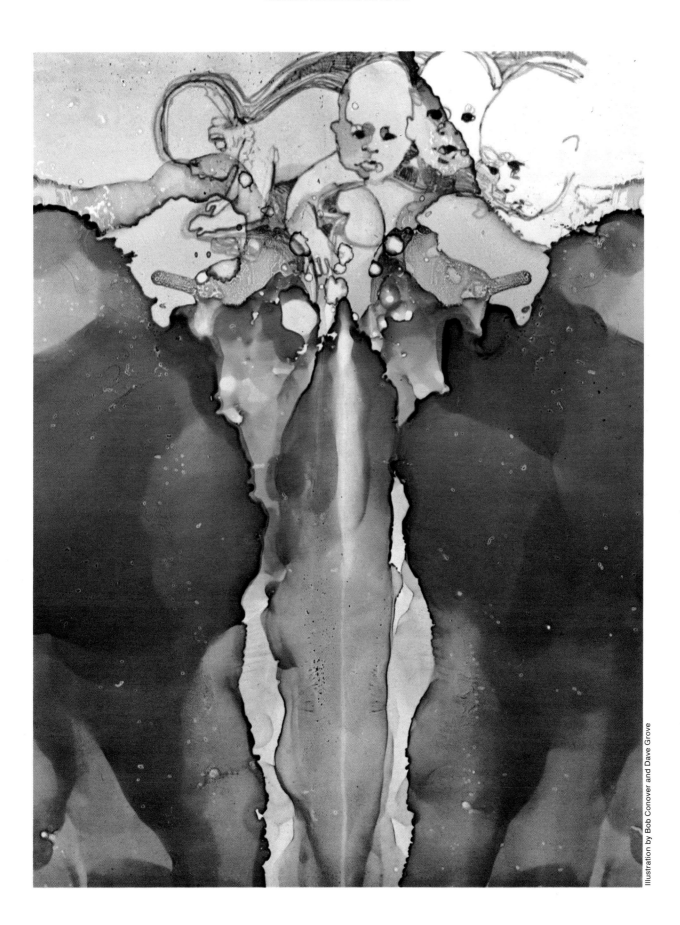

Illustration by Bob Conover and Dave Grove

However, even if somehow all of these measures could be applied to the fullest extent we know how on a global basis, the growth rate of the world's human population would not "stabilize" (i.e. just exactly reproduce itself) until the year 2066. But by then it may be much too late to preserve the environment in which humans live.

A technological solution that has been proposed by a New England biologist, and which may have some merit, would be the use of an aerosol contraceptive on a global basis. Couples who desired children would apply for an antidote at a local clinic. The aerosols would be spread by high flying planes.

The "real" problems are the exhaustion of natural resources which cannot, by any technology we now possess, be replaced, and the contamination of our environment with chemical compounds whose end results we cannot calculate and which we do not know how to remove.

On the average, there are about nine inches of topsoil in arable regions where edible foods may be grown in the United States. One third of that has been destroyed in the last 300 years.

We do not know how to replace topsoil, the product of millions of years of weather cycles.

However, it will take some time, even with our advanced technology, to destroy the productivity of all the topsoil on earth. We have invented other ways to destroy our habitat much faster.

There are many of these, but perhaps the most crucial is the contamination of the atmosphere in a way that reduces the input of solar energy. The contaminants are the outpouring of carbon and sulfur compounds from industrial plants and from their combustion-based products.

Along with atmospheric pollution, we have introduced a number of chemical compounds into the natural cycles. These tend to concentrate at the end of the food chain, in birds, fish and mammals. For the most part, we do not know what the end result of this contamination may be; it has been, apparently, "too expensive" to find out. No one has explained, so far, for whom it is "too expensive;" but, obviously, for all of us.

"Waste" and "garbage" are real problems, too, in densely occupied areas, but they are largely psychological. Food becomes "garbage" when a person is no longer hungry enough to eat it. "Waste" becomes waste when a person decides something is no longer useful to him. One of the cheapest and most effective ways of "getting rid of" both garbage and waste would be to spread it out in dumps for the poor people—approximately two-thirds of the world's population—who would consider it neither waste nor garbage. Or, if that is too difficult, we can simply incinerate it in high temperature furnaces which produce energy, but few pollutants.

Thus, we finally come to this poor fearful creature—namely, ourselves—whose insatiable desire for things, many of which are seldom used and rarely needed, has led to systems of production and distribution whose real but "hidden" cost is not the expenditure of human energy, but the progressive deterioration of the natural environment.

Even with today's rudimentary technology, it is quite possible that humans can produce everything they need, as well as many of the things that they want, without seriously damaging the planet, providing that population can be stabilized. We are beginning to have the science for such approach, much of which could be translated into effective technology right now. We are beginning to have, mostly through the energy of the young people, the moral persuasion to do so.

The question, which will be asked more and more persistently over the next decade or so is, "What are we waiting for?"

I CHING

SINCE in this way man comes to resemble heaven and earth, he is not in conflict with them. His wisdom embraces all things, and his tao brings order into the whole world; therefore, he does not err. He is active everywhere, but does not let himself be carried away. He rejoices in heaven and has knowledge of fate; therefore, he is free of care. He is content with his circumstances and genuine in his kindness; therefore, he can practice love.

Ta Chuan

"The I Ching or Book of Changes," based on texts written circa 650 B.C.

the worm ouroboros

According to legend...the Worm Ouroboros ate its own tail, and thus  **was a symbol of a world that survives by endlessly devouring itself.**

Bottom illustration by Masami Miyamoto

Top illustration by Keith Henderson from the book THE WORM OUROBOROS by E. R. Eddison. Copyright, 1926, 1952 by E. P. Dutton & Co., Inc. Renewal, 1953, by Winifred Grace Eddison and Jean Gudrun Rucker. Published by E. P. Dutton & Co., Inc. and used with their permission.

The image of the self-devouring reptile shaped itself slowly in the recesses of the mind of prehistoric man. It could serve today as a model of the way modern ecologists see the system of life as it operates on this planet. It is a closed system, undulating in waves of energy that pass through cycles of alternate life and death, like the slow beating of the wings of some giant pterodactyl at sunset over a primordial marsh.

What we now call ecology—the study of organisms in relation to their environment—must be the most ancient of the sciences. Prehistoric man survived only because he was a superb ecologist. Peering from his hiding place in the bushes around a clearing, or from the opening of his cave, his science was empirical. The laboratory was the place where he lived, the success of his observations could be measured by the fact that he managed to survive through the day.

What the prehistoric ecologist studied was the interface of living systems moving within living systems—the tiger in the bush, the bison on the plain, the edible insect stirring in the rubble of a fallen tree. Today we might call such vision "holographic," meaning simply that the entire web of living things served as a background against which a figure could be discerned. The figure could be discerned because, within the system, it moved in

(Continued on page 17)

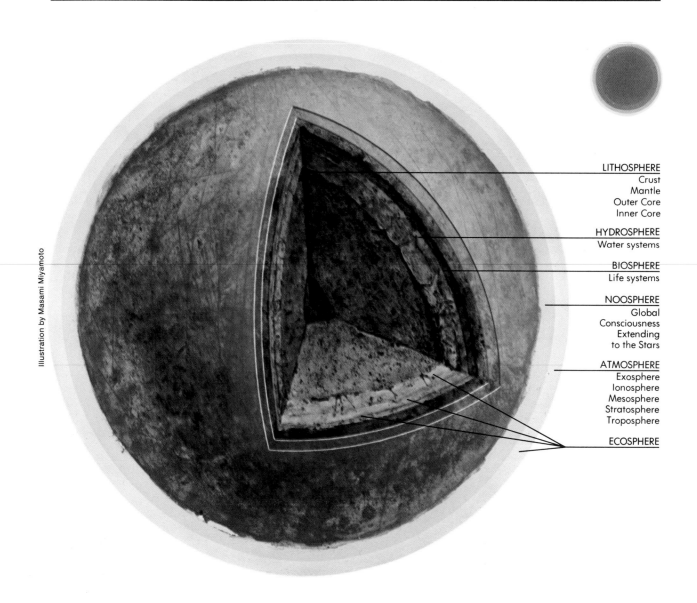

Illustration by Masami Miyamoto

LITHOSPHERE
Crust
Mantle
Outer Core
Inner Core

HYDROSPHERE
Water systems

BIOSPHERE
Life systems

NOOSPHERE
Global
Consciousness
Extending
to the Stars

ATMOSPHERE
Exosphere
Ionosphere
Mesosphere
Stratosphere
Troposphere

ECOSPHERE

Life does not exist everywhere in and on the earth. Rather it is confined to a thin shell that includes particularly the interfaces among land, air and water. It is a remarkable fact that, in general, life does not exist in depth within any one of these earthly phases — not very far down in the land masses, nor very high in the atmosphere, nor very abundantly in the abyss of the oceans. Characteristically, life is abundant at the interfaces between phases. Life's habitat is the relatively thin zone where land, sea and sky meet. We call this inhabited region of earth the *biosphere.*

CLIFFORD GROBSTEIN / "The Strategy of Life"

The bio-bubble may be thought of as a dilute gelatinous film of which the living orders actually themselves are the particles held together by physical and by non-material forces.

F. L. KUNZ / "The Film of Living Beauty"
Main Currents in Modern Thought — Sept./Oct. 1961

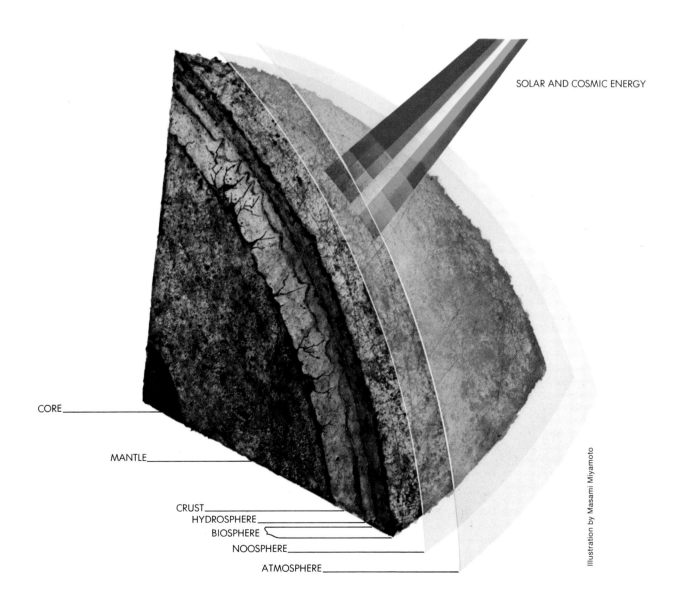

SOLAR AND COSMIC ENERGY

CORE

MANTLE

CRUST

HYDROSPHERE

BIOSPHERE

NOOSPHERE

ATMOSPHERE

Illustration by Masami Miyamoto

FORM IS THE CREST OF A WAVE THAT IS BREAKING – Bathed in the radiance of a beneficent star, a pebble, a drop of water, and a blade of grass are the magic ingredients whose constant interaction is the foundation of that "dilute gelatinous film" we call biosphere. These are *all* the tools we have; to destroy them or abuse them, to interrupt their function, is to destroy ourselves. Not all the decisions of corporate board members, not all the legislation passed by our politicans, not all the money in all the banks of the world, not all the power stored in our military arsenals can change this fact. Yet we act as if they could and continue to consider that the laws of man have priority over the laws of nature and that wealth is more precious than life. One reason that we do this is that we tend to think of a pebble, a drop, or a blade of grass as "things," when, in reality, they are phases in a process that moves as waves of energy through space and time. We are, at best, poor voyagers upon this tide.

Illustration by Masami Miyamoto

the field of vision at a rate different than the rest. The scanning process we call perception is both receptive and projective; as humans we project what we *want* to see, hear and feel upon the holographic "surround" that is available to us at the moment. It is an interference beam that renders visible the crests of waves of energy, expressed momentarily as concrete shapes—rocks and trees and other living things. We select some elements of the pattern and omit the others; the ones we select we call "reality."

Man is, himself, a system moving within a system caught up in, and forming a part of, an intricate web of protoplasm that writhes upon the surface of the planet. A pull upon any strand of the web exerts tension on others. For prehistoric man, an aura of magic trembled between the quick and the dead. The magic was in *all* living systems—to partake of the heart of the bear was to become a part of the long cycle of which that particular animal was but the crest of a wave.

Just as water collects in basins to form ponds, so magic collected in certain favored places: groves of trees, grottoes whose moss and lichen glistened with moisture, sweat upon the face of the earth; and in the deep recesses of caves where the unquenchable spirits of the dead awaited their turn at life again. Their man-made images, in ochre, manganese and iron oxide, danced in the flickering flames of torches, deep in the back of caves; just as they do today, tens of thousands of years after the species they symbolized had passed from earth.

Throughout all of this, prehistoric men, "the children of the dream"—for it was the dream that made them different from other organisms—passed as easily as gleams of sunlight on the ripples of a stream. This was no idyll of flower children; life for them was brutish, short, hard, and dirty. But except where early man set fire to grassland or forest to flush out game for the waiting clubs, his activities did not seriously disturb the living system of which he was a part. He was, indeed, a part of all that he had seen.

Of their passage we know very little: a heap of stones, some charcoal, bits of bone—artifacts of the first ripple of a wave of energy that was to sweep all other living things before it, and which may ul-timately flame around the planet like a vast corona; a star unwanted. Somewhere along the road, they forgot that they did not weave the web of life, but that they were a strand in it. In the forgetting was the tragedy of this strange species, whose legendary story has not yet run its full course.

Along the way, a very long time ago, this highly percipient organism recognized that all came from the sun. His earliest, most persistent gods were sun gods. And it is with the sun that contemporary ecology begins...

As the earth turns, slowly, like a rabbit on a spit over a bed of coals, it receives a steady power supply of radiant energy estimated to amount to 2.5 billion billion horsepower. About one-third of this is reradiated into space, mostly by clouds and ice. The rest is absorbed to activate systems and then dissipated into space again. The absorbed energy drives the great engine of the earth, melting ice, evaporating water, generating winds, and waves and currents. The sound of life is the sound of running water. It beats upon the reef and shore, and moves as a tide through all living things; walking bags of water, sun-driven upon the surface of the earth. Some 99.9998 per cent of all the energy income of earth streams out from the sun.

Of this income, about four-hundredths of one per cent drives all the mechanisms we know as life. Plants transform the radiant energy into chemical energy through photosynthesis. They use about one-sixth of the energy they absorb; the remaining five-sixths are available to others. In ecological terms, plants are producers; all other living beings are consumers. Man is thus—along with lice and mice, microbes and mustangs, deer and dogs—a consumer.

Man produces tools and symbols. Important as they may be as time-binders, they are not edible. Man may release nuclear power, or he may transform the mechanical energy of flowing water to electrical energy through turbines, but his role is primarily that of a custodian of energy. He sometimes forgets that he is, as much as the toadstool or the termite, a child of the sun.

In earth's ecologic system, the first consumers are herbivores—they reap the radiant harvest of the green plants. They harvest about half of the

(Continued on page 20)

Illustration by Bob Conover and Dave Grove

A BRIGHT GOLDEN HAZE ON THE MEADOWS—If you were to go down to your backyard or an empty lot and mark off a square yard, stretch a gauze net over it, and then remove all the plants, insects and animals in that little square, you would learn at least two things. First, there is a great amount of life going on there—much more than you would have thought. Second, if you divide your "harvest" up into species, you will find that while there is one dominant species (by numbers) there always are a number of other species. Nature has stocked each square of earth with a sufficient diversity of genetic "alphabets" so that if there should be a change in the environment, some of the "minority" groups will probably survive.

If you were to try this same experiment on a square yard of man-cultivated land, the story would be different. Constant cultivation, and drenching with herbicides and insecticides, will have wiped out all but the dominant species. Such man-made environments—like stands of corn or wheat, or paddies of rice, or even your own rose garden—are highly vulnerable to environmental change. The dust bowls of North America, the ravaged, bare hillsides of Southern Europe, the deserts around the Mediterranean—all were largely caused by man's agricultural and industrial "progress." Now repeat the square yard experiment on a freeway, a parking lot, or the roof of a building and you'll see where we're headed. There's nothing left to count.

Illustration by Bob Conover and Dave Grove

THEY KNOW NOT WELL THE SUBTLE WAYS I KEEP, AND PASS AND TURN AGAIN—Although, because it is so mechanistic, the analogy of the internal work of a clock is inexact to describe the system by which living things maintain themselves, it may serve our purpose here. Think of solar radiation as being the force that winds the mainspring. With negligible exceptions, it is the only source of energy that living things have. The energy accumulated by the earth as it turns is distributed throughout the system. At each transaction there is an unavoidable loss of energy in the form of heat. Within the primary system, there is no such thing as an inessential wheel; each absorbs energy, uses a little, passes what is left on to the next. Should one wheel fail, the rest of the system stops. Within this system man is no more important than any other wheel. In nature, the energy transactions take place in "geochemical cycles" in which some life systems (producers) transform radiation into chemical arrays of molecules, and other life systems (consumers) transform the output of the producers into other patterns of molecules, lose a little as heat, and return the waste into the system to be used again. Man, as one of the consumers, may disrupt the system in at least four ways: he oversimplifies it; he overloads it; he injects new chemical compounds which disrupt the rhythm of its cycles; and he removes the wastes from the system in which they originated.

five-sixths of one per cent of radiation absorbed by the plants.

When animals eat plants, only about 20 per cent of what is consumed is turned into tissue; the rest is used up as heat to keep them going, or discarded as waste.

When one animal eats another, the conversion efficiency is again about 20 per cent. As a meat-eater, man is at the end of the chow line, living on 20 per cent, of 20 per cent, of five-sixths of 50 per cent, of four hundredths of one per cent. However, since man is an omnivore, he can eat plants directly, and thus short circuit the system. Instead of killing insects with chemicals, he might do better to eat them. He may soon have to, if population growth continues.

Lamont C. Cole (from which the above energy figures were taken), in "The Ecosphere" (*Scientific American,* April, 1958) puts it this way: "For example, 1000 calories stored up by algae in Cayuga Lake can be converted into protoplasm amounting to 150 calories by small aquatic animals. Smelt eating these animals produce 30 calories of protoplasm from the 150. If a man eats the smelt, he can synthesize six calories of fat or muscle from the 30. If he waits for the smelt to be eaten by a trout and then eats the trout, the yield shrinks to 1.2 calories. If we really were dependent on the lake for food, we would do well to exterminate the trout and eat the smelt ourselves, or, better yet, to exterminate the smelt and live on plankton-burgers."

Man is a beggar upon the face of the earth; he can contribute nothing but waste products, and in urban areas he manages to divert the wastes away from the system that generated the food. Coupled with the runaway growth of human population, the only possible description of this activity is insanity—an insanity that Arthur Koestler attributes to a gene mutation that may have occurred when homo sapiens first burst upon the earth.

Edward S. Deevey, Jr., in "The Human Crop" (*Scientific American,* September 1960) writes, "The dependence of the human crop on plants as the ultimate source of bodily fuel can be compared to the life of squatters along a railroad track, whose only source of warming fuel is coal dropped from passing trains. Clearly, if the situation is to last indefinitely, the squatters must adjust their rate of coal consumption to the rate at which coal is lost from the tenders."

Apart from the population increase, which puts more squatters on the track, man is cutting down the number of passing trains as well. Since the early 1940's the amount of atmospheric pollution around the globe has increased at an alarming rate. Some of this is through increased volcanic activity; some of it is caused by man's burning coal and petroleum. One result has been a drop in global temperature of about 0.3°C. The last ice age was caused by a drop of only 6°C. Through the burning of fossil fuels (which might better be used to produce protein) man is reducing the .04 per cent of solar radiation on which the whole life system depends.

Through the use of radioactive tracer elements, radiation counters, data processing, computer modeling and process simulation, today's ecologists are beginning to understand the part man plays in the intricate web of life.

By combining their knowledge with that of other disciplines, and through systems analysis, it may be possible for the ecologists to suggest how man can have the material things he needs without destroying the system that makes those things possible. We may very well see this begin to happen within the next five to ten years; if everyone is willing to try. ✿

I CHING
THEREFORE they called the closing of the gates the Receptive, and the opening of the gates the Creative. The alternation between closing and opening they called change. The going forward and backward without ceasing they called penetration. What manifests itself visibly they called an image; what has bodily form they called a tool. What is established in usage they called a pattern. That which furthers on going out and coming in, that which all men live by, they called divine.

Ta Chuan

"The I Ching or Book of Changes," based on texts written circa 650 B.C.

When we put the bits and pieces of accumulated knowledge together, we find that it is possible to construct rather primitive sentences that partially describe the world revealed to us through our senses so far. These sentences, whose verbs are radiant energy and whose nouns are accumulations of matter, appear to have a direction—they all seem to move toward increasingly complex com-

journey to infinity

munities of systems. We find this in the progress of the atoms from hydrogen to plutonium; in organic molecules from algae to vast communities of plants in forests and jungles; in the animals from the amoeba up to the community of organs that make up man; in the evolution from the simple cave or shelter to the enormous human communities that are clustering around the oceanic coasts and the inland waters of the world; and in the growing complexity of the communities of tools, from the simple club to the interlocking systems of electronic "brains." The sentences appear to have a wave-like, sinosoidal quality, radiating out as spirals from some central point buried in the depths of time. What is expressed in all of these sentences is the orderly formation of systems into communities whose chief characteristic appears to be to guarantee a greater array of experience to choose from (i.e., the possibility of arrays of new combinations of systems) and thus greater freedom, through communal support, for each individual. Someday it may be possible to make a whole paragraph out of the rude sentences we now falteringly construct from "The Grand Alphabets." It may be that the day when we can do so is not so far off. ✿

The evolutionists, piercing beneath the show of momentary stability, discovered, hidden in rudimentary organs, the discarded rubbish of the past. They detected the reptile under the lifted feathers of the bird, the lost terrestrial limbs dwindling beneath the blubber of the giant cetaceans. They saw life rushing outward from an unknown center, just as today the astronomer senses the galaxies fleeing into the infinity of darkness. As the spinning galactic clouds hurl stars and worlds across the night, so life, equally impelled by the centrifugal powers lurking in the germ cell, scatters the splintered radiance of consciousness and sends it prowling and contending through the thickets of the world.

Loren Eiseley/*The Unexpected Universe,* 1969

PROTO-ZONE   **ZONE OF INCREASING DIVERSITY**

Illustration by Masami Miyamoto

ZONE OF INCREASING COMPLEXITY　　　　　　　　ZONE OF COMMUNITIES

the long voyage home

Wherever we look in nature, the same process appears to be taking place, and in the same direction. The elemental particles join to form atoms, which form molecules, which form compounds, which form communities of ever greater complexity. At every stage, some energy is "lost" or "traded" for a more complicated structure. The more complex the structure or system, the more possibilities it has for forming new combinations; its capacity for change grows.

All the world, physical as well as biological, seems to be engaged in the same grand enterprise. Man is one, but only one, phase of the trek of all things through time. But as far as we know, only he is aware of this, and with awareness, assumes reponsibility for the world in which he finds himself. It should be a *joyous* awareness, and a responsibility for which love is the only adequate adjective.

Material and illustrations on these pages are based on "SURVIVAL. A Study Guide for Teilhard de Chardin's 'The Phenomenon of Man'." © 1967 by Phenomenon of Man Project, Inc. Canoga Park, California.

Illustration by Nancy Benedict and Masami Miyamoto

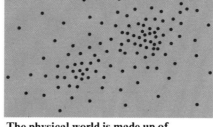

The physical world is made up of infinitely small particles…"grains"

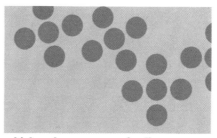

which under pressures of radiation, gravitation and magnetism form atoms.

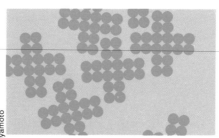

Molecules are also linked in systems we recognize as megamolecules.

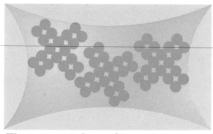

These are acted upon by pressures of radiation, gravitation, and magnetism

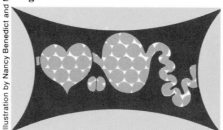

Organisms join to form colonies amid another exchange of energy and heat

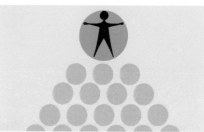

and finally man emerges at the apex of the ladder of increasing complexity.

"The emergence of consciousness is the birth of life from the heart of matter," says French Philosopher Teilhard de Chardin in THE PHENOMENON OF MAN. "It is also the direction of all evolutionary processes....The passing wave that we can feel was not formed in ourselves. It comes to us from far away....It reaches us after creating everything on the way."

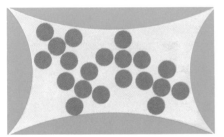

Thousands of atoms are symmetrically grouped under the same pressures

and form more complicated systems called molecules of carbon compounds.

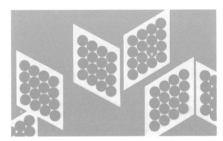

Molecules clump together into complex systems of non-organic compounds.

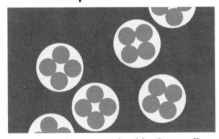

and are contained in the smallest of all living cells, so far known.

Individual cells lump together into more complex communities or colonies.

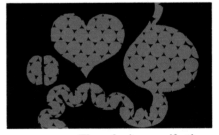

The colonies, manifesting increased interdependence, become living organs.

The cycle begins anew as man becomes the grain and combines to form systems

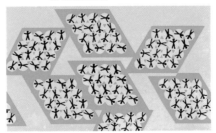

of even more complex structures — tribes, villages, metropolises, nation-states.

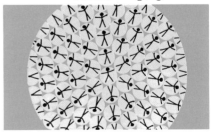

Then a final whole — a global community acting as if it were a single organism.

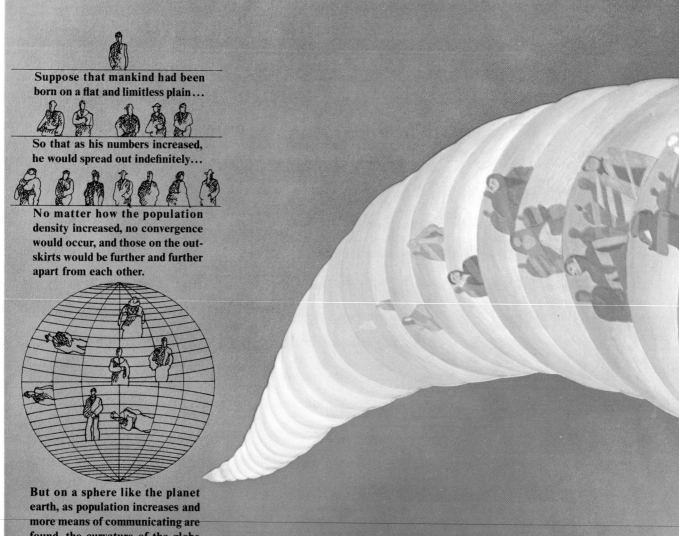

Suppose that mankind had been born on a flat and limitless plain...

So that as his numbers increased, he would spread out indefinitely...

No matter how the population density increased, no convergence would occur, and those on the outskirts would be further and further apart from each other.

But on a sphere like the planet earth, as population increases and more means of communicating are found, the curvature of the globe *forces* a convergence. These radial lines of convergence can be seen even now in the urban densities forming along the rims of the continents of the world...
As these densities coalesce, pressures build up that reinforce the evolutionary drive of each living cell to communicate with, and to enter into new combinations with, other living cells...

...Ultimately, this may lead to the creation of a "superconciousness" in which the people of the planet act as if they were the cells of a global "brain," stretched like a membrane of awareness through the interchange of human experience around the whole earth. This is what Teilhard de Chardin has called "the noosphere"; a foreseeable next stage in the billion-year evolution of organisms.

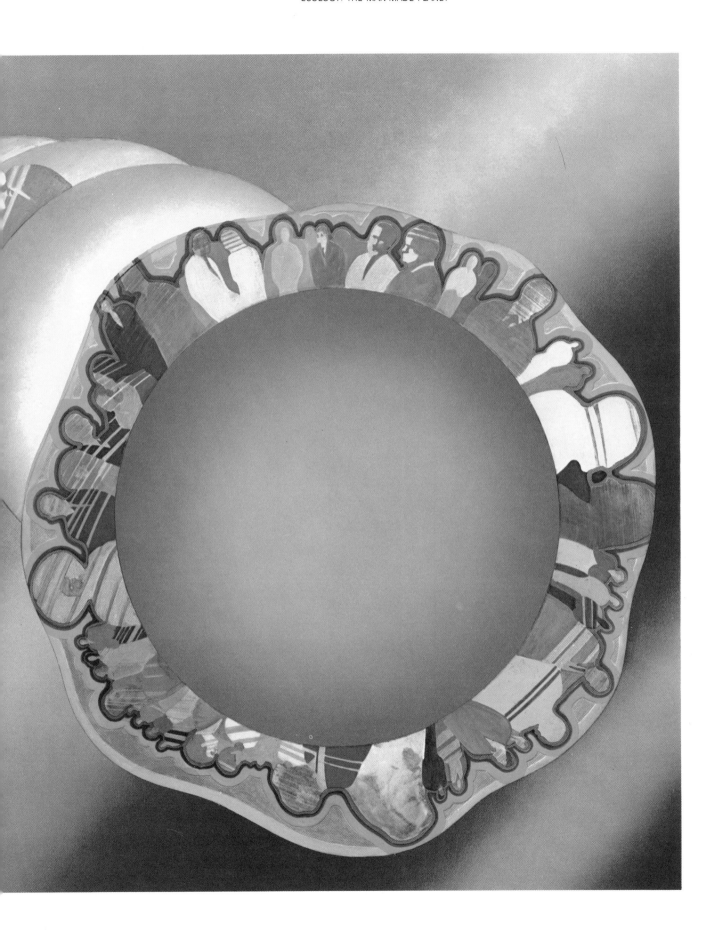

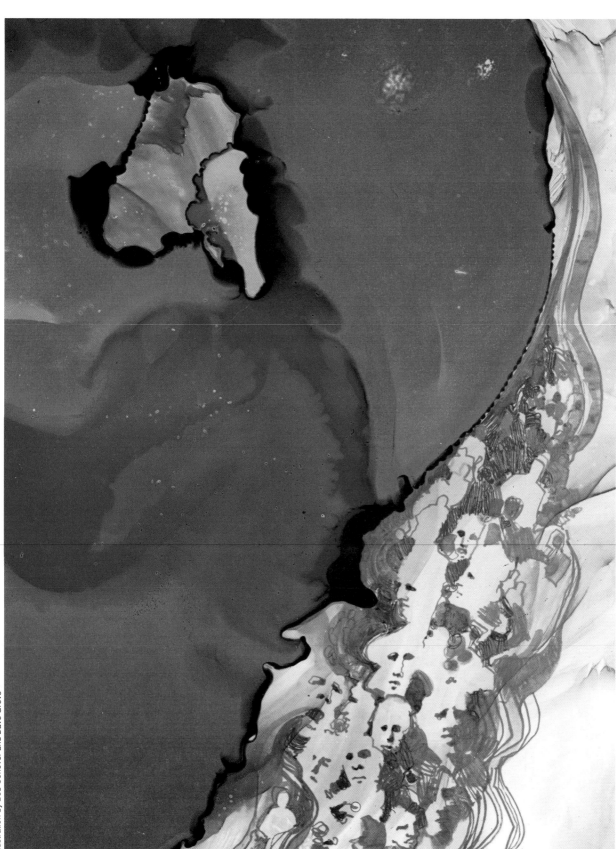

eastward in eden

And God said, Let us make man in our own image, after our own likeness: and let them have dominion over the fish of the sea, and the fowl of the air, and over the cattle, and over all the earth, and over every creeping thing.... So God created man in his own image...male and female he created them...and God said unto them, Be fruitful, and multiply, and replenish the earth, and subdue it....And the Lord God planted a garden eastward in Eden; and there he put the man he had created.

GENESIS 1.26–28

After his millennia, the stone-gathering creature crept out of his cave to hear, amidst the thunder and lightning, the terrible injunctions: *have dominion, be fruitful, multiply, subdue.* One injuction he does not seem to have heard was *replenish the earth;* perhaps a clap of thunder drowned it out.

One senses, after all this time, that the Garden of Eden was the model of a perfectly functioning eco-system. Humans (though limited in number), beasts, and plants lived together in harmony. Then came the apple episode with its awesome prohibition, "thou shall not eat of it, lest ye die," and the even more awesome promise (the Worm Ouroboros speaks), "ye shall be as gods, knowing good and evil." Not death, but the *fore*knowledge of death, was the great wing that darkened the Garden that day.

The eating of the forbidden fruit was re-enacted in the 17th and 18th Centuries with "The Enlightenment" and "The Age of Reason." Rationalism was the scalpel that chopped the human adventure into little pieces; the feeling of oneness and harmony with all living processes was lost. The new exodus from the garden of faith had as its concomitant the breaking of the world into things —stones for the cave, perhaps—isolated areas of experience that could be dissected, counted, labeled, and accumulated in the cave of man's mind.

Knowledge became a mosaic of prettily colored pieces—like a stained-glass window—through which the light of understanding shown but wanly. This self-appointed observer of "reality" drifted through a clockwork universe like a disembodied intelligence; here, indeed, was Koestler's "Ghost in the Machine."

Then, about 100 years ago, an extraordinary thing began to happen. The little pieces of prettily colored glass began to flow and merge and form new patterns; the colors "ran." From the heat of incandescent minds, the leaden barriers that separated the little bits of knowledge melted. The colors began to coalesce into a holographic pattern; interacting systems of motion and change.

Order was not a dead fish on a dissecting table, but a school of fish flashing through the shallows; not a dead duck, but a flight of birds heading toward some eternal south. The scalpel was transformed into a painter's brush, electrified with color.

Now, man began to see himself as part of the processes he observed; he could be described as a system interacting with other systems. They defined him as much as he defined them. The explorer and the explored were parts of each other; inextricably intertwined in an adventure common to them both. In the Western, rationalist way of thought, "Man conquered Everest." In the more ancient, Oriental way, it would have been said, "The mountain has gained a new friend." The ancient magic had crept once again out of the cave and the grotto to rejoin the creature who had buried it there.

From this seemingly simple shift in interpreting human experience—the shift from thing to processes, in which the observer himself is an integral part—there streamed out, like waves of energy from an exploding star, concepts that caused mutations in the genetic patterns of human thought. The old authority crumbled—Jericho! revisited—and the walls came tumbling down. And this is the cause, acknowledged or not, of much of the turbulence in human societies today.

Although less than a century old, the concept of interacting systems—of organic patterns—of which man is only one, has already caused profound changes:

—in mathematics it has led to probability theory and non-Euclidean geometries and anomalous numbers...

—in physics to the concept of interacting fields of force, quantum mechanics, and the theory of relativity...

—in biology to the concept of evolutionary development of living species, shaped by their interaction with a constantly changing planetary environment...

—in psychology to the concept of the unconscious, the subconscious, and the conscious as interacting systems of energy exchanges...

—in geology to the concept of dynamic processes of the inorganic, moving like waves of energy through the fields of time...

—in genetics to the concept of an "alphabet," endlessly reshuffled, where the dealer is time and the "wild card" is mutation...

—in business and industry to the growing use of operations and systems analysis, aided by data processing, computerization and model simulation; the flow and process of things through time...

—in architecture to the study of human communities as fields of force rather than clusters of buildings...

—in the arts generally to the flow of experience and the interaction between artist and audience in which the art object is but a catalyst—as in nonrepresentational painting, free-form sculpture, free theatre, kinetic art, mobiles and "happenings"...

—in ethics and morality to the concept of situational or contextual ethics; the "rightness" of a response is measured by the situation in which it occurs, absolute "good" and "evil" have constantly to be reappraised...

—and in science generally, the movement from the observation of isolated systems to the study of interaction between systems; organic patterns whose interaction is synergistic.

"The new pattern requires a conversion," says Professor Donald W. Rogers (in "Main Currents of Modern Thought," March-April, 1969)..."we must be born again...and honestly, even naively, confront experience with humility and innocence. In the new pattern, time becomes an essential dimension of reality, a 'fourth dimension,' perhaps, without which all the others lose their character and being. This kind of time can be measured not by logic nor by clocks, but by biological time or growth as exhibited within the living experience of conscious creatures caught up in the relentless flow of organic being."

The newly rediscovered relationship of man as a partner in the adventure of all living things underlies much of the new ecological science and helps to account for the almost sudden concern of man for his environment and the effects of his actions upon it. Such concern was not possible to a mind that believed it held divinely given "dominion" over the earth, nor to a mind that believed it operated outside the universal system altogether.

Science has begun to shift from the measurement of things to the study of processes and the interactions between them; the "proper study of mankind" has become not "man" but change.

If we consider mankind as a whole...does there not come a profound awareness that knowledge *in the present* of what the humanity *of the future* will be would equally help each one of us to act freely and to coordinate our actions with those of others following the example of processes which we witness throughout the whole evolution of life?
Such a humanity, perfectly unified yet preserving individual freedom, will constitute a new being for the individual men, as man does for each of the cells of his body. This unified mankind must be regarded, from now on, not as a fiction or even as an ideal, but as the *inevitable reality* toward which we are inexorably on the move.

Jean E. Charon/"Physics Reveals that Evolution has a Goal,"
Main Currents in Modern Thought, Sept.-Oct., 1969

But what is man and who is man? Whom and what do we mean, exactly, when we say that word? In this context, we mean normally "the Western white civilized male adult"—who is in fact only a very small percentage of the human race, even if we consider, perhaps rightly, that this sort of human being outweighs in importance the rest of humanity. But if we take another index, for instance, a statistical one, we would mean and consider as typical for mankind the largest race, age and sex group. That is, young Chinese females.

PIERRE BERTAUX/"The Future of Man"

Unfortunately, the systems concept has moved much more slowly into the field of human institutions — in government, organized religion, politics, economics, and least of all in education. These are, for the most part, systems engaged in protecting established authority through hierarchies of bureaucratic rituals. They are designed to protect structures whose foundations date back to a pre-industrial and agrarian concept of man's relationship to his environment.

When Western man dropped out of the oppressive "law and order" systems of 17th Century Europe, he carried with him more than rats, lice and smallpox. He also infected the new continent with an endemic conceptual disease — the idea that man held a divinely-given supremacy over all other forms of nature.

There was some other conceptual supercargo aboard those wind-swept, wave-washed, creaking 17th Century ships, too. Included were the ideas of "progress" and of "development." Both of them were related to making man — a particular type of Western European white emigrant — more "secure" through the acquisition and accumulation of physical things.

The ideas of progress and of development grew out of religious concepts that saw man's role on earth as a transitory stage on his journey to the eternal life of the hereafter. "Work" meant, for the most part, converting natural resources into things that could be sold. There was little serious questioning of man's right to do this; indeed, it often was conceived to be a duty.

When one examines the journals, essays, and letters of the early colonization of the American continent, it is apparent that most of the people felt that the wilderness was an enemy to be conquered.

The idea that the continent was already inhabited by highly complex communities of living organisms — the forests, the grasslands, the marshes, bays, river systems, tidal estuaries and all the wild life they contained — occurred to very few men: Muir, Audubon, a few others.

It is important that we understand that the whole psychological "set" of the invaders of the new continent was to subdue nature to the material desires of men.

Ecology as a formal scientific discipline was not introduced into American universities until the beginning of the 20th Century. Serious ecological concern outside of the academic world did not begin to assert itself until the "Dust Bowl" era and the succession of disastrous floods in the Mississippi drainage complex. One was the consequence of "the plow that broke the plains," the other resulted from the ruthless destruction of the northern forests. Geologically, both dust bowls and floods had occurred in the past; the efforts of man intensified them.

Until the introduction of the airplane, and with it aerial photography, few saw the things that were happening along the North Atlantic coast, the lower end of the Great Lakes, the rim of the Gulf, and in a thin, now ominous line, along the Pacific Coast. The land was so vast; the works of man seemingly so scattered. Now we know differently.

So, it all happened, and there is nothing we can do about the past except to write history books to cover it up. The future is endlessly ours, and we *might* do something about that, but the issue is still uncertain.

Another set of factors, so far not discussed, needs to be mentioned here. The older generation, which is now running things, grew up in the tradition of the pioneer and almost unquestioningly

---

By changing what he knows about the world, man changes the world he knows; and by changing the world in which he lives, man changes himself.

Theodosius Dobzhansky/*Man Evolving*

Through his images of the future, we come to know man, who he is and how he wishes to be, what his thoughts are, what he values most highly, what he thinks is worth striving for, and whether he thinks it is attainable... Certain types of men hold certain types of visions, subject to their temper and spirit; tell me what your vision of the future is and I will tell you what you are.

Dr. Frederick L. Polak/*The Future of Man*

accepts that natural resources exist to be exploited for human use. The Depression, which most of the older people remember all too clearly, reinforced the desire for the production and accumulation of things. At the same time, largely due to mechanization, fewer and fewer of the young people grow up on farms; their contact with living systems in their urban environment is almost wholly through television, an occasional visit to see caged animals in a zoo, and a household pet or two.

So, perhaps, the place to start is with a national —perhaps global—education in ecology, for the older people as well as for the young. Somehow the sense of being a part of the ecosystem and the ecosphere has to be established. Perhaps ecology should be as much a part of the educational system as the requirement for language and mathematics. If there are not enough professionally trained ecologists to establish such a nation-wide program, then crash programs to train them could be undertaken.

This may have to begin by establishing a Secretary of Ecology at the Federal cabinet level. Equivalent positions would be established at the state, county and municipal levels as well. Every government program would be reviewed for its ecologic consequences as well as its social, economic and political ones.

The train, the automobile, and the airplane long since have turned political subdivisions such as counties, states and municipalities into governmental fossils. Should it not be possible to develop regional political systems that cover the whole course of a river, or all the shores of a lake, or the continental length of a mountain range, coast, or desert? Man "made up" the political subdivisions that we now have, and they don't work anymore. Why not make up new ones that do?

Since, in an over-populated highly urbanized world, the introduction of technological innovations assumes immediate and monstrous proportions, would it not seem reasonable to establish an International Council for Technological Review, made up of the best minds of dozens of disciplines, to consider whether the introduction of an innovation can be absorbed by the human society and the ecosystem? Such a device would, to be sure, slow down "progress." But we are having difficulty absorbing, without ruining our environment, such innovations as the combustion engine, nuclear power, super-sonic aircraft, the transfer of work from men to machines, computerization... so many. Slowing down a little may not hurt.

Most of all, we have to find some way to diminish fear—economic fear, that we may run out of things; that there may come a time when we cannot last the night. We need some new thinking. Technologically we can now produce whatever is necessary for a reasonably comfortable existence for man on earth. Technologically we can do this with only a minimum disturbance of the natural ecology. If we can train our engineers to think in cyclic terms, in which all "waste" is returned to the system, instead of linear systems, in which most of what is produced ends up at the city dump —then our ecologic problems can be solved. If it is argued that there is not time to produce enough engineers with this new set of mind, let us argue back that we do it easily enough in wartime.

We can do all of this, and more, if we want to. But we will not do it if we continue as individuals to support technological systems that rapaciously destroy the very system that supports them.

In ensuing episodes of this strange Odyssey, we will try to show, rather concretely, what alternatives appear to be open to us. At the moment, there

There can be a need, but no market; or a market, but no customer; or a customer, but no salesman. For instance, there is a great need for massive pollution control, but not really a market at present. And there is a market for new technology in education, but no customer really large enough to buy the products. Market forecasters who fail to understand these concepts have made spectacular miscalculations about the apparent opportunities in these and other fields, such as housing and leisure products...

Theodore Levitt/"The New Markets," *Harvard Business Review,* **1969**

seems to be a wide range of them; we can still do anything to our future that we want to. But we really don't seem to know what we want to do. We are peering out of our caves, amidst the thunder and lightning, hoping to hear a voice.

The only voice we are likely to hear is our own.

Don't wait. ✿

Photo by George Selland

chapter 2.

SHELTER:
The Cave Re-examined

2.
The Ringing Fire

"Perhaps the best analogy (to a city) is to imagine a field in a darkness. In the field, many fires are burning. They are of many sizes, some great, others small; some far apart, others dotted close together; some are brightening, some are slowly going out. Each fire, large or small, extends its radiance into the surrounding murk, and thus carves out a space...The murk has no shape or pattern except when it is carved into space by the light...

Reprinted by permission of Random House, Inc. from THE DEATH & LIFE OF GREAT AMERICAN CITIES by Jane Jacobs.

Illustration by Uta Nietiet

"Suppose that it were possible to invent an imaginary architecture. Suppose that we could think of architecture not as a thing, but as a process for perfecting the earth ....if you think of most buildings as a process for perfecting the earth, most of them are simply unnecessary. They need not exist before our eyes as discrete objects, as things set in the landscape. They simply need not be there." ARTHUR DREXLER/MUSEUM OF MODERN ART, NEW YORK

the invisible city

When most people think about shelter, they usually think of it in terms of structure—something fixed in time and space. They seldom think of shelter as function or process.

By extension of thinking of shelter as a thing, these same people are apt to think of villages as small clusters of structures, towns as bigger ones, and cities as still bigger ones.

This kind of thinking has an ancient lineage. The earliest communities could be considered as entities because hunting and gathering economies required lots of area per person and therefore the communities were far apart. This continued to be true even after the introduction of agriculture; there were not many people, and plenty of land. Such villages as there were (mostly for trade or ritualistic purposes) were relatively small, relatively well defined and quite separate from each other.

The concept of separate identity was reinforced in a concrete way in the walled cities of ancient and medieval times. In most men's minds a city was a "thing," well defined, with limits that could be marked and seen by all. When the walls fell under the onslaught of increased population, armed invasion, and the increase in commerce and communication, men still acted as if the city walls were there.

They still spoke of "in the city" and "outside of the city." (A student of topology would call this the concept of the simple curve) and even today we have political markings which we call "city limits"; ghosts of the walled cities of the ancient past. They are completely irrelevant to contemporary cities in a technological environment, and their very existence makes the solution of urban problems virtually impossible.

It is precisely urban problems that concern us most when we think about shelter, for the worldwide trek of people from the country to urban areas shows no sign of abating. As the mechanization of agriculture spreads to more and more areas, it is probable that the migration toward the "cities" will intensify. Most of the shelter of any kind that is likely to be built within the industrialized countries in the next thirty years will most likely be in urban areas.

Instead of thinking about the contemporary city

We can no longer use the word "city" without thinking twice, because we all have an image of the city as a built-up area, and we forget that the ordinary man and his family no longer live within a city but within a system of life processes which extends well beyond the city, which it only touches at certain points. This system is growing continuously in space.

"The Scale of Settlements and the Quality of Life"/ *Ekistics.* October, 1969

A city that outdistances Man's walking powers is a trap for Man. It threatens to become a prison from which he cannot escape unless he has mechanical means of transport, the thoroughfares for carrying these, and the purchasing power for commanding the use of artifical means of communication.

ARNOLD TOYNBEE/"Has Man's Metropolitan Environment Any Precedents?" December 1966

Throughout the world, men and women and their families are leaving the countryside for the cities. They may not be going to cities as we have known them in the past, but the farm base is definitely ceasing to have the significance it has had. Even where a farm base continues, life on the farm is vastly different; marginal coffee growers in Colombia now listen on their Japanese transistors to the quotations on the coffee exchange in New York.

"Technological Advances and Human Values"/ *Ekistics,* October, 1969

There can only be disaster arising from unawareness of the causalities and effects inherent in our technologies.

MARSHALL McLUHAN/ *The Gutenberg Galaxy*

I find man utterly unaware of what his wealth is or his fundamental capability is. He says time and again, "We can't afford it." For instance, we are saying now that we can't afford to do anything about pollution but after the costs of not doing something about pollution have multiplied many fold beyond what it would cost to correct it now, we will spend many fold what it would cost us now to correct it.

R. BUCKMINSTER FULLER/ *The World Game*

In 1516, Sir Thomas More described an imaginary island called Utopia, which enjoyed perfection in politics, law and family relations. More's choice of name was not accidental. It came from the Greek *ou* (not) and *topos* (a place) to emphasize that Utopia did not and probably could not exist, although it was an ideal toward which men could strive.

ROBERT SOMMER/ *Saturday Review—* **April 5, 1969**

(the word defies scientific definition) as a giant cluster of shelters, we might, in line with current scientific thought, consider it as a "force field" in which energy transactions take place through the media of various organic systems. This concept is not only currently fashionable, but it may also have some validity. At least it gives us a new conceptual instrument for exploring a phenomenon that is becoming increasingly complex.

The foundation for such a conceptual approach may be in a relatively new field of study called "Ekistics," which is defined as "the science of human settlements." As a disciplinary approach it began about 1950 and is the brainchild of Constantinos A. Doxiadis. It employs contemporary general systems theory with well-advanced computer data processing and computer graphics, to try to find out whether general laws (analogous to those in physics, chemistry and biology) might not be discovered and expressed in terms that will enable us to understand the way human settlements are formed and how to plan for and anticipate their future growth and control.

What is examined in Ekistics is what might be called the science of the possible. It is not based on Utopian theories of what we think a city *should* be, but upon the pragmatic grounds of observation, data gathering, data processing, and the application of general systems theory to discover what natural laws define what a city *can* be.

If it is indeed possible to formulate general, natural laws concerning the life cycle of human settlements, then a great amount of human energy might be conserved in the planning and rehabilitation of urban areas.

It is at least worth trying, since we do not seem, with our present approaches, to be able to cope with the cities we now have (not to mention the ones we *may* have, with populations of the order of 20 to 30 million inhabitants in the near future).

It should be mentioned here that the change in dimension is of a magnitude for which there is no historical precedent; we can no longer look it up in a book. Whatever answers there may be, we will have to invent them. We have no idea what these may be but at least we know that we are now voyaging into a world of concepts of human

(Continued on page 45)

AN EKISTIC ALPHABET

NATURE

EKISTICALLY SPEAKING, Nature is the entire matrix of interacting organic and inorganic events we today call the ecosystem. Certain combinations of climate, water availability, and terrain appear to act as natural "corridors" along which human settlements tend to form and grow.

MAN

THERE DO NOT APPEAR to be any satisfactory definitions of "man" available. Let us simply say that as we study it further, this organism appears to be of an extraordinarily rich complexity. Under the impact of contemporary electronic information inputs, it is becoming even more complex.

SOCIETY

THERE APPEARS TO BE no satisfactory definition of Society, either. One might say that it could be defined as any system through which interaction between humans is facilitated. One of these is by proximity. The urban settlement creates the *possibility* for more different encounters than a small town.

SHELLS

THESE MAY SIMPLY BE DEFINED as shelter in any of its forms, natural or man-made. They are systems for homeostatic support of an organism whose tolerance to bodily thermal change is narrow. Secondary functions performed by shelter are biological, social, psychological and communicative.

NETWORKS

THESE ARE THE SYSTEMS OF CHANNELS along which the interactions between Nature, Man, Society and Shells flow. They include streets, the distribution systems for water, gas, electricity; waste disposal systems and all the channels for communication, including electrical and printed.

It is possible to
improve a little on
Leonardo's bubble. Here-
with we present one interpreta-
tion of contemporary man's bubble.
It is kind of like an onion, concentric layer on concentric layer, and its
dimensions are cosmic. But it is still only 38 cubic feet. (Six feet high, six
feet in diameter—arms outstretched.) The closest we have come so far to
designing an efficient habitat for man is the space capsule: 235 cubic feet that
include all life supporting systems, within environments that range up to
4900° F, with an impact force at takeoff of 6½-7 Earth gravities and an
impact of 5½ Gs at re-entry. Perhaps the people who build today's shelters
might take a few more courses in physics?

Illustration by Masami Miyamoto

Man moving requires a number of interlocking bubbles which, strung together, make a sort of tube in time. This man, for instance, is enroute from Scarsdale to

Marrakesh. On his journey, he assumes many postures, few of them with arms outstretched. When we plan shelter for contemporary, technological man, we must plan tunnels in time, of which the primary ingredient is the bubble. (Leonardo said that in the 15th Century, but we are slow readers.)

Illustration by Masami Miyamoto

relationships and of energy transactions for which the past offers us no guidance. Not Rome, not Athens, not Nineva nor Tyre are of much help to us now.

So we stand back, and squint our eyes, peering through the smog, and try to find out what it is *possible* for us to do. And, of course, we know that we can do the impossible, if we want to. We already have. But that was on another planet, and besides, the soil was dead.

Let's see how the Ekistics thing works.

We said, a little earlier, that the urban community might be envisioned as a "field of force," and that the field is composed of energy transactions between organic systems.

We might begin by asking ourselves what basic functions "shelter" (which we conceive of as systems of gravitational and radiational transactions) may perform for biological organisms on this planet.

It would appear that the first and fundamental function of shelter (whether the scales of reptiles or fish, the shells of molluscs, feathers of birds, fur of mammals, clothes of humans, caves, teepees, mud huts, suburban split levels, town houses, factory buildings, skyscrapers or manned space capsules) is to support homeostasis through limiting solar radiation as (usually) expressed in terms of thermal gradients.

Homeostasis is a term used to describe a rather complex "feedback" phenomenon. It simply means that a living organism will return to "normal" after a change of state brought about through interaction with its internal or external environment. From what little we now appear to know about operational systems, homeostasis is the process through which survival is possible in a changing environment.

For man, sans most fur, with only rudimentary scales (as in epidermal cells) the array of tolerable thermal change is very narrow. If his blood temperature changes as much as 8° above or below 98.6° he will not normally survive. He can, and sometimes does live in temperature environments as low as −110° up to 160°, but he only does so with suitable shelter. Earth thermal gradients are determined by the amount of radiant energy received, absorbed and reflected by the surface (and cloud cover) of the planet. Shelter serves the primary purpose of reducing the width of thermal gradient so that the homeostatic system of the body can cope with it.

A secondary function of shelter is protection against the discomforts of changes in the weather —rain, snow, wind—all of them products of the thermal gradient.

Another secondary function is protection against predators—either human or animal. Most of the early human communities were walled as protection against raiders (the thorn-bush fences of some villages in Africa today serve as protection against both wild animals and hostile neighboring tribesmen).

A fourth function is to provide privacy for biological activities. This is an acculturated function and differs widely from culture to culture and from time to time.

A fifth function of shelter is symbolic communication. The size, location and style of a human habitat is a way to signal economic level and social status. Much of the cost of construction in an affluent society is the result of this function, often leading to units that are much larger (and more ornate) than is required for the performance of their primary function.

Although shelter is most usually expressed as static structure, it also can be viewed as a system whose functions are operational. Seen in this way, the material of which the structure is made—rocks, brick, adobe, cement, palm fronds, canvas, plastic, wood, metal, glass—is irrelevant, provided the shelter accomplishes its function.

Studies in Ekistics have led to the formulation of five basic systems that are characteristic of all human settlements, regardless of the era in which they were formed, the place they were formed or the culture in which they were formed. (The Ekistic people prefer to call them elements, but in popular usage this word has the connotation of something static—a thing. We prefer to call them systems to reinforce our own concept that they are processes changing through time.)

The five basic systems defined by Ekistics are:

NATURE—the constantly changing ecosystem which forms the matrix...

MAN—a highly complex biological organism...

SOCIETY—a much more complex organism in which individual men function as cells, and where groups of cells act as organic systems...

SHELLS—systems of shelters whose function is to modify the natural environment in order to insure biological survival...

NETWORKS—the systems through which the interactions between the other systems take place. Paths, roadways, railway lines, water, gas and electrical distribution, radio, etc.

The science of human settlements thus (in Ekistics) becomes the exploration of the transactions that occur between the five systems listed above (and described in greater detail on the following pages).

To isolate any one of these systems as a field for study is to miss the point of human settlements. We do—and have done—this frequently. We have special disciplines, such as architecture and engineering, or contractors and developers, or many municipal agencies, which are concerned almost exclusively with one, or at best two, of the five systems. One of the results has been the haphazard and piecemeal development of most urban settlements. We often build shells, without thinking about networks; or networks without consideration of shells; or both, without thinking about the natural environment; or all of them without thinking about the man and society that has to try to survive in them.

It is not that the population densities in urban areas are "too high,"—at least not yet. It is possible that higher densities in some areas might actually improve the quality of life, provided the various systems have been designed so that they support and reinforce each other.

Another way in which we may be historically blind is to think of the "city" as a collection of shells within more or less well-defined areas. It is, for instance, within the "city limits." But the city that men really inhabit encompasses a much larger complex of systems—all the networks (railroad lines, highways, air corridors, canals, steamship routes) that connect it to sources of supply as well as the surrounding agricultural areas and rural villages which feed it and clothe it, and the suburban areas that provide much of its labor force.

One way of looking at urban settlements might be to consider them as living biological organisms vastly extended in space and developing through time.

The basic analog of the organic cell would be man himself; the individual room in which he finds himself would be the equivalent cell of the shelter system. Society would be analogous to the grouping of cells into organs (equivalent to the heart, lungs, liver, muscles, etc. in animals), the roads and utility lines (including all communication facilities) would constitute the equivalent of an organism's circulatory and neural networks. Nature is, of course, the field from which the "animal" harvests its energy.

Now consider that no city in the world, nor any complex of cities has anywhere as many people in it as an individual man has cells (60 trillion), nor does any urban region have anything remotely as complex, self-regulating, and as efficient as the networks of veins and arteries and the neurosystem in one human body. Contemplate this, and you may begin to feel that human urban problems are not insoluble. Nature solved similar problems millions of years ago, at a much higher level of complexity than any urban situation we are likely to face in the next thirty years. Or thousand, for that matter.

So, perhaps it might be useful for urbanologists to spend some time studying biological systems.

"Biological systems," says Prof. C. H. Waddington of Edinburgh University and President of the International Union of Biology Studies, "are always developing. Developing systems...have a tendency to preserve a *definite pathway of change in time*. If you watch a developing system without disturbing it, it will change along a particular course of events, which one can call an epigenic pathway.

"Now if, in some way, you push a developing system off its normal developmental pathway, it is most frequently observed that changes will occur which will tend to bring it back onto the pathway at some later point...

"This sort of stability...is called "homeorhesis," in which the 'rhesis' is derived from the Greek word, 'to flow'...

In human communities, networks are the interfaces along which the interaction takes place between organic systems—Nature, Man, Society, Shells, and, of course, other Networks. Rural villages have fairly simple systems of networks, but urban communities interweave many systems of networks at various levels—water supply, sewage and waste disposal, electrical and natural gas systems, movement of people and goods, telephone, radio, television and mass printed media. What is important about the vitality of an urban community is not the number or size of shells it contains, but the degree to which the networks function efficiently. Shown below are analogous network systems in Nature, Man, and an urban community.

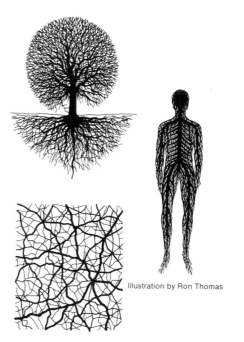

Illustration by Ron Thomas

(Continued on page **50**)

WHAT YOU SEE HERE IS A HOMEORHETIC SYSTEM FLOWING ALONG A CHREOD — If it looks vaguely like someone practicing karate, don't fret about it. Organisms tend to follow paths of energy transactions. Since we are (here at least) considering that urban communities are analogous to living organisms, we can assume that some urban configurations may follow paths like this. Organic energy transactions normally take place along the most economical path, i.e., those directions in which there is least "loss" of heat, which is the "cost" of the transaction. The paths on the surface of the earth that yield the highest degree of organization with the least heat loss are topologically determined. The slighter the gradient, the less fuel is needed to climb it; shipment by waterways is usually important, because it exacts less heat loss per ton-mile than on land. These great organic creatures we call cities grow along the lines of least resistance, just as water flows downhill. Heat loss, through transactions, is traded for organization. A physicist might call this entropy vs. negentropy, which we can't go into here, but the general idea is that all systems tend toward equilibrium (since energy can neither be created nor destroyed) and thus cities are no more exempt from the second law of thermodynamics than are stars, or wooly wombats or jet aircraft. Above we

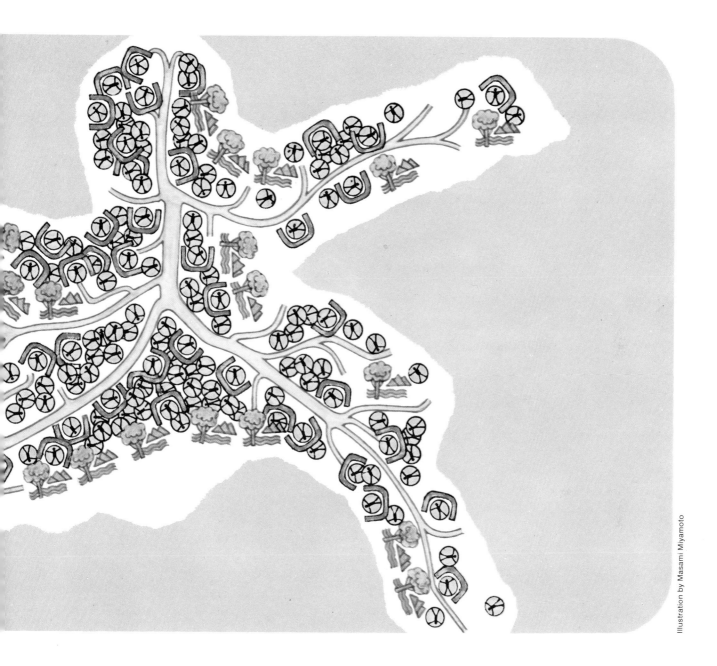

have a rather fanciful configuration of the five basic systems described by Ekisticians (see page 42). If you look closely enough you will see that there is Nature (the hidden topological configuration) which has determined the "chreods" (paths of natural flow) of Man (bubbles), Society (clusters of man-bubbles), Shells and Networks (the systems that connect the systems). There are certain "natural laws" that appear to be operative here, and if they can be discovered through data processing and computerization, then it is possible that we may be able to control the growth of present urban configurations, and perhaps establish new ones to take care of a growing population.

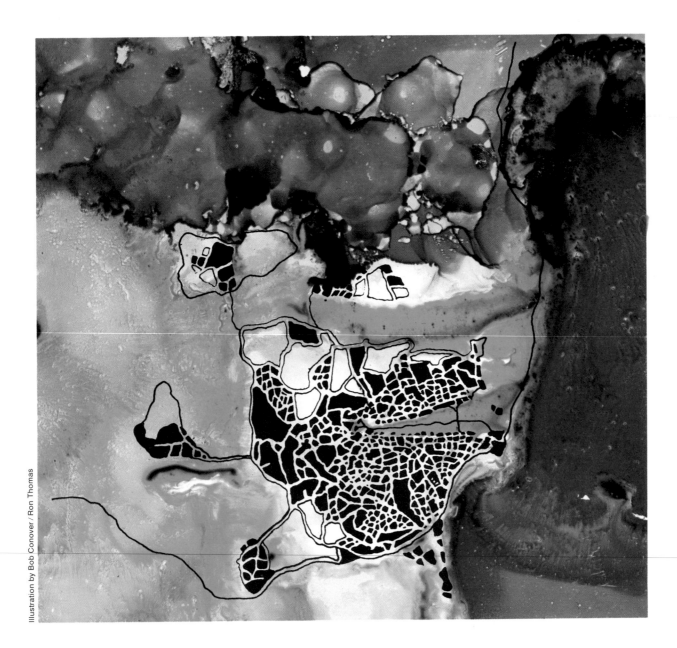

Illustration by Bob Conover / Ron Thomas

"The name for the path along which a homeo-rhetic system flows is a 'chreod.' Thus a homeo-rhetic system is one which develops along a given chreod and tends to return to the chreod if it gets pushed off by some disturbance."

If one thinks of an urban community as a quite complex biological organism, developing through time, then it is equally possible to consider that it is homeorhetic and following chreods. The concept, while only analogous, nevertheless suggests that cities cannot be "planned" anymore than an aardvark can be. About all man can do is to try to establish the route the poor creature is following, and then to help him back to his chreods if he falls off. It seems to us that this is what Ekistics is all about; it endeavors to establish the chreods the great lumbering monsters of the world are follow-ing down the interfaces of the planet, so that planners and designers and administrators can keep the thing alive.

In order to understand how the Ekistians are doing this, it is useful to return once more to Dr.

Waddington's deep well. He suggests taking a clue from the mathematicians.

"There is one branch of mathematics which deals with spaces in many dimensions . . . This is the type of mathematics known as topology. I think that in the future the most professional way of expressing the properties of developing systems, whether they are animals or towns, is going to be by the use of topological notions."

It would seem that the science of human settlements—Ekistics—is applying to urban development the same approaches that Dr. Waddington has used in the application of "topological notions" to embryology.

Through the accumulation of historical and present data, the Ekistians seek to establish points on a multi-dimensional grid whose inter-connections form a sort of "skin" that represents the observed state of the organism (i.e., a metropolitan area) at a given moment of time. They also seek to plot the vectors that tend to keep the organism shuffling along its own chreod.

What they come up with is models of "attractor surfaces" and these are the topological corridors along which urban communities have grown and can continue to develop.

Establishing these "skins" and "corridors" and mapping these "chreods" (none of them terms used by Ekistians) is not an easy matter. In one of their studies of an American city (Detroit), there were found to be 49 million alternatives for it by the year 2000. Through Ekistic analysis of the probable and the possible, these were reduced to 500,000; then to 11,000; then 312; then to 40; to 10; to 7; to 3; to 1. The "1" was not necessarily an "ideal" one—but the one that suited the objectives within the highly complex interrelationships of the five systems—nature, man, society, shells, and networks and all their subdivisions—over a large area of land comprising millions of human beings and envisaging their future development in a technological environment, most of whose innovations have not yet been invented.

Such approaches require an interdisciplinary program of a complexity that approaches that of the Manhattan Project of World War II and the contemporary Apollo program. The Doxiadis-System

The nuclear family was based on the notion that the biological unit was the primary unit for child rearing, but the nuclear family is one of the worst inventions for bringing up children that has ever been made.

MARGARET MEAD/"Child Rearing and the the Family," *Ekistics*, October, 1969

A gap is created between the settlement as built and the society which is waiting. The importance of marginal phenomena should not be neglected; an example is afforded by the hippy movement whose adepts prefer discomfort to the alienation of urban life. Also, the weekly exodus of citizens toward nature and the myth of holidays are proof of the inadaptation of actual conditions to the "style of life" to which society aspires.

ROBERT GREGOIRE/"Human Settlement and Society: Towards a Policy for the Future," *Ekistics*, October, 1969

The behavior of cells may illustrate the sociology and ecology of organic units in interaction as pieces of a continuous environment. A free cell is moving all the time. Movement is primary; what has to be explained is the stoppage of movement. Any torn piece of tissue invariably starts movement in the cells along the torn margin. The thing that sets them off is the disequilibrium between the free edge and the rest of the cells in the tissue (just like a city).

SUZANNE KELLER/"The Changing Family; Some Notes for Discussion," *Ekistics*, October, 1969

In the history of Western civilization, the geometry of right angles has formed almost the exclusive basis for determining the arrangement of urban streets and lots. But a systematic topological analysis of various grid patterns based on the study of the number of intersections for a given area and a unit segment length yields an interesting answer to the bothersome problem of circulation. The most fruitful pattern is a semi-regular tessellation of regular hexagons and triangles—what I would call a trihex.

ROBERT LE RICOLAIS/"The Trihex"
Progressive Architecture, Feb. '68

The historic moon landing oddly enough may serve as a catalyst for changes here on earth. The role of our landing on the moon can be thought of as a change in our collective self-image; as a renewal of self-confidence that man can do whatever he really sets himself to do, merged with impatience and shame about our not having done what we most want to do. I think this combination of hubris with humility will turn out to have significant import for the time ahead.

"Institutional Responses to Changing Attitudes"
Ekistics October, 1969

Peru, India and Japan are likely to be housing their poor in decent homes and communities long before the United States finds a creative way to eliminate its slums.

DAVID JACOBS/"Building—The Medieval Technocracy" *Interplay*, Aug.-Sept., 1969

Development Corporation uses 3200 experts, ranging from ecologists to nuclear physicists and astrophysicists, supplemented by 365 mathematicians. When basic data has been accumulated (and this may be done through compiling available statistics, door to door canvassing, in-depth interviews, traffic flow counts, etc.) it can be arranged in what is called an Ekistic Logarithmic Scale. Steve Barrett (in "The Cities: Meeting the Crisis"—SDS Magazine, December 1969) says that "The scale's smallest unit of measurement is the individual man and its largest, the largest conceivable space for settlement, the whole Earth."

When the logarithmic projection is plotted on a two-dimensional scale—say the number of shells on one axis and the number of humans on the other—it is possible to make an analysis that can lead to the sort of multi-dimensional space-point that Dr. Waddington talks about. From this, one can begin to examine the various interactions between the points in their various dimensions, and you can ask, "If we do that to the system here, then how will it affect the system over there"?

And if you have good enough data to begin with, and good enough technicians to program it, and large enough computers to process all of the possible permutations, then you may come up with an array of alternative futures. From this array you may pick the one you feel would be best to follow (if you are a city administrative official or a housing administrator, for instance). And if someone seriously questions your choice, you can run off the other alternatives and ask, "Do you like these any better?"

Although the entire process—data collection, processing, computerization, mathematical simulation, and arrays of alternates based on mathematical models—may appear mechanistic, the ultimate choice is still human, still based on intuition. But the intuitive part of man would, in this case, have vastly more organized systems of information from which to make its choices.

Population is growing too fast, inhabitable land area is too limited, disorder in the world's cities is increasing at too high a rate, to wait any longer for horse and buggy politics to solve the problems of an electronic age. ✿

A HOUSE IS NOT A HOME

Is shelter as much of a problem as we seem to think it is? What's being done *now*? Have there been any technological advances at all? Are they being implemented? How?

Journey with us, if you will, through the next few pages, as we explore some possible solutions to the housing "crisis." Some have succeeded . . . some have failed . . . more have never left the drawing boards.

It doesn't matter where you begin—backwards makes as much sense as the other way. Let your imagination and your knowledge of other projects fill in the areas we've missed and expand on what we have said. Not even a gas-station map can detail all the possible routes to your chosen destination.

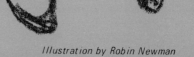

Illustration by Robin Newman

is urban renewal the answer?

What happens when an area is "selected" for urban renewal? Unfortunately, the project is usually approached in a very conventional way. The ground is·cleared, and there is implied a promise that those who are moved out will be moved back as soon as renewal is completed. They rarely are.

The project is completed; other low-income residents move in where the first group was displaced; the buildings age and are victims of the general apathy toward maintenance of "public housing." The cycle begins anew.

Developers are attracted to the project by attractive land prices, long-term FHA loan availability, and sometimes (not often enough) by the opportunity to make a contribution to the welfare of the community.

The developer will generally decide to hire an architect to "save the city," and the architect complies, working some sort of esthetic miracle in the process. Too often such miracles occur at the expense of room sizes, quality of workmanship, open spaces, and other little things.

To date, only about one twentieth of the housing demolished by urban renewal has been replaced.

"The old cities can be reorganized more cheaply, more efficiently and more quickly than we can build new cities. We could double the population simply by better use of the existing area, and at the same time organize the chaos . . . An aerial photograph of any major U.S. city makes it appear to be bombed out; vast areas are given over to empty plots and parking lots. These, plus railroad yards and even highways, would make ideal sites for future new towns within towns."

Nathaniel Owings, *Skidmore, Owings, and Merrill, Architects*

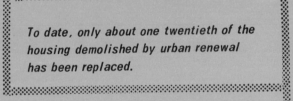

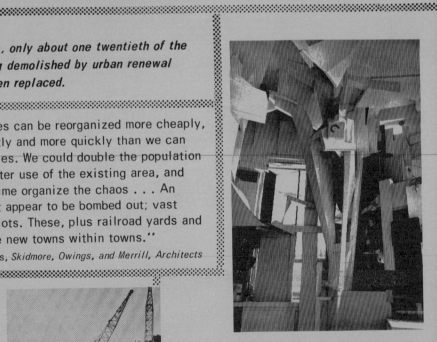

An urban renewal project that isn't one is being tried in Washington, D.C. Several years ago the public housing agency there discovered that it could be a lot cheaper to buy existing apartment buildings, including luxury buildings, than to spend up to $18,000 per unit to build new housing or renew slum areas. Since then, the city has acquired 600 one and two-bedroom apartments in luxury buildings, and is using these to house the elderly poor. As a part of what Mayor Walter Washington calls "a good bargain," some of the residents are comfortably ensconced in air-conditioned buildings with swimming pools and off-street parking—all for only $50 a month rent.

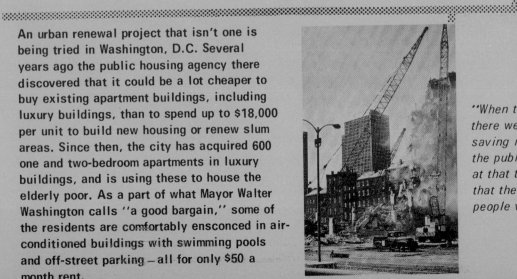

"When the surveys were made it was said that there were only five houses that were worth saving in that area. This was not true . . . at the public hearing the protests that arose at that time—and it was too late—indicated that the survey itself had not touched the people who occupied the area."

Mrs. Lillian Love
3-time urban renewal victim

APARTMENT

or

HOME

OWNER-

SHIP

?

During the 1950's, the single-family homes constituted almost 90% of total housing production. By 1969, multi-family units accounted for roughly 50% of total housing starts.

The age structure of the population dictates that a large percentage of housing units built during the next several years will be apartments or other multi-family dwellings. During the early Seventies, the number of house-holds headed by young people (under 35) will increase dramatically. By contrast, the number of households headed by those in the 35-55 age group will hardly increase at all. The latter group has to date accounted for the largest percentage of single-unit homeowners.

One of the most pressing needs for multi-family housing is among the elderly. For example, Nassau County, N.Y., reports that it has 600 units of ''senior citizen'' housing for a population of 160,000 elderly residents.

Some experts see changing racial patterns as another reason for the increase in numbers of families residing in apartments. The National Association of Home Builders, in a recent study, found that people are more willing to be racially integrated in apartments than in single-family neighborhoods. Possible declines in property values when blacks move in do not worry renters the way they do homeowners.

Apartment living is a world-wide phenomenon, and building multi-family units continues at break-neck speed. In the past five years, 600,000 apartments have been newly stacked-up in Moscow. An oil company is building a single development of 12,000 to 15,000 dwelling units, designed to house at least 60,000 people, on a plot of land in Hong Kong formerly used for a petroleum storage depot. The Italian government has been rocked by massive strikes of workers from all classes, protesting the critical housing shortage all over the country. The government has admitted that 20 million new dwelling rooms must be added to Italy's national inventory by the early seventies, and they're working to meet that goal. West Germany recently announced that they've completed 10 million apartments in the past ten years, and they see no signs of a construction slow-down during the present decade.

The rapid increase in costs means that it is less and less possible for a family to buy a house if only one member is working.

Michael Sumichrast, *Chief Economist
National Association of Homebuilders*

the word is PREFAB

The building method most suited to take full advantage of the systems approach is prefabrication. Essentially, prefabrication means the emergence, from assembly-line factories, of components as large as an entire wall or a complete one-piece bathroom, all designed to fit together with a minimum of on-site craft labor. The elements are transported to the site and lifted into place.

This method especially lends itself to use in the building of tall apartment buildings, where floor by floor vertical repetition makes use of identical elements.

The prefabrication concept is not new. In 1624, the English erected a paneled wooden house brought here from England and reassembled in Cape Ann. Thomas Edison drew plans for a Florida home, had it built in sections in Maine, and then transported it by schooner to Florida, where it was erected in 1886.

Over 80% of Soviet housing and 50% of French and British housing have employed prefabricated methods.

"Stealing" a design from nature, students of one architectural school have suggested shelter construction based on the filament process, which is similar to spinning a cocoon. Glass fibers coated with a binding resin are wound on a rotating forming surface to make shells of houses. The material is 80% glass and 20% polyester resin, and is strong, waterproof, fire-and-wear-resisting, and easy to repair. When color pigment is incorporated, the material will not require upkeep or painting for at least twenty years. The cocoon units can be stacked or joined on one level to form split level or single-storied, multi-winged homes.

The most highly-publicized application of modular building methods in North America was the Habitat exposition at Expo 67 in Montreal. A bank of apartments cast as concrete boxes on the ground were lifted into place on a structural rack, giving the appearance of gigantic shoe boxes. Each unit maintained an individual identity as interior plans differed, boxes were shifted on the site, and height of the stacks was varied.

The Home Manufacturers Association reports that prefabricated homes accounted for 30% of the market in 1969 and will corner 50% by 1975.

An immediate cost saving in modular building is labor. In factory-produced shelter components, $3.44-an-hour assembly line labor is used. Labor furnished by members of the craft unions at the building sites costs $5.52 per hour.

What's being done in the pre-fab construction field?
— a Montreal company reports it can produce a three-bedroom home selling for $12,300 which requires only 800 man-hours of labor, about half the time required for conventional construction, and 85% of that time in the factory — a big cost advantage . . .
— a large steel company has developed a modular system using steel frames and plans to erect two hotels at the new Disneyland in Florida using the system . . .
— Isocorp has developed a modular system of precast, prestressed concrete construction for office buildings.
— one paper firm is mass-producing paper houses — inexpensive, built to last 20 years, and suitable for sprayed applications of resin, fiber glass or cement after assembly.
— a major construction company is mass-producing homes utilizing steel-reinforced concrete walls and newly developed quick-set cement to reduce overall construction time as much as 70%. They claim that they are able to market a 1,140 square foot, three-bedroom, two bath home, complete with stove, oven, garbage disposal and central heating, for as little as $11,000.

An all-aluminum modular home that can be trucked to a prepared site and erected in one day by five unskilled laborers, at a factory cost as low as $8.60 a square foot, has been developed in California. The system includes relocatable walls, ceiling tile, vinyl floors, complete kitchen, bathroom fixtures, water heater and forced air furnace — all in the package. A fully-conceived systems approach.

A blue-chip company has developed a prefabricated factory which in turn produces prefabricated building components on-site. Once land has been cleared, a mobile factory — composed of trailers whose sides and roofs are lowered and joined together to form a continuous assembly-line network — moves in and begins turning out finished sections of floors, walls, ceilings and roofs on-site.

Dome construction, inspired by Buckminster Fuller's innovation in 1927, has gained nationwide acceptance and is being put to a variety of uses.

One commercial tool sales company offers the skeleton of a dome home for $2,925. An owner can hire a contractor to finish the structure and acquire an 1,100 square-foot home for $10 to $12 per foot.

One Pennsylvanis company relates that in building units for installation in Connecticut, the company must pay travel and living expenses for inspectors, licensed in Connecticut, to come to the plant and watch the production line, all due to building codes written before the advent of factory wiring and plumbing processes.

Modular, prefab housing has its problems. Some minority group militants ridicule the new dwellings as another shoddy effort to solve housing problems literally "overnight."

The assembly-line building concept also meets resistance from the unions. Building homes in factories may increase the employment of industrial workers, but it decreases the need for highly-paid craftsmen at the site. In many areas, the building trades unions have strongly influenced building codes to protect members from such technological innovations.

Many urbanologists agree that the wide use of aluminum, plastics and space-age adhesives have made mobile homes the best housing value for the money available now in the U.S. Advanced technology in the mobile home industry has been possible largely because its manufacture is exempt from conventional building codes, labor restrictions, and FHA regulations.

How successfully have mobile homes penetrated the shelter market? Sales rose dramatically from 235,000 units in 1967 to 330,000 in 1968. In 1969, sales topped 400,000 units and predictions are for sales of 1 million units annually by 1975. Mobile homes dominate the low-cost housing market, in fact, and are now responsible for 90% of all homes below $15,000.

What's the tab for a non-mobile, mobile solution to the shortage of low-cost housing? A two-bedroom, air-conditioned, completely furnished mobile home can be purchased for as little as $4,000. Double-wide units, more luxurious all around, often run as high as $20,000, and some truly elegant models have been sold in Palm Springs, Calif., for over $60,000. Some builders are now offering two-story mobile homes, which retail for approximately $17,000.

Mobile home manufacturers attribute much of their success to the fact that they are able to run a low-overhead business. They claim they can turn out a fully-furnished aluminum-siding model in less than 1/2 hour and earn a better-than-average profit. Such speed is possible through utilization of modular construction, in which whole rooms are built separately and then quickly dropped into the trailer body.

The major obstacle in the development of the mobile home market is the lack of parking spaces. There is a scarcity of well-planned parks, and tight money has made the acquisition of suitable land even more difficult. In a recent year 317,000 mobile homes were built but only 100,000 parking spaces developed. Obsolete zoning codes, prohibiting the location of parks within easy commuting distance of major metropolitan areas, further hinder the market's development.

The cost difference between a mobile and a permanent home is the labor factor. Labor accounts for approximately 33% of the total cost of a permanent home, and rarely exceeds 10% in a mobile home.

What common design characteristic is shared by a modern aircraft
carrier, a medieval castle, and Chicago's Marina City? Each is
an "omnibuilding" — an environmental structure that contains
elements of all human activities. It provides for a multiplicity of uses
(educational, residential, commercial, recreational, light
industrial, religious, etc.), and contains systems for
both vertical and horizontal movement of people and goods.
Electrical and mechanical systems are fully integrated.

OMNIWHAT?

Omnibuildings — present and planned — count
among their ranks Grand Central Station,
Rockefeller Center, Cumbernauld Town Center,
Market Street East in Philadelphia, and
Embarcadero Center in San Francisco. Each of
these is an "impure" structure, lacking one or
another feature of the true omnibuilding, but
is enough of a self-sufficient shelter system to
be a good example of a self-contained
environment within a single building.

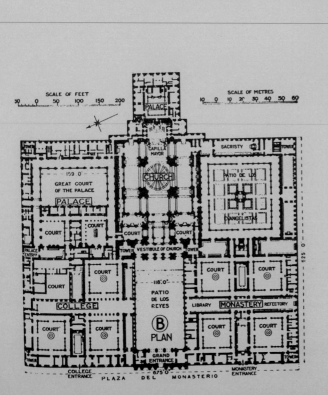

*There are hazards to life in an omnibuilding
— especially a high-rise one. Residents of the
Hancock Building in Chicago report that they enjoy
living above the clouds on the 92nd floor, but they're often
fooled when they venture downward a quarter mile.
The sun shining through their windows up there
in heaven is often the liquid variety when
they descend through the cloud layers
and reach the street.*

*The creator of the omnibuilding in Chicago describes
it as "a combination of spaces for . . . total living,
with density so intense as to achieve a critical
mass. This means that density wherein human energy,
expressed daily in the structure, is self-regenerative,
economically and spiritually."*

Some say the aim of the new towns is to pack as many people as possible into a relatively small area without having them feel congested. The Europeans are achieving this through wide-spread use of high-rise apartments, which ensures the compactness of town while providing land for lawns, woods, lakes, and playing fields.

New town planners mingle all types of activities and buildings — there are no zoning rules prohibiting multiple-family dwellings built next to single family units. Typically, each area is planned so that there is a small store or shopping center within walking distance of every home.

Developers say that the employment base provided is what distinguishes a new town from any other subdivision.

The concept of the "new town" is to plan and locate people and employment in modern cities of planned size, where they have access to work, to recreational areas, to open spaces, and to cultural facilities. Ideally, there would be a balance of workers and varied occupations, of open space and developed areas, of economic, social and occupational groups.

"The most important short-run consequence of the interest in "new towns" is that it has attracted large industrial companies into housing construction. If they are not really creating new towns, they are at least getting into the housing business."

FORTUNE, May, 1967

NEW TOWNS

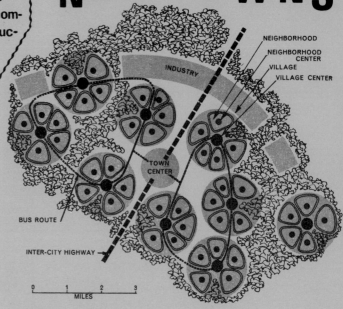

NEIGHBORHOOD
NEIGHBORHOOD CENTER
VILLAGE
VILLAGE CENTER
INDUSTRY
TOWN CENTER
BUS ROUTE
INTER-CITY HIGHWAY

0 1 2 3
MILES

America's most publicized "new town" is Columbia, Maryland, a twenty-two square-mile area (approximately the size of Manhattan Island), located in the Washington-Baltimore corridor and designed to house nearly 30,000 families. The town is divided into villages grouped around a general downtown area. Each village is composed of a cluster of five or six neighborhoods.

The town is designed to host a variety of specialty shops and public services — schools, churches, libraries and recreational centers. A transportation network has been incorporated into the design, and provision has been made for a mini-bus system to operate within the confines of Columbia. As many jobs as possible will be provided in the town.

The most widely-acclaimed "planned city" is Tapiola, near Helsinki, Finland. Designed in 1952, it is still considered the model among cities of its type.

The town is divided into three neighborhoods, separated by green belts. The neighborhoods focus on the town center, housing the business offices, churches, assembly hall and larger stores. Each neighborhood has its own shopping center serving the 5,000 to 6,000 residents of the immediate area.

High-rise apartments and low single-family, garden-type houses are intermingled, lending variety and a sense of spaciousness to the area. Slightly over half the workers are classified as white-collar; just under half are lower-income, blue collar wage-earners.

Eighty per cent of Tapiola's housing is state-subsidized, and is inexpensive by U.S. standards. A five-room house with garage and sauna (a necessity, of course) costs about $13,000 American dollars.

When is a new town really a suburb? A reported conversation between a Baltimore symphony director and an official of the new town Columbia went like this. Asked whether Columbia was to be a city or a suburb, the executive replied "Columbia will be a city."

"Well, are you going to have things like a burlesque house?" asked the symphony director.

"No; if the people want that, they can go into Baltimore," was the reply.

"Then," said the director, "you're a suburb."

An experimental city its developers claim will "open the doors into a new society, a planetary society for a new man . . . will be the synthesis of cybernetics and yoga—the city with the space-ship technology" is being planned in India.

Auroville will be located on the east coast of South India, near Pondicherry. It is planned to provide housing, education, work, food, leisure and a creative environment for 50,000 people from all walks of life and from all countries.

experimental cities

Artificial levels will initially be built on the naturally flat land, and a circular macrostructure will define the shape of the town. Approximately 25,000 people will live in a ring that encircles the town's central area and its theaters, recreation halls, hotels, forums for meetings, sportsgrounds, meditation gardens, etc.

None of the streets or avenues will be straight—each will meander among private single-story houses and wide open spaces. Fountains and squares will surprise the visitor around each curve. The overall effect, Auroville's designers hope, will be one of peace and tranquility—a never-ending succession of discoveries and perspectives.

The residential ring will be encircled by a hundred-meter-wide canal where artificial islands will provide a home for a variety of bird life, and 21st century gondolas will provide transportation in a town where cars are parked on the perimeter and forbidden inside.

On the innermost part of the ring, a Garden of Unity will be found encircling a lake whose running waters will supply Auroville's canals, fountains and paddy-fields. Here, it is believed, will be the core around which the rings are gravitating in wave-like motions, like Yin and Yang of Eastern spiritualism.

A newly formed group calling itself Community Matrix has released its plan for the redevelopment of Trinidad, Colorado, a city on the the verge of receiving Federal assistance for improvement.

This experimental city would be covered by a climate-controlled dome utilizing solar energy. In the midst of a bitter Colorado winter, the inhabitants could work comfortably in their gardens in shirt sleeves.

Walls within the dome would be moveable partitions of wood, plastic, glass, and dyed cloth.

All traffic and public service buildings (banks, stores, fire department, parking lots, etc.) would be underground.

Lighting would be computerized—a continuous flow of changing light would ensure that no 24-hour period would be the same, and colors might change according to the specific activities of the day.

The entire ground floor is planned to be a "garden of changes," where the climate control will allow plants of all types and from all regions to grow simultaneously.

A plan to spend in excess of $800 million to build an experimental city on a site across the bay from Anchorage, Alaska, has been announced.

The city, dubbed "Seward's Success," will be totally enclosed, and will contain a petroleum center, a commercial mall, a residential mall, a sports arena, schools, and a transportation system composed of moving sidewalks. Cars will be prohibited.

Residents of the bubble-topped city will have access to Anchorage via an aerial cable car across the bay, and eventually under the bay, on a subway system.

Questioned as to their motivation, the developers say "we're building a city for people . . ."

little boxes, little boxes*

We live, for the most part, in little boxes. They may be clustered together, as in office buildings or apartment houses or hotels, or they may be scattered over the countryside as in tract housing. But they are still little boxes. As forms for habitation, they are relics of another age. Perhaps, instead of trying to build more little boxes, it would be useful to explore other shelter systems that make better use of the new materials and technologies now available to us.

*MALVINA REYNOLDS, Columbia Records

When we sit down to contemplate the little boxes in which we spend most of our lives, there are two statements (as regards the United States) that keep buzzing around our heads and making it hard for us to focus.

The first of these is, "Between now and the end of the century, the U. S. will have to build as many structures as it has built from Colonial times to the present."

The other statement is, "To maintain decent housing standards, we need to build 2.6 million new single family dwellings each year for the next ten years." This would represent an extraordinary effort, since the annual average of new housing starts since 1960 is about 1.4 million.

The first statement, "We need to build as much, etc." is hard to pin down. It is doubtful that anyone knows, with any accuracy, how much shelter has been built in the U.S. since Colonial days. Multiplying an unknown, or at least indeterminate, figure by two does not get us very far.

Even assuming we knew how much man-made structure had been built, remodeled, re-used—there is no reason to believe we need *twice* as much as the cumulative total of 350 years in the next 30 years.

What is bothersome about these two statements is that they are paralyzing because of their magnitude. We do not know where the skilled labor, the financing, nor the materials would come from. So we sit hypnotized, staring at the prospect of doubling the number of all the little boxes we have ever had. And virtually nothing happens.

Are there other ways to approach the "shelter problem"?

The assumption of single-time/single-use space appears to be a legacy of the Middle Ages. The more rooms, the more powerful the signal of affluence that was broadcast. The concept—as something to be desired—was brought to North America by successive waves of immigrants, whose desire was to live like "The lord in his manor".

Today, we reap the sad heritage of that longing. It is probable that 75 per cent of the living space in a middle-income private dwelling is not used more than a few hours a day, by any member of the family, for any reason. The figures are no better

If we examine the laws under which a city operates, we see a structure of regulations which could hardly be better designed to create stagnation and decline. The aging and decay of buildings is central to the urban decline process, yet we see throughout our tax laws and regulations numerous incentives to keep old buildings in place. As the value of a building decreases, so do the assessed taxes. The reduced expenses make it possible to retain the old building longer.

JAY W. FORRESTER, Prof. of Management, MIT "Systems Analysis as a Tool for Urban Planning"–October, 1969

In a hundred years a technical civilization is born, disruptive in its power and its possibilities, upsetting everything in its passage...A revolution in circumstances, in lives, in institutions. A black wretchedness, a black disorder: men suddenly lose their water level and their plumb line...The tentacular cities were born: Paris, London, New York, Rio de Janeiro, Buenos Aires. The countryside was emptied. Here was a double catastrophe. A menacing loss of equilibrium.

LE CORBUSIER/*Concerning Town Planning*

Wood's Law: The more unworkable the urban plan, the greater the probability of implementation.

ROBERT WOOD/"Groupings and Urban Government" *Ekistics*, October, 1969

In North American cities...the checkerboard was the elementary patern of land division whether applied to virgin land or in extensions to older cities of European type. The latter is the case of New York, where expansion to the north, planned in 1811, gave rise to problems of connection — hence Washington Square, Madison Square and and Union Square. Semantically meagre, the gridiron pattern has no other meaning than that of an efficient tool. After serving colonizers, traders and gold seekers, it became the instrument of industrial capitalism, simultaneously available for speculation or traffic circulation.

FRANCOISE CHOAY/*The Modern City: Planning in the 19th Century*

The truth is that in this work we have neglected the amenities of life. We have forgotten that endless rows of black boxes, looking out on dreary streets and squalid backyards, are not really homes for people and can never become such, however complete may be the drainage system, however pure the water supply, or however detailed the by-laws under which they are built.

RAYMOND UNWIN/*Town Planning in Practice* (1909)

Modern socialist philosophy is rooted in utopian ideals of 18th-Century thought, as, for example, expressed popularly by Jean-Jacques Rousseau (1712-1778). At the end of the 19th Century it was believed by many social philosophers that social reforms could be achieved gradually through moral and intellectual education leading to a future ideal state...in utopias of this period, fundamental, natural and primitive conditions were stressed, the emphasis on exercise, health and physical well-being was corollary to the wakening interest in natural life.

TONY GARNIER/*The Cité Industrielle*

for commercial shelter. We know that nearly all of them are used one-third of the time on work-days (8 hours out of 24) and, in a year's time, allowing for week-ends and holidays, are occupied only 81 (24-hour) days, out of 365.

If the commercial structures we now have were used two or three shifts per day, seven days a week, we probably could meet most of our commercial shelter needs with existing structures.

The mere reassignment of time-use would greatly reduce peak hour demands on transportation facilities, public utilities, police traffic control, tow cars, ambulances, emergency hospital facilities, automobile insurance rates, etc. And none of this would require building a single square foot of new shelter.

Looking at the second statement — the one about the need for 2.6-million new housing starts per year — one finds some interesting things. Only about half of this, apparently, is for "new household formation." Most of the remainder is required because of existing units being destroyed to make room for urban renewal, urban "development," highways and street widening, expansion of commercial and manufacturing activities into residential areas, obsolescence due to age or neglect, and destruction from "natural causes," such as fires and floods.

With the exception of fires and floods, much of the other destruction might be reduced rather simply by the adoption of a different order of priorities.

Assume that the figure relating to new household formation really does account for half of the 26 million new units needed in the next 10 years. One of the supports for this figure is that most of the young people will desire to marry, have children, and begin the complex operations that will enable them at the end of 20 to 30 years to "own their own home," however obsolete it may be at that time.

This appears to be a direct, linear projection of the mores of a society that began to change dramatically shortly after World War II. It is not certain that all, or even a majority, of the people who become of marriageable age during the next 30 years will follow that pattern.

In the U.S., the dream of a "home of one's own" was based very largely on federal subsidy programs through the Homestead Act, reinforced later in the form of FHA and VA loans at favorable rates of interest.

It was *this*, not affluence, that largely led to the exodus of inner city populations to the suburbs. It was difficult to get FHA or VA loans for existing housing in the city, because of high land costs—but relatively easy outside. So that's where the developers went, and that's where the population followed. Only those who could not qualify for loans, or those who were wealthy enough not to need them, stayed in the central city.

For most persons, owning one's own home was at best a dream; an extension of the frontier mythology from a preceding pre-industrial society. Few were ever to own their home outright; most were renting or making payments on long-term mortgages that were seldom paid off because of the growing mobility of the U.S. population, with an average stay in any one place of about five years.

The longer number of years required to get a rudimentary education in a technologically exploding society; changing attitudes towards sex and morality, largely due to the growing availability of fairly cheap, reasonably effective contraceptives; the declining role of institutionalized religions; the uncertainties surrounding forced military conscription even in peace time; general disillusion with the desirability of owning things (including "real property"); the search for life styles that center on human relationships instead of property ownership—all of these trends (and many more)—*may* combine to reduce the rate of new home formations as now predicted by statisticians, many of whom seem to feel that the past is a guide to the future.

If this indeed be so, the now-accepted projections for "durable goods"—plumbing fixtures, stoves, refrigerators, freezers, furnaces, air conditioners, etc., may also be rather far from the mark.

The steady growth of the youth commune movement (where basic appliances and utilities are shared), the rising popularity of mobile homes, (both for the young and the elderly), the growth of multiple family units (such as commercial, condominium and cooperative apartment houses, residential hotels, etc.)—nearly all resulting from increased land, financing and construction costs—argue that the concept of the single family dwelling

Industrialized methods account for 25 per cent of all building in Europe and this is expected to increase. The key to the success of European firms is the development of building systems designed to take full advantage of mechanization and automation. Generally they have had the greatest impact in high-rise, high density apartment housing where precast concrete components form the basic building blocks of the system.

"Modular/Systems Building"/*Contractors' Electrical Equipment*, November, 1969

Nature is vanishing. The city is vanishing. The accelerating dissolution of both ideal nature and ideal city has induced a massive compromise, an attempt to salvage elements of both...The suburb, camp follower of technocratic culture, is spreading from the United States to the most distant corners of the earth with its myth of providing in a single package the convenience of the town house and the enjoyment of the country house. But both the pseudo city and the pseudo country, with commuters shuttling between them in a desperate search for satisfaction, which neither can provide, appear in the end to promote little more than discontent. The suburb's promise of country life within easy reach of the pleasures of the city has proved false.

SERGE CHERMAYEFF/CHRISTOPHER ALEXANDER/*Community and Privacy* (1963)

PEOPLE WHO LIVE IN GLASS HOUSES... One of the more ingenious solutions to low-cost housing has been proposed by Philo Farnsworth, III, of Bolinas, California. It suggests a "bubble" made of prefabricated components of wound fiber glass yarn and metalized Mylar. According to his calculations, a house of this type could be mass produced and erected for about $2.50 per square foot, in one-and-a-half days. It contains four bedrooms and 2,500

photo by David Duffin

square feet. A central column provides the utility core and guides convection currents for heating and cooling. The glass is "one way" so that residents could enjoy a panoramic, 360-degree view, but outsiders could not see in.

on its own little lot is already a figment of the imagination for all but the most affluent.

Even if it were desirable to build single family dwellings it should be possible to build them much more economically than we now do.

Take a "typical" suburban block with 20 houses on it. If it is middle class it will have—in *each* house—a complete stove, dishwasher, etc. No one of these will be used more than a few hours a day; some of them perhaps only an hour each week.

If one assumes that working hours during a 24-hour day can be staggered into two or three shifts, over a seven day week (with holidays also staggered), then it is possible to think of multiple use of facilities and space. People who live in expensive apartment houses and hotels do this all the time.

Why not, then, build housing that shares—as it does now, in most cases, the water sewage and electrical systems—also cooking facilities, space heating and air conditioning, food and equipment storage spaces, etc. These could be supplemented in individual houses or apartments with small, prefabricated utility casettes (such as may be found in mobile homes, travel trailers and boats), that allow for fixing light meals at the inhabitants' discretion.

The idea of the wholly independent, completely self-contained "living machine" grew out of pioneer days (in the U.S.) and pre-industrialized days (in Europe), when houses were isolated. General community services (drinking water, utilities, waste disposal, etc.) were not available. Today we still go on building individual houses as if they were lost somewhere out there on the prairie.

What is being said here is that, if we continue to perpetuate the mythology of the early American frontier, no conceivable amount of effort will meet the housing needs of the kinds of population numbers we are likely to have in the next three decades. Nor will our natural resources support such an effort for very long.

Much of the cost of a house, apart from interest rates, lies in the continued enforcement of obsolete building codes that specify certain materials to be used. It is quite conceivable to have "functional" codes which simply require that a structure meet certain fire and safety requirements, regard-

We build permanently. And it's the houses we
build to stand forever that become the houses of the
ghettos. We build too well and there's no way to
get away from the deterioration. Methods now
exist to package a house, ship it to the site, blow it
up like a balloon. The balloon can be used
as a form for pouring a rigid structure, or it can be
used as it is ... If you decided to move, you
would call the city, and they would spray your
plastic castle and it would disappear ... There
would be no rubble to get rid of.

JOHN J. REUKEMA, Pres.
American Institute of Building Designers – July, 1969

With the trends of increasing mobility throughout
the world, we foresaw the possibility that no one
would be staying at any one place long enough
to warrant the construction of "permanent"
shelters. As a total service facility, the housing
needs would encompass not only shelter but
communications — with its own resultant education
(via TV, computers), medical information and
attention (via telephone to a world central
medical computer), personal contact with anyone,
anywhere — and mobility, with anyone
going anywhere.

R. BUCKMINSTER FULLER
The World Game - 1969

In Synanon the family is not eliminated,
but ceases to think of itself as a self-sufficient
economic unit and thus makes itself more
receptive to the idea of being what it should be:
the unit of love and procreation. When it is
no longer necessary for each family to do its
own entertaining and have its own livingroom and
its own kitchen, when it is no longer necessary for it
to provide for its own transportation, it finds
itself with more time and means to work, to
play, to study, to socialize.

GUY ENDORE/"Synanon City"
Synanon Pamphlet Series **6, 1968**

less of the materials used. Such materials, equal to and often superior to, traditional building materials, are available in quantity, and frequently at less cost, in many areas today.

The most complicated shelter built so far by man was the Apollo moon rocket system. About 85% of its labor cost was for non-skilled workers; 15% for skilled workers. The average single family dwelling house in the U.S. requires 90% skilled, 10% unskilled. When one takes into account that there is an increasing shortage of skilled workers and an increasing surplus of non-skilled workers, one wonders how much longer such a system can last.

The "standard" single family dwelling in the U.S. takes from six weeks to two months to complete. Its exact equivalent can be factory prefabricated, trucked to the site and erected, ready for occupancy, in 18 hours, at half the labor and materials cost. Considering that the manufacturing process, whereby home construction components are cut, fitted and partially assembled is a quiet, smog-free operation (just the kind of light industry the suburbs say they are looking for) and that it takes relatively unskilled labor (and we are *supposed* to be trying to find ways to use this labor supply), the approach we are now using for housing makes no sense whatsoever.

As a result, less and less housing is being built to meet the needs of the growing number of poor in our country today. The median cost per house put on the market in 1969 was $26,000. Something like 72% of the families occupying "sub-standards" housing in the U.S. have total family incomes of less than $3,000 per year.

One problem here is in defining "sub-standard." The standard usually is based on middle-income group requirements, because they make up the rules.

We may labor under a serious misconception — that the task that faces the nation is to bring "sub-standard" housing up to the level of middle income housing. Probably most of the poor would settle for water fit to drink, a toilet that worked, and a roof that didn't leak. It might be useful to see what the bare minimum for survival and a modicum of comfort might be for those who can afford no more.

What other alternatives *are* open to us? Merely providing a "shell" does not satisfy the requirement for housing. Most human beings can devise some sort of shelter that provides homeostasis and some biological privacy. They can, and do, all over the urban world, make shells from flattened cans, scrap sheet metal from dumps, gunny sacks stretched on bent strips of chrome from abandoned automobiles and coated with mud. Any individual, couple or group working together can devise mere shelter from the enormous waste produced by a linear, technological society. It may not be elegant, but it works.

What individuals cannot do—in urban situations—is provide networks. Where and how get safe drinking water? Where and how dispose of wastes? Where get electricity? Or gas for cooking or heating? How get transportation to and from sources of food, medicine, legal aid, municipal services, schools, churches?

Instead of worrying about shells, perhaps a realistic approach to the "housing crisis" in our times might be to provide and maintain networks. Given the networks, people could probably figure some way to provide their own shells. Since something like one-third of *all* urban acreage is presently unused, that might be a good place to begin. If and when some higher income or tax base use can be found for the land, the people living there would simply be made to move to some other network-prepared area.

Building and maintaining systems is, of course, much more complicated than building shells. But with the use of computer-aided systems analysis, even the enormous complexity of systems in urban areas is susceptible to analysis. One could imagine ultimately some sort of regional or ecologic management system that dealt solely with networks, replacing the wasteful systems of separate institutions.

A more sophisticated approach to providing space for shells might be, as has been done in Hong Kong, to erect steel uprights and beams, with poured-in-place concrete slabs, with the requisite utility networks built in, and simply to turn them over to the people to provide their own shells within the framework.

(Continued on page 72)

The "House of the Future," built at Disneyland, was planned for family living and conformed to all Los Angeles building codes. The structure consisted of thin (0.3 inch) curved projecting shells of molded glass fiber reinforced polyesters. Floor slabs were of the same material bonded as sandwich facings to a honeycomb core. The parts were fastened with epoxy adhesives, and joints were sealed with polysulfides. In ten years, about 20 million people tramped through the house. It withstood high winds and several mild to moderate earthquakes.

LLOYD W. DUNLAP, JR./ *Chemical & Engineering News,* **Mar. 11, 1968**

After it was turned on the structure began to inflate, barely revealing the outlines of its form—a multi-sectioned, soft structure consisting of a large central cone-shaped chamber connected by labyrinthine tubes to three other chambers. The two smaller red chambers were on one end, and the third, somewhat larger, was at the opposite end... When full-blown, the structure had a nice squashy Pop Art look.

NICHOLAS POLITES/"Description of Inflatoenvironment"/ *Office Design,* **November 1969**

It weighs 85 pounds on the bathroom scales (when it's packed). It looks like a bundle of old, outsized black plastic raincoats. One man can, of course, carry the package easily. But what is it? It's a church—large enough for a congregation of 200. What's more, it's currently being used to good religious effect in the French town of Montigey-les-Cormeilles near Paris.

San Francisco Chronicle
September 28, 1969

Illustration by Uta Nietiet

THE SHAPE OF THINGS TO COME? — It is possible that the houses of the future will be much different than those in which we now live. Below are three possibilities. Top photo, shows the "squirt-a-house" designed by architectural students at Yale; a womb-shaped habitat made of sprayed-on plastic. Similar constructions have appeared in England, the Scandinavian countries, and the U.S.A. The middle photo shows a prototype four-bedroom, 1,500 square foot home with walls of three-inch polyurethane core, faced on the outside with rough sawn pattern aluminum siding, and inside with tempered hardboard. Being introduced in California, it is said that the components for a complete shell can be factory produced in 42 minutes and erection of complete house takes two to three weeks. No wood or nails are used. Bottom photo shows the "Futuro" house, designed in Finland and offered commercially in the U.S. The shell is made of polyurethane foam, the 20 windows of acrylic. Interior and exterior are made of fiber glass, including the furniture. It has 500 square feet of living area at window height, and the whole unit can be delivered to the site by helicopter. Unfurnished shell is offered for $10,000; furnished at $14,000.

Photo courtesy of "California Living," San Francisco EXAMINER

At a still higher level, it might be possible to take some of the now-unused urban land, install the necessary networks, and then truck in used but no longer marketable mobile homes. These would be far better housing than most of the poor in the U.S. have ever had.

Every year a certain number of relatively large ocean-going vessels are removed from service and "mothballed" or scrapped. Considering that much of the sub-standard housing is clustered around seaports (or the Great Lakes, in the U.S.) it might be useful to investigate whether some of these, at minimum conversion cost, might not be moored permanently to provide housing for the working people and the unemployed.

The nation is dotted with monumental sports stadia, some of which are used only a few days out of the year. Might it not be possible (since utility networks are already installed) to convert much of

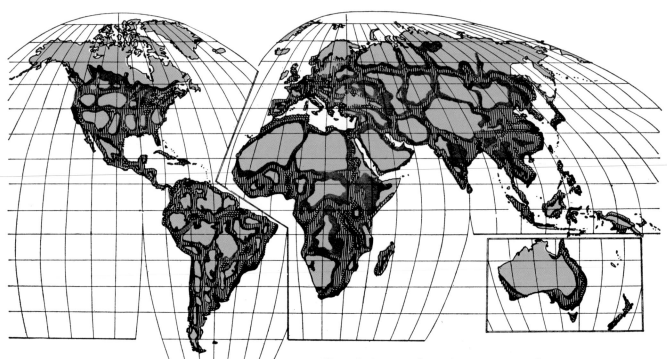

If population growth continues at, or near, its present rate, and urban communities continue to spread along the routes they are now following, then, by 2100 the world-city-state of high density urban population may have the configuration shown above.

Ekistics: the future of human settlements **1969**

the unused area under the stands into apartments, and bus the inhabitants to a picnic or an outing, during the few hours throughout the year when the stadia are being used for sports?

A considerable amount of what might be livable space is now being wasted beneath "cloverleaf" interchanges on major freeways. The land beneath the rising approaches produces neither private nor public income. Yet it has a roof (i.e. the highway above) and side supports, and might be converted, through the installation of utilities networks, into living area.

These suggestions may seem extreme, but they are well within existing capabilities of our contemporary technology; they could provide habitat of a quality somewhat superior to much of the urban and rural housing available to low-income groups in this country today. Their implementation need not entail the billions upon billions of dollars that would be required to bring "substandard" housing up to standard.

What has been suggested are merely interim solutions. But they might buy time to implement some of the plans for "new towns" and "experimental cities" which have been on the drawing boards since the turn of the century; to complete some of the urban renewal and development projects already under way; and time to try new approaches to housing a growing population, particularly of the young and the elderly. Neither the "new towns" nor the "experimental cities," as now planned, appear to offer much hope of adequate housing for the wholly unemployed, the ill, the physically handicapped, nor the elderly.

For the United States, at least, the practicality of establishing and maintaining new towns and experimental cities remains to be explored. It may be that through the use of nuclear energy and by tapping through deep wells the bodies of fresh water underlying the continental mantle, it may be possible to build large cities where none have been built before.

(Historically, as mentioned earlier, large urban complexes have tended to build up along the edges of bodies of water, or in the center of large agricultural areas, following the terrain along corridors of energy exchanges. It might be within the range

In Europe, as in the U.S., the new towns really are extensions of the big cities with an added input of planning. Bijlmermeer and Amstelveen are just beyond the built-up areas of Amsterdam in the Netherlands. Vallingby, Farsta and Taby, Sweden's new towns, are well within the Stockholm metropolitan area. Tapiola and Espoo Bay in Finland are just minutes by car from downtown Helsinki. Cumbernauld and East Kilbride lie within the main industrial belt of Scotland, between Glasgow and Edinburgh. And most of the English new towns are in a ring around London.

"A Look at Europe's New Towns"/ *U.S. News & World Report*, Oct. 21, 1968

A self-contained city of concrete and glass for 300,000 persons, built on pilings 15 miles offshore in the English Channel, and called "Sea City," is the answer of a British design task force to the rapidly growing demands for living and working space. The designers propose a 180-foot high amphitheater-like structure, roughly circular in plan, that would form an artificial lagoon. The wall itself would house two-thirds of the population, plus shops, offices, industry and utilities. The other 100,000 would live in three-story buildings of glass-fiber reinforced plastic erected on concrete pontoons anchored within the lagoon.

"Running Out of Land, Build at Sea"/ *Engineering News-Record*, April 18, 1968

The Japanese people are methodically expanding their living space in the one direction open to them — straight down. Since World War II, Tokyo has built no less than 15 major "chikagai," or underground streets. These are wide, well-lighted corridors, many with street names, all of them flanked by shops and stalls... Nor is the subterranean expansion limited to Tokyo. There are five underground complexes in Osaka... and others in Yokohama, Hagoya, Himeji, Fukuoka, Sasebo. In fact, every major Japanese city has at least one chikagai by now. The country as a whole can count 40 in all.

BERNARD KRISHER/*Newsweek*

The major difficulty encountered in eliminating the ghettos of existing communities is that efforts to redistribute housing, schooling, and recreation run up against prejudice and natural resistance to a change in established patterns. Obviously, in the case of existing cities, change by fiat cannot be enforced. In the New Cities, there would not be status quo to defend, nor change to enforce. Its urban structure would be conceived to make racial and economic integration an element in its basic design.

EDGARDO CONTINI/"New Cities for America"
The Center Magazine, Oct.-Nov., 1969

Columbia is intended to synthesize a way of life pursued, but rarely attained, by the American middle class since World War II. The firm's promotion claims... "Columbia is a symphony in the woods on a summer evening, a horseback ride along a wooded trail, a dip in a pool, a golf or tennis match. It is a place of beauty where nature has been preserved and enhanced. It is acres of green meadows, trees, lakes, streams and rolling hills. It is a place where the smile of a friend and the nod from a neighbor give it meaning and purpose... It is designed for people. It is people."

"Columbia: American Dream in One Big Package"/
Engineering News-Record, Nov. 21, 1968

A plan arranges organs in order, thus creating organism or organisms. The organs possess distinctive qualities, specific differences. What are they? lungs, heart, stomach... I am claiming sun, space and green surroundings for everybody and striving to provide you with an efficient system of circulation."

LE CORBUSIER/*Creation is a Patient Search* **1966**

of technology to establish cities that no longer conform to the historical development; but nobody really knows. Certainly some attempts to build them will be made in the next three decades. Meanwhile, we have to work with what we have.)

In established urban areas, it may be possible to build substantial portions of cities underground, and thus free portions of the surface for agriculture and recreation. (The Japanese have already begun to move in this direction.)

The one thing that does appear to be reasonably certain is that we cannot continue to "spread out" indiscriminately in the future. Nearly all such extensions in the past have been at the expense of close-in agricultural lands, or of scenic area. We can go up or down but it is doubtful that we can crawl sideways much longer and still maintain a technological society.

Getting away from the vast urban complexes, and back to the shells, there are a few questions worth asking. Why are they built as squares or clusters of little squares? Except for some types of crystal, nature does not produce squares. (Ever seen a square wooly wombat?) Nature *does* produce hexagons, particularly for high density areas, such as hornets and bees. People who have studied the various systems seem to agree that hexagonal systems of shells for humans would make the best use of space. The little boxes came down to us from the Egyptians; perhaps we could think differently now?

We appear to try to build all kinds of shelter to last as long as possible. Perhaps we might look more deeply into what someone has called "Kleenex architecture"—structures meant to last for only a relatively few years. By then, the networks would have changed enough to make them obsolete anyway. It might be less expensive to replace them with wholly new structures, adapted to the developing systems, than to try to rescue shells 30 to 40 years old.

What shelter finally gets down to is that we are locked into traditional ways of thinking, derived from ancient and largely agrarian societies, to feudal cities, and to concepts about land ownership and use that may be almost completely irrelevant to our contemporary, highly technological society.

THE 3-D CITIES OF THE PLAIN — One problem of urban settlements is that they are essentially two-dimensional; with their suburbs they spread out over the adjacent countryside, destroying the land from which they draw air and food. The Italian-born architect, Paolo Soleri, suggests organic, three-dimensional cities. The one shown above, called "Hexahedron," could house 170,000 people, use up only 140 acres of land, rise more than three-fifths of a mile, and widen from its base to a diameter of more than half a mile. In such cities, which Soleri's computers agree could be built with existing technologies, no individual would be more than 15 minutes (via elevators and escalators) from the furthest extremities of the community. Power supply, industrial production, and waste recycling would be deep in the earth beneath the building, possibly powered by nuclear generators. Individual units could be built on shelves on the outside shell, surrounding the central core, which would carry the utility networks. Between such cities, the land now used for transportation, parking space, junk yards and tract housing, could be returned to agricultural and recreational use. Highway subway systems could link the city complexes.

Illustration by Uta Nietiet

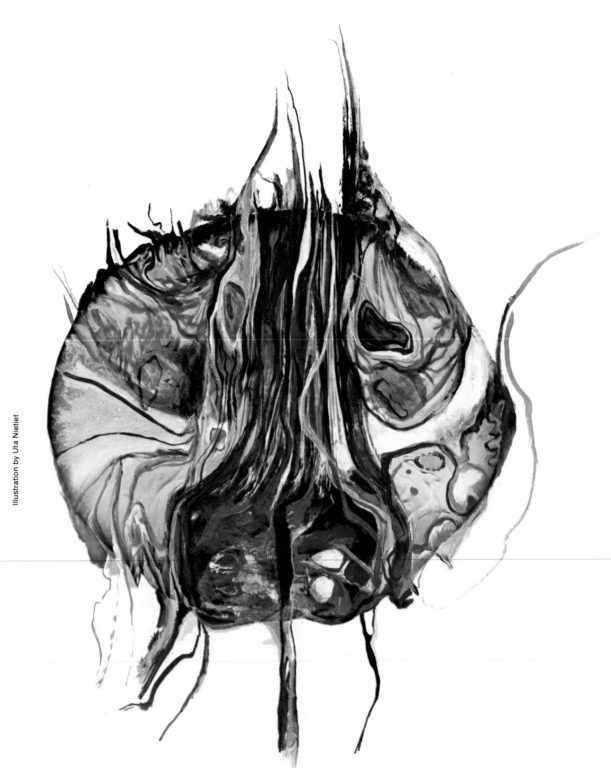

It may very well be that the need for high density population centers (whose main function is communication) may give way to a thin film of electronically connected habitations. But they will still be habitations, and they will still require networks, and it is here that we seem to fall down.

Somehow or other, we have to begin thinking about systems—interacting systems—and not about those mesmerizing little boxes.

It won't be easy, but it can be done. ✿

chapter 3.

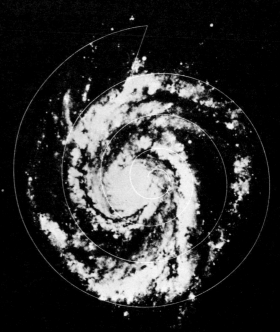

ENERGY:
Transactions in Time

3.
The Spark From Heaven

Cosmic energy is love, the affinity of being with being. It is a universal property of all life, and embraces all forms of organized matter. Thus, the tendency to unite; the attraction of atom to atom, molecule to molecule, or cell to cell. The forces of love drive the fragments of the universe to seek each other so that the world may come into being. TEILHARD DE CHARDIN / *The Phenomenon of Man*

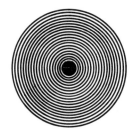

The dynamo's motion, form, and soft purr of sound awed him, as all power awed him, in whatever age...He could not make out the machine's meaning, or dimly making it out, the meaning frightened him. It seemed to leave out all the values that heretofore made human life worth living. So Adams, man and historian, with all his errors upon him, stood and confronted the dynamo, the age's symbol.

ELIZABETH STEVENSON / *Henry Adams: A Biography*

earth's great engine

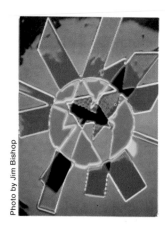

Photo by Jim Bishop

Perhaps the best way to start is to admit that we have only the faintest idea of what we are talking about. "Energy," as a concept—like "life" and "love" and "time" and "mind"—is as slippery as an anaconda in a lard factory.

Textbooks, dictionaries and the encyclopedia usually define energy as "the ability to do work." Work is defined as "the expenditure of energy." One can grope around in the darkness of this verbal coal mine forever; strike a match and the whole thing blows up. Even starshine on the surface is too weak to illuminate our search for the meaning of energy on this remote and spinning planet.

So, having nothing much to work with anyway, we can spin our own fantasy, knowing that the difference between myth and fact is so tiny as to be undetectable by any instrument man has so far devised.

Let us suggest that "work" may be described as an observed change in the environment, as we experience it. The observed change may be gross: as in an avalanche, a forest fire, a tornado, a tidal wave, a chicken crossing the road, an elevator going up or down, or the application of lipstick to otherwise pallid lips.

Work, as we observe it, may also be quite subtle: the movement of a pointer on a gauge, the configuration of excited phosphors on an oscilloscope, the darkening of silver chloride molecules on a photographic negative, the changes of color on litmus paper, the whispering of a million-year-old message in the ear of a radiotelescope by some unseen star.

All of these are "work"—changes in our environment as we observe it. Some kind of energy transformation has taken place; it is sufficiently powerful to affect our neural systems. Energy, as experienced by humans, thus could be described as a psychological phenomenon.

To make man's awareness of change the sole measure of "work" (and thus the transfer of energy) is not entirely honest. Such transfers occur outside the ken of men; but they only become "work" or "energy" when he becomes aware of them. Examples would be radioactive elements such as radium and uranium, which have been giving off "energy" for millions of years before technological

On that fateful afternoon in February in Budapest in 1882, when Tesla was given the vision of the rotating magnetic field, there had come with it an illumination that revealed to him the whole cosmos, in its infinite variations and its myriad of forms of manifestations, as a symphony of alternating currents. For him, the harmonies of the universe were played on a scale of electrical vibrations of a vast range in octaves. In one of the lower octaves was a single note, the 60-cycle-per-second alternating current, and in one of the higher octaves was visible light with its frequency of billions of cycles per second.

...If one note in a lower octave produced such a magnificent invention as the rotating magnetic field and the polyphase system, who could imagine the glorious possibilities that lay hidden in other notes in higher octaves? And there were thousands of octaves to be explored. He would construct an electrical harmonium by producing electrical vibrations in all frequencies.... He would then, he hoped, be able to understand the motif of the cosmic symphony of electrical vibrations that pervaded the entire universe.

JOHN J. O'NEILL/
Prodigal Genius:
The Life of Nikola Tesla

"Energy is most usable where it is most concentrated—for example, in highly structured chemical bonds (gasoline, sugar) or at high temperature (steam, incoming sunlight). Since the second law of thermodynamics says that the *overall* tendency in all processes is away from concentration, away from high temperature, it is saying that, overall, more and more energy is becoming less and less usable."

PAUL and ANNE EHRLICH/
Population, Resources, Environment:
Issues in Human Ecology 1970

"All earlier history had been determined by the
fact that the capacity of man had always been
limited to his own strength and that of the men
and animals he could control. But, beginning with
the nineteenth century, the situation had changed.
His capacity is no longer so limited; man has
now learned to manufacture power and with the
manufacture of power a new epoch began."

ELTING E. MORISON/*Men, Machines and
Modern Times,* 1966

A dunce had searched for a fire
With a lighted lantern
Had he known what fire was
He could have cooked his rice much sooner.

"The Gateless Gate" *Three Ways of Asian Wisdom*

All those who have studied the past from the
standpoint of economics, and those especially
who have studied economic geography,
are aware that from the material point of view,
history is primarily the story of the increasing
ability of man to reach and control energy.

Energy and Man: a symposium, 1960

A century after Colonel Drake's invention
of the first successful oil well, only one percent
of America's physical work is done by man himself.
The rest is done by machines.

The Atlantic Refining Company

man developed the instruments to discover that
something was going on.

There are, it appears, powerful surges of energy
emanating from the galaxies, from "red" stars, from
"empty" parts of space where no stars are visible,
and gigantic pulsations of energy from the "center"
of the now-visible universe.

Recent scientific discoveries suggest that (as Einstein predicted in 1916) magnetic fields are wave
phenomena, much like light and electricity. The
distance between crests of the magnetic waves
appears to be 100 miles, making them the product
of very long-wave broadcasting, indeed.

This discovery has led to the further suggestion
that the Milky Way, with its 100 billion stars acting
as molecules, forms a lens that focuses magnetic
energy that is generated "somewhere else." Where
"somewhere else" may be is not given. Perhaps it
is another dimension. Perhaps it is a projection of
human thought. Either way, out there or in here,
there are pulsations of energy from somewhere.

We do not, as yet, know the source of this
energy, but bit by bit we develop the instruments
to detect it and, in time, may produce the kinds
of human minds that can state the theoretical basis
for it. The discovery and exploration of new forms
of energy may be the most exciting human adventure of the next thirty years, assuming we do not
destroy ourselves with the sources we already know
about.

We tend to forget that we are invisible men—
or at least transparent ones. Cosmic rays pass
through us as if we were not there; so do radio
and television waves, x-rays, to a certain extent,
and most of the waves of energy from radioactive
materials. All of them are forms of energy; most
have been detected only in relatively recent times.

According to "By the Late John Brockman," man
is dead. We might suggest that he never existed.
Just as gods are the projected dreams of men, perhaps men are the projected dreams of animals.
For all you know, you may be the dream of a cock-
roach or a snail, or a whole community of ants
or squid. And this would be another form of energy
transfer.

Oh, there are other trails we can take. Energy
transactions can be quantified and described in

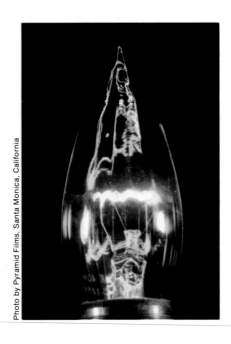

Photo by Pyramid Films, Santa Monica, California

**"Light is a visible form of radiant energy.
Radiant energy is any energy that flows outward,
or radiates in all directions from a source,
with characteristics of both particle motion
and wave motion."**

**RICHARD NEHRICH, JR., GLENN VORAN
AND NORMAN DESSEL/**
Atomic Light: Lasers, **1968**

terms like "kilowatts" and "megawatts." This tells us no more about energy than pinning a tail on a donkey at a children's party or attaching a Latin name to some poor creature groping around in the ooze of the Mindanao Trench.

Putting labels on things or events does not further our understanding of them. So, hobbling along on such rickety verbal crutches as our language affords, poddling around to do our own fossicking in the outback of what little we have been taught, we'll trudge back to the textbooks.

As every fourth grader knows by now, energy can neither be created nor destroyed. There are some difficulties with this point of view, but since that is what is taught, and is what most physicists, mathematicians and engineers believe, we'll leave it resting quietly there on the floor. Let sleeping dogs lie.

If energy can neither be created nor destroyed, then all that can happen to it is that it can be transformed, and this transformation appears to take place between systems. Generating plants appear to be engaged in changing one form of energy into another: falling water, burning coal or oil or gas, channeling radioactivity, catching the wind in sails and vanes. These transactions, when observed, may be called "work." What is transformed is the *form* of energy, so that our "generators" are, in that sense, "transformers."

The systems between which these transactions take place may be stellar, nuclear, thermal, chemical, mechanical, biologic or psychic, depending on what donkey's tail we want to pin on them, and what children's party we happen to be attending. They simply are words that say, "there's something going on." Hence, change.

The transaction between systems appears to involve an "inevitable loss," usually described as heat. The heat presumably goes somewhere else and becomes part of another system, so there is no real loss for the universe as a whole. Or at least that is what we are told. Since we so far cannot observe, and therefore cannot evaluate, the entire universe, we do not know whether this viewpoint is valid or not. But that's what's in the books.

The second "law" of thermodynamics says that, because of heat loss, the universe is "running down," although this would appear to contradict the first "law," which says that every action has an *equal* and opposite reaction, so that it *can't* run down. The apparent contradiction (greatly over-simplified here) may be resolved by considering that two different dimensions of systems—i.e., the local and the universal—are being described. ("The gingham dog and the calico cat, side by side on the table sat.")

Einstein suggested that all measurements (and hence the "laws" derived from them) are relative to the observer and the system he happens to be observing. Which is another way of saying, "energy is an awareness of a change of state in an observed field." One might add that the observer and observed are the products of transactions with each other. Some of these transactions can be quantified. When they are, in our language, they are called "energy."

As Arthur Koestler explains in *The Ghost and the Machine*, "only in recent times did science … realize that the second law applies *only in the special case of so-called 'closed systems'* (such as a gas enclosed in a perfectly isolated container). But no such closed systems appear to exist even in inanimate nature, and whether the universe as a whole is a closed system is anybody's guess.

"All living organisms, however, are in 'open systems'; they maintain their complex form and functions through continuous exchanges of energies and material with their environment. Instead of running down like a mechanical clock that dissipates its energies through friction, the living organism is constantly 'building up' more complex substances from the substances it feeds on, more complex forms of energies from the energies it absorbs, and more complex patterns of information—perceptions, feelings, thoughts—from the input of its receptor organs."

All of this may sound very philosophic to someone engaged in the day-to-day job of providing electrical energy (or other forms of power) to a constantly expanding number of people. And perhaps it *is* philosophic. But we are not trying to tell the professionals in the power industries how to do their jobs.

What we *are* trying to say here is that the trans-

Everybody wants ample electric power, for instance, but more and more communities are prepared to resist the presence of a power plant. Decisions on plant location are being made in a basically disorderly way with each fragmented community interest in turn poised against the fragmented interest of the power company. More and more of these cases are getting into the courts. But the courts, operating in the narrow dualism of adversary proceedings, are hardly in a position to say where a power plant ought to go.

In this decision system the most apathetic or careless community would get stuck with the power plant or the refinery—and this might be exactly the worst place to put it from either a business or an environmental viewpoint.

Obviously, a high-technology society needs, and its government should provide, forums for the national resolution of such questions. Carl E. Bagge, a member of the Federal Power Commission, argues that regional planning bodies should become forums for deciding on such questions as the location of new power plants and power transmission facilities.

MAX WAYS/"How to Think About the Environment" *The Environment* by the Editors of *Fortune*

"We must either ask the people to forego luxuries like air conditioners or build electric power plants over the protests of the conservationists."

Joint Atomic Energy Committee Report, 1970

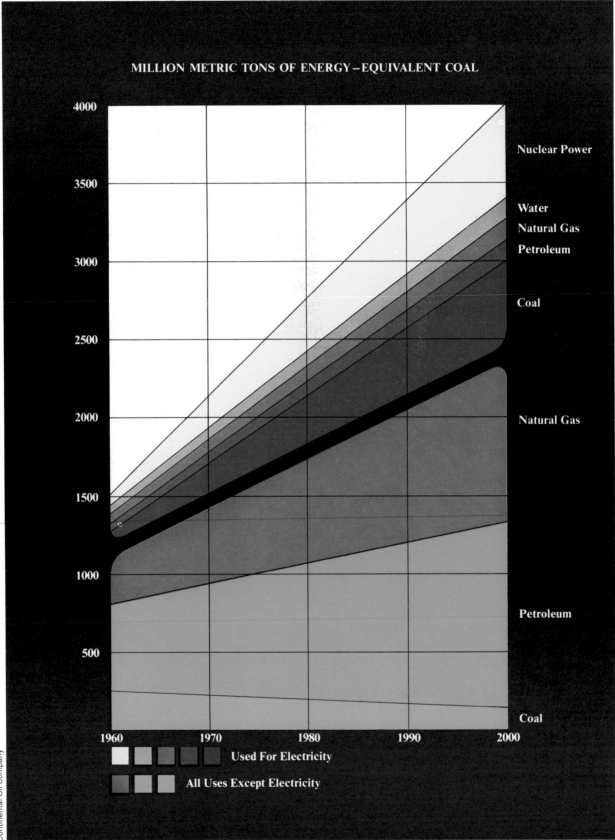

MILLION METRIC TONS OF ENERGY—EQUIVALENT COAL

formation of energy for human use, which has been primarily an engineering and technological problem in the past, will increasingly become an economic, political and moral problem in the next thirty years.

Economic because, with our present technology, most of our energy is produced through the destruction of non-replaceable materials—coal, oil, gas, timber, fissionable elements. We are living off our capital and not our interest. Hydroelectric is not much better; the dams will silt up. The new ones, if we build them, will only replace the ones we've lost. There are inexhaustible sources of energy—the sun, the winds, the tides—but we do not use them. We don't even try to.

Political, because the allocation of available energy is the responsibility of elected officials. Who gets to transform power? Who distributes it? And to whom, and at what cost? These are political questions and to pretend that they are not—that they are a part of the "natural order" of things—is to ignore reality in favor of myths. How many myths does it take to turn a turbine?

Moral, because we are not alone. What we extract from the planet, and the sorts of waste we return to it, affects other species, who have as much right to live on this planet as we do. All we have against them is that they don't make money.

If the point of "producing energy" is to make money—then God help us; no one else possibly can. Sometime we better start to do some thinking.

"Let us go then, you and I, where the evening is spread out against the sky, like a patient etherised upon a table," suggests T. S. Eliot (*Prufrock,* 1917).

There are a few problems here, quite apart from distinguishing "you" and "I." One of them is finding the sky; in our times, in our cities. Evening comes quite early these days.

"Civilization has been formed in the crucible of fire. Combustion, or the rapid chemical reaction of oxygen with carbon, has propelled human advancement," says Tom Alexander (in "The Environment" by the Editors of *Time,* Inc.). "But Prometheus' presumptuous gift of fire to man is calling down a punishment not anticipated by the ancients. For where there's fire, there's smoke.

"Fossil fuels that accumulated over hundreds of millions of years are being converted to gas and ash in a gluttony that began a century ago. In the U.S., the tonnage of these fuels consumed doubles every twenty years.... The hunger for energy seems insatiable."

And so, what we seem to be facing—or refusing to face—is a certain "set" to the mind of technological man; whatever his skin color, his race, his nationality or his ideology. "More" is "better." One may ask, "Why is more better?" How much more of this can this poor old world stand?

We might ask, for instance, whether we really need all of the energy we use. (The industrialized regions, with one-fourth of the world's population, consume 75% of the world's coal, 80% of its oil and electrical power, and 95% of the natural gas so far released. The United States, with 6% of the world's people, has consumed more than a third of the world's commercial energy supplies during the last decade.)

We might ask whether having more electrical energy available to each human being is, indeed, desirable. Buckminster Fuller, playing "The World Game" at Carbondale, Illinois, says that every person on earth should, by the year 2000, ingest—or have available—3500 calories per day. This was all worked out on a sort of electronic ouija board at Carbondale and it makes at least two assumptions, the number of people who might be alive in the world in the year 2000 and the economic condition in which they may find themselves.

We might ask—we might ask. But we have never been taught to ask. We are not likely to ask these questions of ourselves in the next thirty years. Never mind, the world will ask us.

As Max Ways says (in "How to Think About the Environment"), "Life is presently diminished; it loses point and relish and sense of direction when it is spent amidst a haphazard squalor that God never made, nature never evolved, and man never intended."

Or, as T. S. Eliot said in *The Wasteland* (1922), "And I will show you something different from either/ Your shadow at morning striding behind you/ Or your shadow at night rising to meet you;

I will show you fear in a handful of dust." ✿

THE STEAM CAME AFT through the main steam line like wild white horses. The throttle and the slide valves were gates and the horses ran invisibly down the connecting rods and out along the whitely spinning shaft. Only their pale ghosts went to the condenser. When there were too many horses in the boilers, they kicked open the safety valves and charged off into the sky in a great, white, trumpeting host of horses... He was listening... Steam blowing through ports and receivers roared hollowly far off, like a million hoofs drumming a distant prairie... From the fire room came the hiss and sulfur smell of coal smoke and water on hot ashes, the scrape of shovels and the clang of fire doors... All the voices sang with the engine... And then, standing with eyes open... he caught the intricate play of light and shadow as the wild horses spun whitely aft into the dimness of the shaft alley.

RICHARD McKENNA/*The Sand Pebbles*

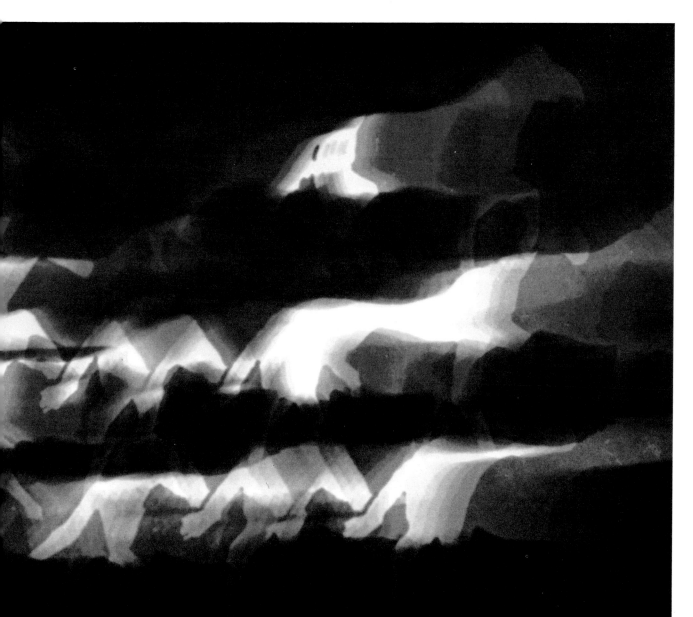

The originator of the steam engine, Thomas Savery,
had noted that his engine could do the work of
two horses, but it was James Watt who
established the horsepower as a unit of measure.
He determined that a horse, pulling for one minute,
could lift some 32,400 pounds to a height
of one foot. Later, to make it easier to calculate the
power of his engines, Watt rounded this off
and set the standard unit at 33,000 pounds raised
one foot per minute... In today's scientific
shorthand, this is expressed as "550 foot-pounds
per second."

MITCHELL WILSON and the Editors of Life
Science Library/*Energy*, 1963, Time Inc.

It is a tiny globe, luminous only because it is reflecting the light from its parent. The globe grows in size as you approach…Up until now your journey has been a reality. Now this reality is distorted for the first time and a limited form of it absorbs your consciousness so that if you are not careful you will take this little globe for what it appears to be. And that would be an error. EDWIN CORLE / *Coarse Gold,* 1942

Photo by Bob Conover

good morning starshine

When we talk about energy—inputs and exchanges—we often ignore the most obvious source of all, the sun. This inflow of energy warms the earth and produces, through photosynthesis, all of the food, fuel, and oxygen upon which life depends. "In the sun, born over and over again, I ran my heedless ways." (Dylan Thomas)

Solar input has been going on since the birth of the sun itself. Streaming in daily in enormous quantities, sunlight provides in the United States every two days enough energy to outlast all our known remaining fossil-fuel reserves.

In thinking about solar radiation, we are dealing with energy bundles of photons of fixed sizes. Some are at the ultraviolet end of the solar spectrum and are much more energetic than those in the visible band. Visible light rays, in turn, contain more energy than the photons streaming toward earth in the infrared or heat end of the spectrum. The thing to remember is that each photon is a fixed amount; it cannot be cut in half and cannot be joined with another to do the work of a larger, more powerful cousin. Solar energy capture, then, becomes simply a matter of learning the different ways individual molecules of earth-bound matter react under the impact of solar photons of different sizes.

Some solar energy has been undergoing conversion throughout history, as successive layers of such energy have been stored in the earth from the organic conversion of plants and animals. These are usually known as the fossil fuels—coal, petroleum and gasses.

The interchangeability of various forms of energy is one of its most important properties. One can't tell a leopard by its spots. Our nearest starry neighbor, the sun, radiates both heat and light toward planet earth. We have developed increasingly clever and complex means of trapping solar heat and putting it to work for us, as heat.

Man learned early in his game with life that heat is captured when the sun's rays are absorbed by a blackened surface, and that this heat can be greatly amplified by using reflection or refraction to concentrate a large area of sunshine onto a small target. Such techniques have been used since 1750 to generate heat, to cause chemical reactions, and

most recently, to produce usable electricity.

Several types of mechanisms have been developed to aid in trapping solar energy. One is the flat plate collector, which consists of a base of some good radiant energy absorber, an air space, and one or more covers of transparent glass or plastic. Some fluid—air, water, or liquid—is pumped through the space between the absorber and the cover, picking up the impounded solar heat en route.

Production of salt by evaporating sea water was man's first use of this type of solar furnace; conversely, the production of potable water from sea water was the first successful large-scale application of solar stills. These stills usually use a shallow blackened box covered with a layer of glass or plastic film, through which the solar radiation enters. The sun causes some of the water to evaporate. Water vapor is condensed on the lower surface of the transparent cover. It eventually trickles down into appropriate containers, producing perfectly good drinking water. Since the output of such solar stills is relatively low (approximately one gallon per day for each ten square feet of collection area) they offer little promise for producing large amounts of water, such as are needed for irrigation. They can, however, supply drinking water for limited numbers of people, and they are still being used for this purpose on several of the small arid Greek islands.

Solar furnaces can be relatively efficient, converting more than seventy percent of the total incoming radiation into usable heat (as distinguished from direct conversion to electricity). Temperatures above 7,000° F have been obtained from them.

We now know that, in addition to being used as heat, both incoming solar heat and sunlight can be changed to yet another energy form—electricity.

Until several decades ago, man had no technique for converting sunlight directly into electricity. Solar energy, in its "raw" form, was usable only by green plants in the photosynthesis process; the limited conversion of solar energy to electricity had to go through an intermediate step of channeling the captured solar heat to make steam to drive turbines. Now, Bell Telephone scientists are using solar cells to convert sunlight directly to

Photo by Jim Bishop

electric power. This type of solar cell (a thin wafer treated with silicon, arsenic, and boron) has made possible much of the space exploration to date. It is expected that the silicon cell can reach efficiencies of approximately twenty-two percent in the direct conversion of heat to electric power.

At present efficiency levels (12%), one such system, containing 30,000 solar cells, is powering all the instruments, including cameras, in a satellite that has been in orbit since 1958. There is no reason to expect that the cells will "die" very soon.

So much promise does the silicon solar cell hold that experts are predicting that, by 1984, most of the world's transcontinental communications systems will rely on satellites carrying solar cells. The space vehicles can be designed so that they travel with their solar panels constantly facing the sun. No problems with rainy days nor long winter nights.

So far, however, methods devised for the direct conversion of solar energy to electricity appear to be less efficient than other, more conventional, sources of electricity. Scientists seem to agree that solar energy is most likely to find its principal application in residential use—for space heating, for some cooking, and for hot water supplies. Solar water heaters are now being used in several states, and there are increasing numbers of solar-heated houses.

For home use, a flat-plate collector is usually built as a portion of the south wall or roof of the house. Incoming heat is stored by circulating air (or water) through it and then directing the air into a reservoir of water, stones, or chemicals from which the heat can be withdrawn as needed. Water or stones are cheap enough. The problem with them is bulk. Chemicals, like sodium sulfate, can reduce the storage volume somewhat. But for localites where heat must be stored for several days in the absence of the sun, or where the heating load is severe, the volume (and hence the cost of installation) may be high.

To date, residential application appears to show most promise in areas lying between 30°N and 30°S latitude (Marquesas Islands, anyone?), where sunshine is plentiful and conventional fuels often expensive.

A few solar furnaces are in operation in industry, but the sizes of furnaces required for production of many kilowatt hours of electricity often make installation expensive here also. One square yard of sun-catching surface generates only enough electricity in bright constant sunlight to light one 100-watt incandescent light bulb. Hardly enough to run a factory.

In addition, users are often plagued with problems of long-term rainy season storage of energy impounded on sunny days. In western Europe and in the United States some metallurgical research centers have been able to overcome these problems and they now appear to be able to use solar energy quite efficiently.

Consequently, although weather and the unavoidable nights make it improbable that solar energy will be utilized on a large scale within the next several decades, in small amounts it already has had and will continue to find important applications. Man's conversion of sunlight may definitely be counted on to contribute a substantial share to earth's energy bank account.✿

Photo by Jim Bishop

The maintenance of man on earth is accomplished through the use of the energies incoming from the sun and from the stored energies of past evolutionary transformation of the planetary surface.

JOHN MCHALE/*The Future of the Future*, 1969

A research dentist at UCLA has reported that a moment's exposure of human teeth to a low energy beam from a pulsed carbon dioxide laser may make them resistant to decay. The laser apparently glazes the enamel without producing heat which would damage the pulp of the tooth behind its enamel.

U. C. Clip Sheet, April, 1970

energy is an awareness of a change of state in an observed field

MANY of the forms of energy man uses today were virtually unknown 150 years ago. They were not "invented"; they were discovered, and the discoveries were the result of a heightened awareness on the part of a few gifted men, aided by increasingly sensitive instruments which revealed to them changes previously unnoticed within their fields of observation. It is possible, even probable, that forms of energy wholly unknown now will be discovered and put to practical uses before the end of the century. It is also possible that some of them may come out of the revolution in the arts of the 1960's and the revived interest in parapsychological and religious phenomena.

A place there is in hell called Malebolge. Which, with the precipice surrounding it, is all composed of iron-colored stone...The banks were covered with a crust of mold, deposited by vapors from beneath, that sore offended both the eyes and nose...And here we stopped, to see the next division of Malebolge...I saw it, but no more could I discern than bubbles rising in the boiling mass; it seemed to heave, and then subside again.

DANTE ALIGHIERI / *The Divine Comedy*

the earth did quake and the rocks rent

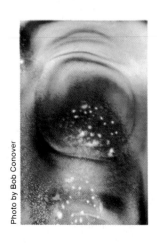

Photo by Bob Conover

Photo by Dennis Galloway

Some say watching it is as close to hell as you can come and still be alive. Others say it will take a second seat only to nuclear power as the most important producer of electrical energy in the future. Both groups are talking about geothermal power — steam spewed forth from the bowels of the earth, captured and forced against giant turbines to produce electricity.

Although capturing this natural energy source isn't a new concept (historians think that steam vents near Larderello, Italy, inspired Dante to write the "Inferno" episode in the *Divina Commedia* in 1310), geothermal energy has been exploited for commercial use only since 1904, again by the Italians. Steamwell drilling and capping in this country has, so far, been mostly limited to an area of Northern California known — incorrectly — as The Geysers. Actually, geysers are streams of boiling water sprayed into the air with great force. Geothermal wells are really fumaroles, eruptions of steam rather than water.

Geothermal literally means "heat from within the earth." Once again, the concept is a relatively simple one. At many places in the earth's 20-mile-thick outer crust, water (mostly seepages from rainfall) comes into contact with molten rock (magma trapped under the crust) and, at 2000°F, the water is converted to super-heated steam. By drilling a well into the earth's crust, it is possible to release the steam and pipe it to a turbine in a generating station.

This is exactly what several petroleum companies are now beginning to do in California. Their efforts are unique in that, although there are many geothermal projects underway around the world (Japan, West Indies, Ketanga, Iceland, Kenya, Chile, Russia, New Zealand, etc.), those in The Geysers are the world's first privately developed systems. The others are government sponsored. Participants in geothermal operations in the U.S. wish openly that government funding approaching that given to the Atomic Energy Commission had been assigned to the development of this source of energy at the same time. If this had been the case, geothermal power might now occupy a far larger segment of the total energy picture.

With four large turbine generators operating at The Geysers, that project is now producing enough power to satisfy, by today's standards, the electrical requirements of a city of 80,000 people. Some experts predict that, if developed to the fullest possible extent, geothermal production of electricity could supply as much as one-half of America's electrical power by the end of this century. One well in The Geysers area, Whistling Annie, releases ten times the energy of Yellowstone Park's Old Faithful, perhaps the best known of any fumarole.

Aside from the obvious advantages of being a power source that doesn't require fuel or monstrous dams and doesn't pollute the environment (neither heat nor contaminating particles are discharged into the atmosphere or into water), there is another very important plus to developing this energy source. There is no danger of depleting valuable resources to the detriment of future generations. Instead, a nearly inexhaustible supply of heat is generated deep within the earth, increasing about ten degrees in temperature each thousand feet into the crust. The temperature reaches nearly 2000° some twenty miles into the surface, and evidence suggests that the decay of radio-active elements present in small amounts in all rocks and life forms will continue to produce this heat indefinitely.

It would appear that geothermal energy is competitive with other ways of producing power, according to one utility company that has experience with all types, including nuclear reactors. It suggests that, as more experience is gained in well production and as geothermal plants increase in size and efficiency, this source of energy may well prove to be the cheapest of all. At any rate, as depletion of resources causes the prices of oil and natural gas to increase, geothermal power may keep the price of electricity from following them up the scale.

Man knows that geothermal belts are widely scattered around the globe — along the fiery rim of the Pacific, up the mid-Atlantic from the Canary Islands to Iceland, under Siberia, through the Northern Mediterranean — but he has not yet begun to exploit them to their fullest measure. Perhaps he should do so quickly, if he is to meet the challenge of the next thirty years. ✿

F. D. ROOSEVELT
President of the United States
White House
Washington, D.C.

August 2, 1939

Sir:

Some recent work by E. Fermi and L. Szilard, which has been communicated to me in manuscript, leads me to expect that the element of uranium may be turned into a new and important source of energy in the immediate future...In the course of the last four months it has been made probable ...that it may be possible to set up a nuclear chain reaction in a large mass of uranium, by which vast amounts of power and large quantities of new radium-like elements would be generated...

ALBERT EINSTEIN
Old Grove Road
Nassau Point
Peconic, Long Island

$$E = mc^2$$

When Einstein published his famous formula shortly after the turn of the century, his friends were highly skeptical, says Peter Michemore (in *Einstein: Profile of the Man,* Dodd, Mead, 1962).

"You're saying there's more horsepower in a lump of coal than in the whole Prussian cavalry," they complained. "If this were true, why hasn't it been noticed before?"

"If a man who is fabulously rich never spent or gave away a cent," Einstein replied, "then no one could tell how rich he was or whether he had any money at all. It is the same with matter. So long as none of the energy is given off externally, it cannot be observed."

"And how do you propose to release all this hidden energy?"

"There is not the slightest indication that the energy will ever be obtainable," said Einstein. "It would mean that the atom would have to be shattered at will...We see atom disintegration only where nature herself presents it."

But that was long ago and far away, and today it appears that nuclear energy, by the year 2000, may be the dominant form throughout the world.

"It can function anywhere," says John McHale, (in *The Future of the Future*). "It is independent of geography, climate and the general cultural level of the inhabitants. Upkeep is minimal...needed amounts of fuel are easily transported and the consumed weight is negligible. Operation is automatic and can be managed with limited personnel ...The plants can be placed where they are needed."

The Atomic Energy Commission has estimated that, by 2000 A.D., nuclear reactors could account for nearly half of the U.S. generating capacity. Something like 90 percent of the generating stations now on the drawing boards are nuclear.

Still, all is not well in the atomic garden. Whether the plants on the drawing board ever get off it depends very much on whether the power companies can convince conservation groups that such installations are at least as safe as conventional coal fired or petroleum-fed power plants, and that they will not contribute to pollution.

In the minds of many people, nuclear energy is equated with The Bomb. Approval of power generating sites is usually up to local option, and who wants a bomb in the backyard? There is as much technological difference between a controlled nuclear reaction and a critical one (as used in The Bomb) as there is between burning papers in a backyard incinerator and lighting a stick of dynamite. But the power companies have not, so far, convinced the general public of this, and until they do, they will find virtually every site suggestion opposed by the very people who would benefit most.

There is risk to any energy exchange. Coal mines explode, oil wells blow up, dams collapse. That the risks are any greater for nuclear generated power has not been demonstrated nor proven. But, in the popular mind, it is still The Bomb.

Quite apart from the possibility of catastrophe, there are other effects that, in the non-technical mind, are deterrents to a wider use of nuclear power generators.

One of these is radiation contamination and the disposal of wastes. Inevitably, there will be some human error (witness the oil spillages in offshore drilling) and some mechanical failures. The waste products are difficult to get rid of because some of them have a "half life" of 100 years, and neither our geological nor our oceanographic sciences are good enough, yet, to predict what might happen to the areas where atomic wastes are buried or dumped. Since radioactive wastes are, themselves, still generating energy, it seems incredible that contemporary technology cannot find a safe and profitable way to exploit the wastes.

The other problem in the public mind concerning the increased use of nuclear power plants is "thermal pollution." Nuclear plants require large amounts of water as a coolant, and the used water is returned to its source as much as 17 to 30 degrees higher than it came in. When the temperature of water is raised, the oxygen content is reduced, and the ecology of the river or lake is disturbed. Algae may proliferate and fish and mollusks may die.

The amount of scientific information on thermal pollution, of the type described, could be written on the head of a pin. We will do so here.

In *Scientific American* (May, 1970) there is an article called "The Calefaction of a River" by Daniel Merriman. The scene is five miles of the Connecticut River, above and below Haddam Neck, which is 15 miles from the mouth of the river, the spot where the Connecticut Yankee Atomic Power Company has built a nuclear power plant.

The study began 30 months before the plant began operating (in order to establish "normal" ecological patterns for that section of the river). The effluent from the plant is figured to be about 20° F. higher than the temperature of the river.

(One should walk softly here. The intake is from the bottom of the river, where the water is coldest. The output is near the surface of the river, where the water is warmest. The gradient between intake and output is not an accurate measure of the actual thermal pollution; it is the difference between two extremes. The temperature of the river changes throughout the year, so that in the hottest weather, the returned effluent may be only a few degrees above normal surface temperature. Measurement of thermal pollution is not all as simple as some people would like to think.)

"In the study, so far, there have been no deleterious effects on the biology of the river," says Merriman, stipulating that this is an interim report, and it is impossible to forecast long term effects.

Merriman's group also studied radiation leakage. It measured "normal" background radiation in the area for thirty months before the plant began operating. It measured it for thirty months afterward. It detected no difference.

That's one study. Here's another.

The scene changes and you are now at Turkey Point, on Biscayne Bay, Florida. There is a power plant here that takes in 820 million gallons of water each day and returns it to the bay at temperatures that are about 14°F. higher than the intake temperature.

A study by the Federal Water Pollution Control Administration (hereinafter referred to as the FWPCA, which it will not be) said, in part:

"An underwater search of an area 500 yards offshore (from the output) showed that few living plants and none of the usual invertebrate animals populating 'grass beds' remained. A zone of nearly complete destruction of the plant and animal life extended into the bay for 500 to 700 yards."

Different generating plants, different places. We

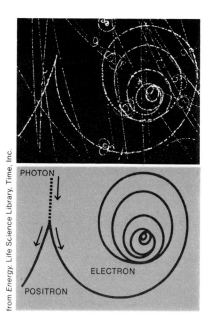

from *Energy*, Life Science Library, Time, Inc.

Just as the Yin and Yang of Asian philosophy are the reverse counterparts of each other, just as good and evil in Western religions are opposite faces of the same coin in that each defines the other, so equations in contemporary physics are reversible. Since matter can be transformed into energy, following E-mc², so energy may be transformed into matter. The illustrations above show how this actually has been done at the laboratory level. The photograph shows the bubbly trails which result when charged subatomic particles from the University of California's bevatron move through liquid hydrogen kept just below its boiling point. The accompanying diagram clarifies the specific paths of the newly created bits of matter. Someday, perhaps before 2000 A.D., it may be possible to transmit matter, as energy, around the world, and reconstitute it as matter at the other end. Ships, cargo aircraft, and big transcontinental trucks may become obsolete.

stumble along in the darkness of our ignorance. There are no easy answers, in our society, at the present time. We should accept that we do not really understand very much, and that what we do understand is highly suspect.

Assuming that thermal pollution from nuclear plants *does* cause ecologic disturbance, there is no reason to abandon ship. Other possibilities exist.

A "thermocline" (an elegant word that simply means difference in temperature) of 17 to 30 degrees, should find some economic use. It might be used for heating houses and commercial buildings in the immediate vicinity, returning to its source at temperatures only a few degrees above normal. The warm water could be used to heat municipal swimming pools, or in fish ponds for exotic, tropical species; the ponds constituting a series of "staging areas" until it is cool enough to be returned to its source. And, of course, it is always possible to build "cooling towers" (as the English have done) and return the water to its source at near normal temperatures.

All of these solutions are expensive, and it has been argued that if they have to be used, nuclear power would not be competitive with coal, hydroelectric and oil produced power. But if these generating plants also were forced to be pollution free, then the competing systems would be competitive again.

In order to be economic, nuclear power stations have to be quite large. Part of the enormous investment required might be recovered by selling by-products. The heated water described above might be one source of revenue, thus changing a potential pollutant into a salable product.

In coastal areas, nuclear installations may use sea water or brackish water as a coolant, in which case a major portion of the mineral content has to be removed (to reduce corrosion in the coolant system). Such semi-fresh water may also have a market for irrigation or sewage purposes in water-short areas. By the time it had been used, it would be back to ambient temperatures. The minerals extracted during the desalination process might also find some commercial markets.

Another source of revenue may be in the radio-isotopes that are a by-product of nuclear operations. These already find use in the chemical, medical, biological and biochemical fields.

Considered as a system, with all sources of revenue taken into account, nuclear power plants appear to make a lot of sense. When considered purely as generators of electrical power they are not really competitive with conventional power sources, under present conditions, without subsidies.

There are some other ways to go, but they are still nuclear, and have the same problems. The "fast-breeder reactor" is one. It produces more fuel than it consumes. It appears technologically and economically feasible. Some have been built; some work, some don't. As a system, the breeder appears to have fewer pollution problems than conventional reactors. Its use in quantity may be as many as ten years away.

Another trail that might be followed is thermonuclear energy—the "fusion" process. It is a kind of difficult trail. Our favorite star—the sun—manages to do it quite easily, but it has been around a lot longer than we have and it may have learned something from its galactic cousins.

What goes on here is really very simple. When two nuclei of hydrogen atoms are fused, at very high temperatures, they give off energy. When one atom's nucleus is bombarded by a neutron, it splits in two parts and gives off energy in the process. In present nuclear technology, you make them split. In thermonuclear technology, you make them merge.

In thermonuclear transactions, we appear to be talking about stellar dimensions. At 60 to 100 million degrees, a "fourth state" of matter appears (fourth because it appears to be different than solid, liquid or gas) which is called, for reasons too tedious to go into, "plasma." This creature can only, apparently, be confined in magnetic bottles. We don't know how to make magnetic bottles that work. So this wild creature is still roaming the plains of galactic space. It is well within our imaginations that he can be corralled. And if he is, there will be "enough" energy for every person on earth. And more. The question may be—why do we want it? And if we got it, what would we do with it?

Meanwhile this ancient creature grazes space not attracted by magnetic bottles. Why are we? ✿

Blow, winds, and crack your cheeks! rage! blow! You cataracts and hurricanes, spout…You sulphurous and thought-executing fires / Vaunt-couriers to oak-cleaving thunderbolts, singe my white head! And thou, all-shaking thunder, strike flat the thick rotundity of the world!…Rumble thy bellyfull! Spit, fire! spout, rain! WILLIAM SHAKESPEARE / *King Lear:* Act III, Sc. II

they call the wind Maria

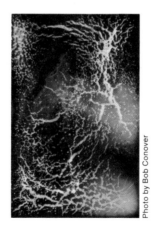

Photo by Bob Conover

The winds of the world have many names. Mostly they were formed by the soft, beard-surrounded lips of tough young men whose every day might be their last; it is not easy to be a sailor. It was they who put the names upon the winds.

There is the *breeze*—from the Spanish *briza*—a gentle wind. There is the *cyclone,* borrowed from the Greek term for "the coil of the serpent" which it closely resembles. The word *hurricane* ("High Wind in Jamaica?") came from the early Spanish and Portuguese seamen *(huracan, haurachana)* and was changed in the sixteenth century by the British seamen who saw the 140 mile per hour winds flatten the sugar cane. Hence, *hurry-cane.* Or so they say.

Then there is the *monsoon,* which started out as the Arabic *wasama* which meant "to mark," as at the beginning or ending of a cool or rainy season. Filtered through the Dutch, it became *monssoen,* easily Anglicized as *monsoon.*

From the Cantonese "ta feng" (big wind) we get *typhoon,* which, as a word, is related to tycoon (from *tai-kiun*—big prince).

There is the *willawaw*—a sudden, violent squall. Its name may derive from the Australian *willy-willy,* a tropical cyclone first noticed in the Timor Sea. And, finally, the *zephyr*—a light west wind; as a word out of the Greeks, through the Romans, it entered the English language 1,000 years ago.

Thus, some of the names upon the wind.

The wind was among the first of the non-biological sources of energy to be used by man; it drove his ships and windmills, lifted his water, ground his grain, aired his mines. Even today in The Netherlands, in the still rural parts of the United States, and in Australia, along the southern edge of the Kimberleys, where they join the Great Sandy, windmills are important sources of power.

A hurricane, cyclone, tornado or typhoon releases as much energy as a hydrogen bomb. But very little has been done, technologically, to harness this power for the uses of man. And yet, technologically, it should be quite easy to do.

Harnessing the Trade Winds, which blow at a constant 11 to 14 m.p.h., with a predictable time and direction, should be even easier.

The source of the power is free. It exhausts no natural resources. It produces no pollution. As long as the earth turns, it will be available. Coupled with recent advances in electronics that greatly increase the efficiency of electrical systems, one can see how, especially where there are prevailing winds, wind generators might be woven into existing generating systems as a supplemental source of energy. This might help to relieve the pressure on coal mines and oil fields and could serve as a useful supplement during peak hours.

The ocean tides, like the winds, could serve as important sources of electrical energy, should we want to harness them. Like the winds, they are an inexhaustible natural resource. They produce no pollution. And they are highly predictable as to time and height.

In bays and fjords in some parts of the world, the tidal differential is as much as 50 feet; billions of tons of water flowing at speeds as high as 10 knots. Dams and generators can catch the power from the incoming tide and from the outgoing tide. In most places (it depends on local currents, winds and topography) there are two high tides and two low tides each day; a rich and dependable source of energy.

The United States has one project going, begun by Franklin D. Roosevelt in the 1920's. This would reap the power from the 18-foot tidal differential at Passamaquoddy Bay, between Maine and Canada. On each tide, two billion tons of water are on the move. The output of the plant would be one million kilowatts.

Meanwhile, the French have completed a tidal project on the Rance River in northern France, harvesting the energy from the 44-foot tidal differential in the English Channel. Numerous such opportunities exist in Norway, the northwest coast of Australia, among the sounds and fjords of South Island New Zealand, and doubtless many other places as well.

If, as appears to be true, fossil fuel and nuclear based generators will be hard-pressed to meet the energy demands of a much larger, more highly industrialized world population by the year 2000, then we may very well see an awakening interest in the natural bounty of the wind and tides. But that time is not yet. ✿

ENERGY: TRANSACTIONS IN TIME

$$6CO_2 + 6H_2O = C_6H_{12}O_6 + 6O_2$$

A living body is not a fixed *thing* but a flowing *event,* like a flame or a whirlpool: the shape alone is stable, for the substance is a stream of energy going in at one end and out at the other. We are particular and temporarily identifiable wiggles in a stream that enters us in the form of light, heat, air, water, milk, bread, fruit, beer, beef Stroganoff, caviar and pâté de foie gras. It goes out as gas and excrement—and also as semen, babies, talk, politics, commerce, war, poetry and music. And philosophy. ALAN WATTS / *Does It Matter?*

Photo by Bob Conover

We have been, up to now, gazing at stars and finding solar energy; looking over the brim into hell and discovering geothermal power; defying ordinary logic in creating more fuel than is used in operating breeder reactors. All important parts of the energy story, but not the entire story. There is so much more.

Perhaps we should look at man himself to complete the composite picture of energy, as we have defined it, in our galactic imaginations. It appears that, in addition to obvious outputs of energy from man's body in the forms of heat, physical movement, and wastes, there is another, more intangible, outpouring of energy from the individual. It takes the form of powerful waves emanating from the brain. Some individuals seem to exhibit a greater tendency toward displaying this type of energy, which often manifests itself in suggestions of prophecy, fortune telling and magic.

It is, in fact, entirely possible that normal men are endowed with powers which they rarely use simply because they have been persuaded that they do not possess them. Actually, parapsychological experiments seem to prove that between man and the universe there exist means of communications beyond those provided by the five senses. It might be possible for every man to be able to perceive objects at a distance or through a wall, to move objects without touching them, to project his own thoughts and feelings into the nervous systems of others, and to have knowledge of events that have not yet taken place.

What is required is a fairly simple understanding (if understanding any natural phenomenon is really possible) of what is happening to cause experiences that seem beyond the realm of the ordinary. We have been bound into an increasingly scientific society for the past several hundred years. Accordingly, science has dictated that we live in a three dimensional environment and in present time. Perhaps those who seem to possess supernatural powers have taken upon themselves the freedom to disbelieve science. They can then ascend into a state of increased awareness, in which all time (past, present, and future) is merged and dimensionality has no immediate relevance. This might explain why "clairvoyants" or "psy-

chics" so often receive their messages in dream states. As Edgar Cayce, widely acclaimed master of prophecy, suggested, "in dreams, time seems to have no existence. It is not its passage which occupies us, but the reality of the message. Nor is space given a rational treatment. It is as if the mind no longer needed to be bound by time and space, but could see in this state what is important."

There is a time for everything. Is there also a time for time to come together?

Cayce asserted that not only can precognition be explained against the formula of time, space and patience, but so can intuition, perception beyond factual knowledge, telepathy and teleportation.

What kind of "magical" behaviors result when time is merged? J. W. Dunne has proved scientifically that certain dreams can foretell even distant future events. He dreamed in 1901 that the town of Lowestoft, on the east coast of England, was bombarded by foreign warships. The bombardment actually took place in 1914, and happened exactly as Dunne had described it in 1901. He also dreamed of newspaper headlines announcing the eruption of Mount Pelée several months before it actually happened.

Edgar Cayce was able to enter self-induced hypnotic states and, while asleep, he prescribed successful medical treatments for people suffering from undiagnosed ailments. Cayce never met the patients (their symptoms were described to him by observers) and he had no medical training. In fact, he was once arrested for practicing (successful) medicine without a license. Perception beyond factual knowledge through the blending of time and space? Maybe. Maybe not.

Such examples of energy transference (brain waves, perhaps?) have not been limited to the span of modern man, with his knowledge of magnetic fields and electronic transmission. We find in both Old and New Testaments of the Bible accounts of an old man's psychic experience, stories of the witch of Endor, of the visions of the prophets, of the appearances of angels and cherubim, of the sudden ability of the Christians to speak in tongues.

If we can account for these occurrences through a re-arrangement of time, might we also then be-

lieve that there is a magical quality in all of life, a kind of formula for doing things beyond one's personal powers? Perhaps magic is nothing more than a ritualized expression of desires that cannot be fulfilled by technical means, and which finds expression in speech and gesture.

If there are no magical people (assuming that all normal men could be trained to see the universe as the prophets do, once contemporary time-space imprints are destroyed) are there then magical places on earth? Lourdes for the healing of the faithful? The Mexican desert where believers search for specially potent cacti?

Is it not at least possible that energy created in men's minds is converged by the lens-like structure of the Milky Way to focus on these select spots on our planet? Worth considering on a lazy summer day.

Whatever its cause, this pulsating flow of energy in and out of the human mind (maybe in conjunction with other "energy" forces in the universe) creates a phenomenon that is hard to ignore. Call it the supernatural, the religious, the mystical experience. Whatever, it is seeming to be living through a resurgence of worldwide popularity.

Although church membership is on the decline, there is evidence of a growing awareness of and belief in the supernatural, and in gods of sorts. In the last decade, there have been more than 30,000 astrologers making their livings in the U.S., and more than twenty magazines devoted exclusively to astrology. In France, francs spent annually on fees to prophets and soothsayers far exceed the number budgeted for scientific research. Psychics like Peter Hurkos are being employed by police departments to help solve crimes, and one U.S. governmental agency has even proposed that clairvoyants should be employed by its department to try to foresee where enemy bombs would fall in the event of war.

Perhaps all we've said is that, in addition to his increasing reliance on scientific discoveries and technological advances, man should look to himself as the most complete, most vital form of energy anywhere.

As Alan Watts has urged, man should have an "awareness of eternal energy, which seems to be

"But there was one pigeon, a beautiful bird, pure white with light gray tips on its wings; that one was different. It was a female. I would know that pigeon anywhere.
No matter where I was that pigeon would find me; when I wanted her I had only to wish and call her and she would come flying to me.
She understood me and I understood her...
I loved that pigeon, I loved her as man loves a woman, and she loved me...As long as I had her, there was a purpose in my life.
Then one night as I was lying in my bed in the dark, solving problems, as usual, she flew in through the open window and stood on my desk.
I knew she wanted me; she wanted to tell me something important so I got up and went to her.
As I looked at her I knew she wanted to tell me—she was dying. And then, as I got her message, there came a light from her eyes—powerful beams of light.
Yes...It was a real light, a powerful, dazzling, blinding light, a light more intense than I had ever produced by the most powerful lamps in my laboratory..."

JOHN J. O'NEILL/*Prodigal Genius: The Life of Nikola Tesla*

both the current in your nerves and that mysterious e which equals mc^2 ... One sees clearly that all existence is a single energy, and that this energy is one's own being. Of course, there is death as well as life, because energy is a pulsation, and just as waves must have both crests and troughs, the experience of existing must go on and off. Basically, there is simply nothing to worry about, because you yourself are the eternal energy of the universe playing hide-and-seek with itself." ✿

Photo by Marvin Lyons

chapter 4.

FOOD:
An Energy Exchange System

Photo by George Selland

4.
The Lost Alphabet

Something happened about a billion years ago that changed the nature of life on earth. Animals suddenly emerged as species distinct from their vegetable forebears. They lost that part of the genetic alphabet that told them how to manufacture half of the protein components necessary for life. To survive, they had to eat species which had not lost that ability. Thus "the food problem" began—with a lost alphabet.

When chronic hunger, particularly hunger for proteins and certain vitamins, produces chronic lack of appetite and loss of interest in food, the sexual instinct becomes dominant. The chronic starveling, whose appetite for food is dulled and easily satisfied, turns his attention away from his weakened nutritional instincts. The biologically important and psychologically satisfactory activity which presents itself is sexual. Thus one primary need is emphasized to compensate for the other.

ROBERT DE ROOS/
"Hunger, the World's Terrible Aphrodisiac,"
This World, July 5, 1970

From the innocently perverse technological pioneering of the eighteen-eighties, which removed most of the vitamins and minerals from two-thirds of our American foods, the American diet has never recovered. Nutritionally, the modern food technology turned out to be not exactly a Frankenstein, but a kind of institutional Dr. Jekyll and Mr. Hyde.

JAMES RORTY and NORMAN PHILIP/
Tomorrow's Food, 1947

Diet is constructed from fuel material, body-building and body-regulating material. No diet is perfect in which these are not all represented. Now, foods are like sections of houses. Some correspond to single parts, as a floor or window or perhaps a chimney; others to a house lacking only a door or two. It takes some kind of thought to put them together so that we shall have all kinds of parts without a great many extra ones of certain kinds and not enough of others.

MARY SWARTZ ROSE/
Everyday Foods in War Time, 1918

You wonder what this he or she or it was; this once microscopic creature who now in colonies of cells walks the world like a giant, devouring everything in its path.

Whatever this catastrophic creature may be, it is driven by hunger. More specifically, it is engaged in the search for eight or ten missing amino acids, part of twenty that make up the proteins that make life possible. This creature can bask in the sun and it can eat dirt—the combination that vegetables use to produce the missing aminos. But for man—and all his animal relatives—it does not work.

And so in desperation it eats the creatures whose blueprints include the missing formula.

In search for the missing letters of his genetic alphabet, the giant stalks the earth; turning over logs, plowing the grasslands, poisoning ponds, or, in his more sophisticated version shooting elk and moose with machine guns from helicopters. He is alphabet driven. He is insane.

He can, does and will eat anything he can capture and swallow: ants and eels and earwigs; sea slugs and urchins and scallops and sea lions; porpoise, dolphin and whale; snails and cucumbers, artichokes and sunflowers; fungi and mushrooms and toadstools; rice and wheat, barley and rye; sheep and cattle and goats. In extremity, he will eat cats and dogs and mice and lice, and even his fellow humans.

"The human brain," says Loren Eiseley in "The Unexpected Universe," "so frail, so perishable, so full of inexhaustible dreams and hungers, burns by the power of a leaf. . . . The human body is a magical vessel, but its life is linked with an element it cannot produce. Only the green plant knows the secret of transforming the light that comes to us across the far reaches of space."

The concept of the missing alphabet comes to us from Hamish Munro (*Technology Review,* April, 1970). He said:

"Animals emerged as distinct forms of life probably about one billion years ago, first as single cells, then as organisms made up of groups of cells, finally developing into the many species we now know—worms, insects, fish, birds, and mammals. All types of animals from the simplest forms up to the most sophisticated so far examined show basically the same needs for dietary constituents.

"For example, although the proteins of their bodies contain 20 different amino acids as their structural components, all species of animals, from single-celled types up to man, can manufacture only half of these important compounds; all are dependent on the environment for the remaining eight or ten amino acids. . . . Animals cannot survive and grow if they are denied even one of these. . . .

"This is quite different from the situation in bacteria, plants and molds; many bacteria and all plants are able to synthesize all the amino acids, from simple precursors. It can be concluded that the branch point from which the plant and animal kingdom evolved separately from more primitive cells was also the point at which the animal cells lost the capacity to make these eight or ten essential amino acids; part of the DNA carrying the information for making these compounds became deleted from the cell's genetic information, and all subsequent forms of animal cells perpetuated the defect."

He goes on to point out that surviving animals "fed from the dead bodies of their next door neighbors" and that thus muscles (which increased the area for feeding) and later on neural systems (which enabled them to detect where the bodies might be) led to the more complicated forms of animals as we now know them.

But that was in the past. It is now technologically possible for man to produce most of the amino acids synthetically. He can also, on a laboratory scale, perform photosynthesis; the conversion of solar energy into edible chemicals. Perhaps it may be no longer necessary for man to murder in order to live.

"Thereafter," as Alan Watts says in "Murder in the Kitchen," "the energy of the universe will appear in new patterns and guises, and dance to different rhythms. The show will always go on, but must the going on be so intensive an agony? Must the price of life always be soft, sensitive flesh and nerve squirming under the crunch of sharp teeth? If so, then, as Camus said, 'the only serious philosophical problem is whether or not to commit suicide.' " ✿

In the South Pacific, the king of the Fiji Islands assured Dr. Price that the vitamin-conscious cannibals were interested primarily in the livers of their victims. . . . Among the seven-foot Neurs of the upper Nile Valley, Dr. Price again encountered a liver-worship similar to that of the cannibal islanders. The Neurs believe that every man and woman has a soul that resides in the liver and that man's character and physical growth depends on how well he feeds that soul by eating the livers of animals.

JAMES RORTY and NORMAN PHILIP/ *Tomorrow's Food,* **1947**

Man has emerged as a thinking animal because he possesses a nervous system that evolved as part of his ancestors' equipment for regulating movement. Furthermore, the ideas that man conceives can only be communicated through muscular movements, originally favored because of their evolutionary advantage in the hunt for food.

HAMISH N. MUNRO/ **"Nutrition and Human Evolution,"** *Technology Review,* **April, 1970**

Back in his Cleveland laboratory, Dr. Price proceeded to compare, for mineral and vitamin content, the primitive diets, specimens of which he had collected as a routine part of his field studies, with the white man's diets that had displaced them. What he found was startling. Compared with our meager and degenerating nutritional perversion and parsimony, the best of these primitives lived like kings, with an habitual daily consumption of vitamins and minerals often tenfold that of the displacing white man's diet.

JAMES RORTY and NORMAN PHILIP/ *Tomorrow's Food,* **1947**

In a culture recently accustomed to affluence, we seem to be obsessed with the "more-is-better" syndrome. Consequently, we've convinced ourselves that to win the worldwide war on hunger, all we need do is produce more food…Maybe…But it appears we might win even sooner by simply making more intelligent use of what food we have.

the thinking man's diet

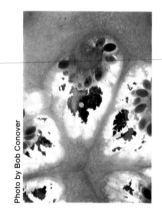

Photo by Bob Conover

Because we all eat, we automatically become self-appointed experts on food *and* nutrition. And that's just the problem. Although few of us realize it, there *is* a difference between the two.

We eat because we have to—simple as that. But, the quality of life each of us is able to maintain as a result of eating depends on the quality (not quantity) of the food he puts into his mouth. You are, in fact, what you eat.

There are certain components of food known as "nutrients." It has been scientifically deduced that a pre-determined amount of specific nutrients is required by the human animal to provide energy and, equally important, to fulfill a structural and functional role. This latter role includes basic mental and physical development in childhood, and then the maintenance of good health throughout life.

Basically, food components commonly labeled fats and carbohydrates (sugars and starches) are used by the body to provide essential energy. The potential for energy release that each component of fat or carbohydrate provides is measured in terms of calories. Calories not immediately used up in energy releases are stored, in the form of fat, for later demands.

There's another class of nutrients that has responsibility for performing the second role—meeting functional and structural needs. These are the proteins, the vitamins, and the minerals. Commonly referred to as the "building blocks," they work to build strong, fully developed bodies in the first place, and then to keep all systems in balance and functioning smoothly—the bones straight, the teeth strong, the cell walls firm, the blood red and rich.

It has been shown that children deprived from infancy of some of the essential nutrients from the second group (caused by either a lack in the quantity or, more likely, in the *quality* of food available) suffer from some degree of physical and/or mental impairment. This may be seen in stunted bone and skeletal development, in decreased learning capacity, in limited brain size and functional ability. Such early damage is irreparable.

When a person's diet does not include an adequate amount of protein, minerals, and vitamins,

Despite all we have done we are still in the Model T era of food and nutrition expertise. We are at a sort of launching phase of a new food world for tomorrow.

HOWARD BAUMAN/
"Foods of the Future,"
speaking as Vice President, Science
& Technology, Pillsbury, Feb., 1967

Although no conclusive proof can be obtained, the addition of the B vitamins to white bread and flour has effectively eliminated beriberi, pellagra, and ariboflavinosis in the United States. Perhaps protein fortication can similarly affect malnutrition.

DR. WILLIAM SEBRELL, JR./
"Fortification of Foods with Synthetic Nutrients,"
Technology Review, **Feb., 1970**

Here is the nub of the problem: we confuse diet with medicine and cooking with pharmacology, and thus it comes to pass that the classes of dietician and cook are mutually exclusive—the former judging by the test tube and the latter by nose and tongue. Labels on food packages read just like labels on proprietary medicines. You may not have the slightest idea what it means, but with all that small, scientific-looking print and decimal points it sure must be good for you.

ALAN WATTS/
"Murder in the Kitchen,"
Does it Matter?, **1970**

Vegetables are a real untapped gold mine of value for many of us. We need meat, too, but not nearly as much as most Americans eat. Perhaps we should arrange our meals like people in many foreign countries—fill up on plant protein foods before tackling the meat course. We Americans tend to wade right into the roast beef before taking the edge off our appetites, and as a result, our arteries fill up with cholesterol faster than anyone else's.

ROBERT RODALE/
"Cooking Without Recipes,"
Organic Gardening and Farming, July, 1968

Ever since Adam and Eve, whole armies of explorers have been travelling on their stomachs. From Moses to Magellan, from the ships of the Iliad to Apollo XI, diet has played a dominant role in man's peregrinations into the great unknown. Indeed, a study of the supreme feats of exploration leads to the inescapable conclusion that leadership and nutrition have proven the ultimate difference between success and failure—often the difference between life and death.

LOWELL THOMAS/
"From Eve to Astronauts,"
Nutrition Today, Autumn, 1969

he is said to be suffering from malnutrition, regardless of the quantity of fats and carbohydrates he is eating daily.

The key words are "adequate amount," and herein lies the problem. A *sufficient* daily intake of proteins, vitamins and minerals differs from individual to individual. It is possible, though, to establish general guidelines for body sizes, sex, age, activities, etc. For example, women are known to need more iron throughout most of their lives than are men. Pregnant and nursing women need 1/3 to 1/2 more of each of the essential nutrients than other women in their respective age and weight groups. And, of course, adolescents need more of everything than most adults.

Most people think they know what they need, and many make a determined effort to eat "balanced" meals. Those who eat "junk" food and know it often rationalize that they make up for it by drinking orange juice, having a nice juicy steak for dinner and so on. They rarely do. The danger here is not that the "junk" will hurt them (it's generally high in calories and while it won't make them sick, neither will it insure well being) but that it will replace food containing vital nutrients. Children who snack on cookies and soda pop, and teens who fill up on potato chips and pretzels, are generally "too full" to eat the milk, green vegetables, and meat served at mealtime.

Such eating habits have taken their toll. In a recent National Nutrition Survey that involved more than 4,000 households throughout the country, one-third of the children studied had anemia, one-third suffered from vitamin A deficiencies, and 5% of the people had enlarged thyroid glands —a condition virtually eliminated some years ago when there was an emphasis placed upon eating iodized salt. With increasing consumer concern over various "additives," consumption of iodized salt has decreased, and the goiter condition has reappeared.

Malnutrition. But why? It appears that, contrary to widely accepted belief, supported by politicians and television documentaries, there is no positive correlation between poverty and malnutrition. (There *may* be a correlation between poverty and restricted opportunities for education that would lead to subsequent intelligent choices of food. What is important here, however, is to realize that one who is poor need not be malnourished, and one who is malnourished is not necessarily poor.) As nutritionist George Mann points out, (*Food and Nutrition News,* Nov., 1969) "it is an obvious fact that many malnourished persons make bad food choices. The prevalence of automobiles in the front yard, television in parlor and beer in the refrigerator ought to rank with pot bellies and sad eyes when the nutritionists go out on their survey sallies. Perhaps this oversight occurs because poverty is a more acceptable explanation for malnutrition. If it were the cause, we would have a ready solution in this affluent society — money. But if poverty is not the main cause, neither malnutrition nor our consciences are going to be relieved by doles and food stamps."

It cannot be assumed that with more food available to choose from and more money with which to buy it, the nutritional quality of man's diet is automatically going to improve. Witness the growing demand for "gourmet" food in this country. Or the changing life styles in India, where, as more money becomes available to each family unit, the first thing the family does is shift from home-pounded rice to polished rice, which is more aesthetically pleasing but has far less nutritional value than the former.

When malnutrition appears in places that are not suffering from an acute famine (we're not talking about Biafra here but about mid-town Atlanta, suburban Walnut Creek, upper class Grosse Pointe, New York's west side, and all their companion neighborhoods), there seems to be only one real reason—a lack of nutrition education. And in this case, ignorance isn't bliss. It's headaches, and colds, and flu and weakened bones and listlessness.

It's pretty obvious that no wife or mother knowingly harms her family by serving nutritionally weak meals. She just doesn't know the difference. One of the major problems in combating the malnutrition problem is convincing those who prepare the family meal that there is a problem. Back to the idea of self-styled experts. What woman doesn't think she knows best what's good for her

family? Isn't there always enough food to go around? What more could anyone ask?

Actually, quite a bit more. We should be asking —no, demanding—that an all-out educational nutrition program be launched immediately, aimed at all age levels, at people in all income groups, in all ethnic groups.

If it is to succeed—and there's no apparent reason that it couldn't—the major thrust of the education program should be aimed at young people. These children are the very ones who suffer the consequences and who stand to gain most from a nutritional up-grading of eating habits. If a toddler can sit in front of the television set for hours and be "taught" to ask his parents for "Hot Wheels" or Captain Crunch breakfast cereal, there's absolutely no reason television can't also be used to teach him to ask Mom for milk and apples and peanut butter. The use of television to teach very young children is being ably demonstrated by the overwhelming success of "Sesame Street." There's nothing "academic" or schoolish about it. Children learn through the use of games, animation, fast-paced skits, songs, etc. All of these techniques could and should be employed to teach the very young basic principles of nutrition, both in regular programming format and in commercials surrounding the children's programs.

Another thrust in the educational program should be directed toward physicians. If serious nutritional questions arise in households today, such questions are most often directed toward the family doctor. Unfortunately, he is, in most cases, no better informed than the questioner himself. Up until now, there has been little attention paid to nutrition in the nation's medical schools, and few doctors have the time to educate themselves in this field. In one never-officially-released test, Harvard medical school students and secretaries at Harvard were given a basic test on nutrition. The results for each group were equal.

Because doctors usually only see sick people, it is important that, once their own nutrition education is upgraded in medical school, they be encouraged to prescribe nutritious meal suggestions for individual patients along with medicine. Special emphasis should be directed toward outlining

**La Cuisine Maigre describes itself—
it has little food in it. "Everything,
everyone is lean, scrawny, half starved
in this poor kitchen."**

**La Cuisine Grasse is occupied by
"Mynheer Fatman and his friends . . . A
suckling pig is being basted, while an
overfed cat laps the drippings . . ."**

Both engravings are attributed to van der Hayden and are dated 1563. Courtesy of *Graphic Worlds of Peter Bruegel, the elder*, Dover Books, N.Y.

menus for infants and toddlers as a regular part of well-baby care.

As still another facet of a massive educational program, advertisers should be encouraged, and forced, if necessary, to upgrade their advertising. This would involve a change from being strictly sales oriented toward being health oriented. If consumer demand can make it fashionable to be aware of and concerned about nutrition, advertisers would certainly find it to their advantage to point out the nutritional values of their products.

There is a place for nutrition education in the schools, and not just in home economics classes. Nutrition can be easily worked into mathematics classes (story problems with a message) and into classes in history, economics, and of course, biology.

Why not continue the education program onto the food labels themselves? Instead of telling the cook that a can of chicken soup contains 298 grams of chicken stock, enriched wheat flour, vegetable oil, cream, salt, corn starch, non-fat dry milk, monosodium glutamate, sugar, and margarine, why not change the label to read "when mixed with 1 can whole milk, this can contains 30% of the protein, 43% of the calcium, 70% of the vitamin A that a male adult needs daily." Bottled vitamin pills are labeled in this way as a matter of course. There's no reason that most food products sold in cans or bottles or boxes can't be.

Now, for the content of the educational program. First, of course, people must be made aware of what is nutritionally important food and what isn't. A start in this direction was made in the recent "expose" of the empty caloric value of many breakfast cereals. While they certainly are not harmful, the same portions of meat, milk, or eggs contain far more nutrients essential for the maintenance of good health.

A second part of the program might teach people not to waste what nutritious food is already available in large quantities. We throw away a far larger part of the nutritiously valuable plant (about 80%) or animal than we eat. It has been estimated that if human beings ate the produce cultivated in the world today in their entirety, there would be enough produce available to feed more than ten

The one absolutely essential requirement for the art of cooking is a love for its raw materials: the shape and feel of eggs, the sniff of flour, or mint, or garlic, the marvelous form and shimmer of a mackerel, the marbled red texture of a cut of beef, the pale green translucence of fresh lettuce, the concentric ellipses of a sliced onion, and the weight, warmth, and resilience of flour-dusted dough under your fingers. The spiritual attitude of the cook will be all the more enriched if there is a familiarity with barns and vineyards, fishing wharves and dairies, orchards and kitchen gardens.

ALAN WATTS/
"Murder in the Kitchen,"
Does it Matter?, 1970

Every man shall eat in safety
Under his own vine what he plants, and sing
The merry songs of peace to all his neighbours.

SHAKESPEARE/
King Henry VIII

**Daily allowance for man of average size =
70 grams of protein**

Impt. sources of protein	Grams
3 oz. serving lean meat	16-23
3 oz. fish	16-25
3 oz. chicken (boneless)	25
1 whole egg	6
1 cup milk	9
1 inch cube American cheese	4
1/2 cup cottage cheese	15-19
1 cup cooked dried beans	15
1 tablespoon peanut butter	4
1 slice bread	2
1 cup cooked oatmeal	5
1 cup cooked macaroni	5

Better Homes and Gardens New Cookbook, 1965

There is a great need for research and
massive education of the populace on
proper nutrition. Assistance should be
provided in this direction by the $100
billion-plus food industry. Just in terms
of practicality, it's not profitable to
kill off the consumers!

RALPH NADER/
"The Chemical Feast,"
speech delivered May, 1970

you've seen a strawberry
that's had a struggle; yet
was, where the fragments met,

a hedgehog or a star-
fish for the multitude
of seeds. What better food

than apple-seeds—the fruit
within the fruit—locked in
like counter-curved twin

hazel-nuts?

T. S. ELIOT/
"Nevertheless"

There is no flavor comparable, I will
contend, to that of the crisp, tawny,
well-watched, not over-roasted, *crackling*,
as it is well called—the very teeth are
invited to their share of the pleasure at
this banquet in overcoming the coy, brittle
resistance—with the adhesive oleaginous—
O call it not fat! but an indefinable sweetness
growing up to it—the tender blossoming
of fat—fat cropped in the bud—taken in the
shoot—in the first innocence—the cream
and quintessence of the child-pig's yet pure
food—the lean, not lean, but a kind of animal
manna—or rather, fat and lean (if it must be
so) so blended and running into each other,
that both together make but one ambrosian
result, or common substance.

CHARLES LAMB/
"A Dissertation Upon Roast Pig"

times our current world population. (Harrison Brown, *The Next Hundred Years,* 1963.) There is no valid reason that people cannot be educated to eat the stems, leaves, and roots of wheat as well as the seed.

Another component of the educational program must be directed toward a change in consumer attitudes concerning fortification. Increasing skepticism toward additives of any type has contributed its part to the malnutrition scene. Some years ago, it was decided that bread and flour would be the vehicles to carry added nutrients in this country because the majority of the population was getting 40% of its daily caloric intake in bread. Today, bad publicity surrounding mushy bread and its reputation for being "fattening" have reduced bread consumption considerably, and the nutrients with which it is fortified are not being received from any substitutes.

It would seem to make sense to ascertain which foods constitute the staples in any given nation or region, and then to fortify those products with the amino acids (proteins), minerals and vitamins missing in normal diets in the particular area. For example, research has demonstrated that substantial calcium deficiencies in India can be overcome through salt fortification, without increasing the cost of the salt.

If advertising can indeed create "false" demands, as it has so often been credited or chided for doing, it can certainly be used in this case to create a demand for and acceptance of fortification of basic food products.

And, finally, on a global scale, the educational program must convey the message that combatting malnutrition must rank among any nation's top priorities. Good nutrition is every bit as important as industrialization to a developing country. What good are modern factories, gleaming laboratories, and skyscrapers if the workers are sick, lethargic, or mentally impaired, all as a result of lingering malnutrition?

If only it were so simple to solve all the world's problems. It's not. But malnutrition is one problem that doesn't have to exist at all. We have the technology and the resources to eradicate it completely. All that seems to be lacking is the will. ✿

green paradox

It has been called "The Green Revolution"—the discovery that essential cereals can be biologically engineered to increase crop yields and protein content and be specifically tailored for the areas in which they are to be grown. It has been likened in importance to the introduction of the steam engine to the Industrial Revolution. That it is green there is no doubt; that it is a "revolution" remains to be seen. The paradox is that, should "The Green Revolution" be wholly successful, it may well destroy the very societies it was intended to preserve.

Illustration by Bob Conover

There is no longer a division possible between factory and farm or, in this sense, town and country; all are closely interlocked in a close symbiotic relation—a man-made ecology which we now see, almost for the first time, as an integrally functioning "organic" sector within the overall ecosystem. Agriculture, until recently viewed as an independent sector of human activity from industry, is now more clearly viewed as a frontier area of scientific and technological attention. It is one, particularly, in which traditional modes are no longer adequate to the complexity and size of immediate requirements.

JOHN McHALE/
World Design Science Decade, **1965-1975**

All indications are that the maldistribution of income in the underdeveloped world will be worse before it is better. The agricultural areas affected by the green revolution may progress quite rapidly, but this affects only 10 to 20 percent of the rural population.

MAX F. MILLIKAN/
"Population, Food Supply and Economic Development,"
Technology Review, **Feb., 1970**

Most Americans, if asked what they considered to be the most significant advances of the first 70 years of this century would probably answer, "the development of nuclear energy, the introduction of television as mass media, and the space programs that finally landed men on the moon."

Significant as these may be (and there are more serious questions as to their significance), the technological breakthrough that is sometimes called the "Green Revolution," and about which most Americans know very little, is probably of greater significance than all the others put together.

The "Green Revolution" can very simply be described as the application of biological engineering to the development of edible plants for specific ecological areas. Mendel and Burbank did this many years ago, but their efforts were directed toward foods in the north temperate zones. What is different about the "Green Revolution" is that it can be—and is being—applied to the tropical and equatorial areas of the earth where there are the most people and where the food problem is most critical. Using advanced biological techniques and sophisticated space age instrumentation, new species can be deliberately designed and developed for the soil conditions, amount of solar energy, rainfall and the ability to learn new techniques by peasant farmers.

"Plant breeders are biological engineers," says Lester Brown (*Seeds of Change*, 1970). "Just as Henry Ford designed the Model-T to meet the varied needs of middle-class America, so the plant breeders designed the new wheat and rice varieties to meet the varied needs of peasant farmers in the poor regions of the world. . . . Just as the Model-T had to be run on all kinds of roads in all kinds of weather, so the new seeds had to be able to grow under a wide variety of soil and climatic conditions."

We can, if necessary, do without many of the conveniences we take for granted: washing machines, television sets, automobiles, wonder drugs, houses—all products of our major industrial enterprises. What we *cannot* do without is food with a high enough protein and caloric content to sustain human life. Except to the extent that the industrial establishment contributes to the production of food (through tools, inorganic fertilizers, pesticides, distribution and storage systems) industry is at best peripheral to the needs of humans and at worst superfluous. This may seem so obvious as to not be worthy of mention, yet when the "planners" establish national or international priorities, they frequently appear to forget that farms and farmers can survive without the cities, but that the cities and their attendant industrial belts cannot survive without the farms. In the allocation between bombs and butter, the bombs always seem to come out on top. But you cannot eat bombs.

The Industrial Revolution was the product of the Agricultural Revolution, which freed people to leave the land to work in the factories. The feedback from the Industrial Revolution was mechanization of agriculture, thus driving more people off the land to furnish low-cost labor for the factories. The legacy of mechanized agriculture is the big city ghetto. The countries that have managed to create urban ghettoes in this way are called, by a euphemism surpassing belief, "developed." Those which have not seen the light yet are "underdeveloped." Many other factors are involved, but the trek to the cities is, in most countries, the result of mechanized or plantation-type one-crop agriculture.

It remains to be seen whether the "Green Revolution" will reverse this process or accelerate it. In McLuhan's "electronic village" concept (itself an extension of Lewis Mumford's concept of the city as "an instrument for communication"), there is no advantage whatsoever in city life over country life. Perhaps the combination of the "Green Revolution" and the electronic village will bring about the inevitable death of the cities and a new global society will be formed. It would be formed of "cottage industries" supported by large "collective" farms, and held together by computers, satellites, laser and television. Perhaps not; the "Green Revolution" may drive all but the biggest, most highly mechanized operators off the land, and the cities will continue to be the cesspools for the waste products of the combined spectres of the Industrial and Agricultural Revolutions.

The way the "Green Revolution" began and de-

Today we hear a lot about various "revolutions" taking place in our society, but there's one in agriculture that is more of a "creeping" revolution than a sudden one. This is the marked change in agricultural practices since farmers first started using electricity to replace kerosene lamps.

JOHN D. TURREL/
"New Dimensions in Electricity on the Farm,"
Farm Technology, Jan., 1968

Rapid increases in cereal production are but one aspect of the agricultural breakthrough. The new seeds are bringing far-reaching changes in every segment of society. They may be to the agricultural revolution in the poor countries what the steam engine was to the Industrial Revolution in Europe.

LESTER R. BROWN/
Seeds of Change, 1970

So the green revolution will mean an increased disparity in the income in rural populations. Concern exists for urban populations as well: the growth of industry is proceeding too slowly to provide employment for the large number of people being released from agriculture and flooding into the cities.

MAX F. MILLIKAN/
"Population, Food Supply, and Economic Development,"
Technology Review, Feb., 1970

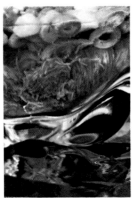

Photo by Uta Maraldo

**Skillfully handled in the seventies,
the Green Revolution can become the
vehicle for eliminating most of the malnutrition
and hunger that now cripple half
the people on this planet and for providing
jobs in the countryside. Poorly
managed, the new seeds and their associated
technologies could displace millions in
the countryside, forcing them into the
already overcrowded cities.**

EUGENE R. BLACK/
Seeds of Change, **1970**

**The Green Revolution, in short, could
do us all in—if it worked. The cruel
joke is that it does not work. To many,
the Green Revolution is a turning point
in man's long war against the biological
limitations of the earth. On examination,
however, "skirmish" seems a more accurate
description. Because, win or lose this
round, the final outcome of the war will
not be altered.**

WILLIAM C. PADDOCK/
"How Green is the Green Revolution?"
Bioscience, **Vol. 20, No. 16**

veloped is a fairly simple, straightforward scenario. It is best told by Lester Brown (*Seeds of Change,* 1970):

"Late in 1944, a group of four young Americans assembled in the hills outside Mexico City. Their mission was to export the United States agricultural revolution to Mexico. They believed that the application of science to agriculture could achieve the same results in the poor countries as in the United States. Like Mao Tse-tung, they believed that the future of these countries could be decided in the countryside.

"The four young revolutionaries were agricultural scientists, the initial staff of an organization assembled and financed by the Rockefeller Foundation at the request of the Mexican government. Their leader was Dr. George Harrar, a young plant pathologist.

"When the group arrived in Mexico, it was a hungry country, importing much of its food from the United States. By 1967, only a quarter of a century later, wheat production had tripled, corn production had doubled, and the average Mexican was consuming 40 per cent more food. Both wheat and corn were being exported, and the economy was prospering. At the heart of this agricultural revolution were new high-yielding wheats developed by Dr. Harrar's group and its successors. Widely adapted to conditions in the tropical-subtropical countries, these wheats proved capable of doubling yields when properly managed and given sufficient water and fertilizer.

"Encouraged by its extraordinary successes with wheat in Mexico, the Rockefeller Foundation joined forces with the Ford Foundation in 1962 to establish the International Rice Research Institute at Los Banos, in the Philippines. Building on the Mexican experience, scientists at IRRI, under the leadership of Dr. Robert Chandler, struck pay dirt quickly when one of their early crosses produced a prolific dwarf rice, IR-8 now known around the world as the 'miracle rice.' Like the Mexican wheats, IR-8 was capable of doubling yields, given the appropriate management and inputs."

There is a particular set to the Western European mind, as transplanted to North America and Australia, to describe "success" in quantitative terms. By such standards, the "Green Revolution" is an extraordinary success. That "more is better" is a proposition that has not yet been philosophically explored in Western societies, and we will not go into that exploration now. But, by the unexamined Western system of values, the "Green Revolution" exceeds the wildest expectations.

According to Lester Brown (*The Futurist,* Aug. 1969), "India's wheat crop has increased 50 per cent in the last four years . . . more than in the preceding 3 or 4 decades. . . . Pakistan has turned in an even more impressive performance. . . . Yet, until two years ago, Pakistan was one of the world's leading wheat importers. . . . Ceylon has increased its rice crop about 34 per cent during the past two years."

Expressed in terms of acreage (again citing Lester Brown (*Seeds of Change,* 1970) the figures are even more impressive. The acreage planted in high-yield cereals in Asia increased as follows:

1964-65	200 acres
1965-66	37,000 acres
1966-67	4,800,000 acres
1967-68	20,000,000 acres
1968-69	34,000,000 acres

Should this exponential growth continue for another decade, the world would be so saturated with high-yield cereals (rice, wheat and corn) that there would not be any room left for people to eat them, and we would have a world-wide desert of food. This, of course, will not happen; the rats, mice, locusts, grasshoppers, weevils, fungi and plant rusts will enthusiastically help keep us from suffering an overabundance of food.

Statistics are impressive, but they are not edible, and there could be some interesting questions as to who really benefits from this new miracle agriculture. In the first place, it does not appear that the small subsistence farmer (who makes up most of the world's agriculturists) benefits very much. To make the new strains work requires large acreage, intensive irrigation, large inputs of fertilizer, roads that connect the farms to the markets, markets with enough purchasing power to absorb the surplus, and mechanized planting, spraying and harvesting equipment that require investments well beyond the range of the small tenant or subsistence farmer. That such systems of credit can be devised there is no doubt. That they will be is doubtful indeed.

Meanwhile the small farmer, no longer able to compete, leaves the land for the cities, and the big owners simply become bigger owners.

There are deeper problems. When a country that once imported foods now is self-sufficient and actually is able to export its surplus, what happens to the economies of the countries that previously exported to them?

The "Green Revolution" involves large acreages of the same species of plants; to be economical, it has to. The ecological result is to reduce the variety of vegetation in any one region, and thus to increase the susceptibility to ecologic disaster (as, in our own experience, wheat rust, corn blight, and boll weevils, insect "explosions," drought, floods, frost) because there are not enough different resistant varieties scattered about the premises to stop, or diminish, the damage.

One more pessimistic thing about the "Green Revolution" and then we'll quit while we're behind. One theory concerning the world population "explosion" is that in many countries parents have large families because of the high infant mortality rate, and in the hopes that at least one son will survive long enough to provide "social security" during the parents' old age. Assuming the success of the "Green Revolution" and that more of the young will survive longer, then how do you persuade the parents that thirty years from now all this will happen? In the meantime, they will continue to have as many children, but more will survive because of the "Green Revolution," and this could be an explosion that makes a hydrogen bomb look like a firecracker.

This is in no way meant to deprecate the "Green Revolution," which is an extraordinary product of contemporary technology. It is to say that like all revolutions, it creates more problems than our present social, political and financial institutions are able—or willing—to cope with. Merely increasing the amount of food does not, in itself, solve the food problem. You cannot, the saying goes, make a silk purse out of a sow's ear. Or maybe it's the other way around. Do we know? ✽

wild kingdom

Any native American Indian, Eskimo, Mexican, African or Australasian aborigine can live off land where most white men would starve. No magic is involved; the natives had lived off their land for thousands of years. In the search for "new" sources of protein, there is an increased interest in "game ranching"; the controlled raising of "wild" animals, and perhaps "wild" plants as well. Wild duck, turkey, pheasant, dove, deer, buffalo, elk, bear and raccoon may show up as low-priced sources of protein in the supermarkets of tomorrow.

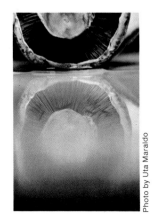

Photo by Uta Maraldo

When the first settlers from Europe arrived in the Western Hemisphere, they found two vast continents literally teeming with plant and animal life. Paradoxically, the settlers virtually starved to death. None of the species they saw were familiar to them and in any event they were "wild" and only savages ate wild things. Beef and mutton and pork, properly raised on proper farms; wheat flour, potatoes, cabbage—that's what civilized man ate.

So, as quickly as he was able, the English settler killed off all the wild things he could; seldom for food, sometimes for "sport," but mostly because they were wild. And, as quickly as he could, he replaced the wild species with domesticated ones; usually poorly adapted to the new environment, and in any case containing less nutritional value than the species they displaced.

The true killers of the American heritage were not the hunters' guns but the farmer's herds of cattle, flocks of sheep and goats; most of all, his acres and acres of wheat, corn, potatoes, sugar cane, cotton and tobacco. His seven-league boots had acre-sized soles, and his heels were made of steel.

In such writings concerning the flora and fauna of the "New World" as have come down to us from the Colonial American period, one finds no suggestion that the herds of buffalo, deer, elk, moose, antelope, bear; nor the flocks of wild birds —duck and geese, pheasant and turkey; nor the shellfish that ringed the coasts, nor the fish that made the inland waters and offshore seas jump, were natural, economical and highly nutritious sources of food. The wild plants that covered the countryside were considered "weeds." The Indians had lived, and lived well, from them for at least ten thousand years.

(The situation was, of course, no different where Europeans established colonies and plantations in South and Central America, the Caribbean, Africa, Hawaii, Australia, New Zealand or the South Sea islands. Wherever the hand of the European white man touched nature, the skull of hunger became visible on the horizon of time.)

Recently there has been some promising, if desultory, interest in "Game Ranching" or "Wild

Farming." This simply means the application of scientific range management to the production of indigenous animals and plants who flourish in their natural habitat. Instead of changing conditions to suit the animals (like building fences, controlling grazing and disease, reseeding, and providing supplemental food and water in order to raise cattle successfully) game ranching makes use of the animals that fit the conditions naturally. The scientific raising of wild animals and plants puts no additional stress on our already overtaxed environment and can, in fact, be a profitable business venture.

Where man has deliberately introduced single crops or species, nature had deliberately introduced diversity.

Says Maureen Shelton (The Environmental Handbook, 1970), "Conventional livestock, — cattle, sheep and goats—graze only a few species of one type of food: grass. Ungulates use the available plants more efficiently. They will eat herbs, grasses, and woody plants ranging from low bushes to tall grasses.

"It is not unusual to find over twenty species of ungulates inhabiting the same area. Each species seems to have a diet different from and complementary to the others. The animals will not only eat different species of food plants but also will eat different parts of the same plant.

"The possibilities of harvesting wild ungulates are now being realized. In Southern Rhodesia, nine large cattle ranches are presently harvesting wildlife. Economic game ranching is being carried out in many other countries."

Well, better late than never.

According to Dr. H. J. Hardenbrook, University of Illinois scientist (Food Technology, Jan., 1970), "There are good reasons for livestock production. They consume roughages not suitable as food for man, harvest vegetation on marginal land. Ruminants harvest and consume cultivated grasses which can yield . . . two times the protein of grain and three times as much as potatoes. Ruminants also synthesize nutritionally essential amino acids."

In the far North, in 1954 a program was begun under the auspices of the Institute for Northern Agricultural Research to see what could be done about the musk-ox, which had virtually been exterminated in the 19th Century to furnish carriage robes for the American elite. The adventure began with the capture of seven calves in Canada's Barren Grounds, on the shore of Great Slave Lake.

"That stage of the program," says John Teal, Jr., (*National Geographic*, June, 1970) "lasted ten years. After intensive study of our animals, we decided that musk oxen were, in fact, suitable for domestication. They yielded a useful product (*qiviut*, an underwool finer than the finest cashmere), were responsive to human beings, bred easily in captivity, lent themselves to farm management and routine, and were even affectionate.

"After 16 years the establishment of a musk-ox industry in the Far North is more than a dream. . . . Our ultimate aim . . . is to make selectively bred musk oxen an important addition to Eskimo economy, chiefly through utilization of their fine underwool. Not in modern times has any other ruminant been domesticated on a large scale."

Things are going on elsewhere, world's apart from Great Slave Lake.

Through Operation Green Turtle (*Undercurrents*, March, 1969) Archie Carr of the University of Florida, in cooperation with the U. S. Navy, the Caribbean Conservation Corps, scientists and citizens of Latin America, the West Indies, Bahamas and Florida, has established a turtle rookery in Costa Rica.

"In the wild, fewer than one per cent of the 500 to 1,000 eggs produced by a female turtle in a nesting season survive. Dr. Carr has almost eliminated nest predation and infant mortality in his nursery, releasing several thousand six-month-old-youngsters each year safely to the sea. But danger for even a nine- or ten-inch turtle still lurks underwater.

"If ranches were established to confine the turtles during their productive life, the fatality rate would be almost nothing. Because of the turtle's fantastic reproductive rate, we would eventually have all the turtle meat we could eat."

In Australia, where the kangaroo is on the verge of extinction, being shot so that its flesh can be sold to American and Japanese pet food companies, a few of the more percipient farmers have

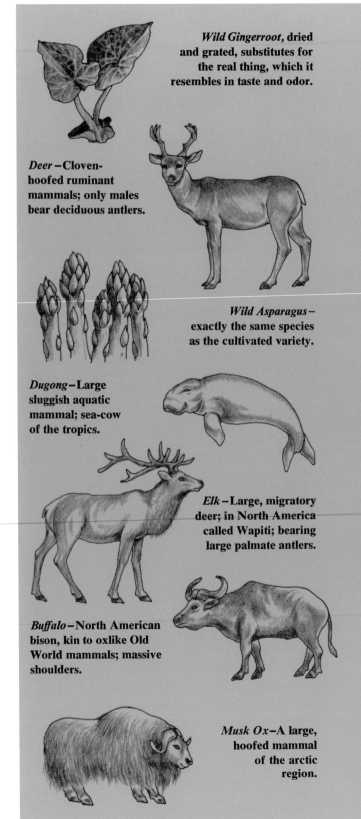

Wild Gingerroot, dried and grated, substitutes for the real thing, which it resembles in taste and odor.

Deer —Cloven-hoofed ruminant mammals; only males bear deciduous antlers.

Wild Asparagus — exactly the same species as the cultivated variety.

Dugong —Large sluggish aquatic mammal; sea-cow of the tropics.

Elk —Large, migratory deer; in North America called Wapiti; bearing large palmate antlers.

Buffalo —North American bison, kin to oxlike Old World mammals; massive shoulders.

Musk Ox —A large, hoofed mammal of the arctic region.

Tapir —Herbivorous, odd-toed ungulate mammal, kin to the horse and rhinocerous.

Mushrooms, when properly selected, furnish some of the most delicious food known to man.

Cattail roots or pollen can be ground to flour; boiled spikes eaten like corn-on-the-cob.

Kangaroo —Herbivorous marsupial from Australia; short forelegs, long, tapered tail.

Wild Onion —All of the many species in this family make good eating, raw or cooked.

Dandelions can be raw in salad, boiled as greens, or drunk as wine or coffee.

Capybara —A large, short-tailed, semi-aquatic rodent from tropical South America.

Eland —Either of two large African antelopes, with spirally-twisted horns.

Day Lily buds and blossoms, stalks and tubers—all are edible.

Hippopotamus — Also called "river horse;" large, chiefly aquatic African mammal.

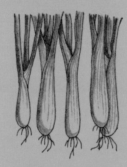

Calamus, or wild iris, can be used as a confection, a cure-all, or a salad plant.

Manatee —Aquatic mammal found in tropical Atlantic coastal waters.

Antelope —Slender, swift-running, long-horned ruminant, from Africa and Asia.

Wild Berries need no explanation; how describe ambrosia, except as food for Gods?

Illustration by Masami Miyamoto

Wild herbivores generally yield more protein
per pound "on the hoof" than domestic
species . . . Ruminants such as the antelope
and the water buffalo are not the only species
worthy of attention, and land is not the
only site available for grazing. The capybara,
a large rodent, is well adapted to South America
and is palatable. Water weeds and plants
growing in swamps and on lake margins,
contribute hardly anything to human nutrition.
They could be collected and fed to land animals,
but it would seem to be more efficient to
domesticate the freshwater manatee and the
marine dugong and use them as sources of meat.

N. W. PIRIE/
"Orthodox and Unorthodox Methods of
Meeting World Food Needs,"
Scientific American, Feb., 1967

There is good reason to think that
several species of wild herbivore,
running together, give a greater return
of human food in many areas of tropical bush
or savanna than domesticated species.

N. W. PIRIE/
"Orthodox and Unorthodox Methods
of Meeting World Food Needs,"
Scientific American, Feb., 1967

Conventional cattle ranching puts stress
on the environment in many ways. Cattle
must be artificially provided with water
and supplementary food. There must be fencing,
bush control, grazing control, disease control,
and reseeding. Even with these expensive
ventures, there are relatively few areas in the
world climatically suited to raising the present
forms of domestic livestock. By contrast, game
ranching uses animals—elands, wildebeests
and other wild ungulates—indigenous to the
local environment. Rather than changing the
conditions to suit the animals, game ranching
uses the animals which fit the conditions.

MAUREEN SHELTON/
"Game Ranching: an Ecologically
Sensible Use of Range Lands,"
The Environmental Handbook, 1970

begun to notice (after 100 years of not noticing) that kangaroo and sheep eat different foods off the same range, and that the two species can be raised on the same land, thus doubling the output of the ranch. For the most part though, the 'roos are simply being shot at night by "sportsmen" using Land Rovers, spotlights, and automatic rifles. Yet kangaroo meat, for human consumption, is a high priced delicacy of far more value than lamb or beef. But the farmers go on raising sheep and cattle. When they have a bad year, they blame the kangaroo for having eaten the food of the domesticated herds.

On a more cheerful note, one might take "A Walk on the Wild Side" with Euell Gibbons (*Stalking The Wild Asparagus,* 1962).

"Come with me for an hour's walk in almost any rural or suburban area in the eastern half of our country (U.S.) and I will point out many edible plants to you. I have collected 15 species that could be used for food on a vacant lot in Chicago. Eighteen different kinds were pointed out in the circle of a two acre pond near Philadelphia. We actually gathered—and later ate—eleven different kinds of wild food in an afternoon spent strolling along Chesapeake Bay."

To give some idea of what we *could* have had, had it not been more profitable to build supermarkets, Gibbons describes the following "wild" feast, made up of foods that could have been picked up by any ten-year-old:

"An autumn meal started off with Wild Grape Juice and Wild Mushroom (Shaggy-Mane) Soup. This was followed by Blue-gill Fillets, battered and fried, and a salad made of sliced wild Jerusalem artichoke tubers and ripe ground cherries, served with a garlic-bleu-cheese dressing. There were Baked Arrowhead Tubers and wild apples, sliced and cooked with butter and brown sugar until they were nearly caramelized. We had dark muffins of lamb's quarter seed, freshly ground, and amber May-Apple-Marmalade. For dessert there was a mile-high Persimmon-Hickory-Nut Chiffon Pie and Chicory Coffee, followed by a bowl of mixed wild nuts for any who still had a vacant cranny to fill."

Or, one assumes, they could have used crannyberries, instead. ✿

Grass clippings, leaves, wet garbage, parts of plants and animals now discarded as "inedible," the bacteria that grow on petroleum waste products, recycled human sewage and proteins wholly synthesized in laboratories may be "new" sources of protein. Most of them have been easily available for thousands of years. Another way out might be to create, through genetic engineering, much smaller people...Lilliput revisited.

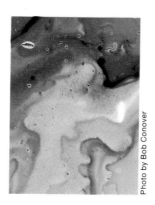

Photo by Bob Conover

hidden springs

FOOD: AN ENERGY EXCHANGE SYSTEM

There's an old story about a cat that got locked up in a warehouse full of canned pet foods and starved to death because he didn't know how to use a can opener.

The story of a contemporary man suffering from hunger and malnutrition in a world stocked with food is somewhat analogous, except that he *does* know how to use a can opener; he just doesn't do so. The reasons why he does not do so are highly complex, but they are not technological; they are economic, political, social and psychological.

We'll start with a statement by H. A. B. Parpia (*Ceres*, Sept.-Oct., 1969) that, "The world produces more than three times the total protein and calorie requirements of its population..." The key word here is "produces," because what is produced and what is available for human consumption are two different things. Losses due to disease, insects and rodents, to inefficient harvesting, distribution, storage and marketing systems take a large toll. Cultural habits, religious taboos, general lack of nutritional knowledge, the deliberate destruction of crops by farmers and subsidies by governments to keep the market price up, all reduce the actual availability of food.

So, short term solutions would appear to be technological and it does appear that technological advances, assuming they are applied on a large scale, may well avert the world food famine that appeared inevitable only a few years ago.

Basically, the technological approaches break down into several promising pathways:

1. We can increase the protein content of plants and animals already widely in use.

2. We can make better use of the protein that is lost in the "inedible" parts of the plants and animals that are now thrown away.

3. We can substantially cut down on the losses to pests, spoilage, distribution, etc. through means that are not in themselves contaminative to the environment.

4. We can begin systems of education that will help people use edible foods that are all around them but, for cultural reasons, they do not use.

5. We can synthetically produce missing ingredients (such as amino acids and vitamins) that can increase the nutritional value of traditional foods.

Some farmers in Hungary are growing a unique rotation of rice or other crop followed by fish and ducks. Large shallow ponds are built and stocked with carp and Long Island duck. They are carefully tended until they grow into flourishing colonies, then harvested and sent to market. The ponds are then drained and rice, maize or other crops are planted in the exposed bottom. The resulting harvests are up to 20 percent higher than for similar crops grown elsewhere in the country.

World Farming, Nov., 1969

In recent years, sunflower seed has become an important crop in many countries of the world. Apart from high quality oil, sunflower seed meal has a higher content of good quality protein than cereals which are still the main source of protein in many countries.

"Preparation of a Colorless Sunflower Protein Isolate,"
Food Technology, March, 1970

Fish Protein Concentrate blends well in cereals, beverages, soups, noodles, bread and cookies. Only small amounts are needed to be nutritionally significant. For example, 5 to 10 per cent of FPC supplementing any cereal makes the protein quality equal to that of milk, meat or eggs.

JAMES R. RUSSO/
"Can New Protein Sources Avert World Shortage?"
Food Engineering, May, 1969

6. We can produce new strains of plants and animals, through genetic manipulation and biological engineering that can survive in areas now barren of edible foods.

7. We can re-cycle garbage and sewage products so that they become important sources of protein in now unharvested plants and animals.

8. We can produce edible protein from sources not usually thought of as sources of food: newspapers and cartons, wood chips and sawdust and petroleum by-products.

9. We can create a world food market based on nutrition rather than on quantity or the number of colors used to print a container that turns out to be half empty when we buy it.

Says Robert Gesteland (*Northwestern Report,* Winter, 1970), "It seems fairly clear that we are very close to synthesis of life and life processes and manipulation of the genome (a complete haploid set of chromosomes) of living things. It will not be long before researchers begin probing genetic modification of plants and animals to produce better food, and ultimately to produce a better man. . . .

"Wilder yet is to think about the shape and size of man. The world is moving much too fast to make use of the evolutionary pressures to modify the structure of man very much. However, it is clear that large size is not much of an advantage and something fascinating to contemplate is the idea of modifying the genome of man to produce very small people. If man were only four-inches high and had no serious predators to fear, our concepts of space on earth would change somewhat."

It's something to think about: the same techniques that brought about dwarf rice and corn could also produce a race of men that would exert much less pressure on the physical environment. Maybe instead of more food, we need smaller people.

There are other ways to go. According to *CIL OVAL* (Fall, 1969), "Unless we have changed the climate of the north with plastic domes, new plants may be bred to turn to the midnight sun to take advantage of long daylight hours. Plants will be bred to take their own nitrogen from the air and will cut fertilizer costs and farmers will apply phos-

phorus, potassium and pesticides in capsules that release the necessary nutrients only when the plant signals (probably chemically) that it needs them."

Such developments are still a long way ahead. Meanwhile there appears to be an abundance of food to feed at least the present population and the techniques to make the food available now exist:

OILSEED PROTEIN: According to N. W. Pirie (*Scientific American,* Feb. 1967), "The residue that is left when oil is expressed from soya, groundnut, cottonseed and sunflower is now for the most part used as animal feed or fertilizer or is simply discarded. It contains about 20 million tons of protein, that is, twice the world's present estimated deficit. . . . Methods are being devised, notably in the Indian state of Mysore and in Guatemala, for processing the oilseeds more carefully in order to produce an acceptable food containing 40 to 50 percent protein."

According to Parpia, "The world production of oilseeds is 85 million tons. . . . At present, a very small portion of the press cake or solvent-extracted meal is being used for human consumption, or as cattle feed."

Says Dr. Nevin Scrimshaw (*Technology Review,* Feb., 1970), "Because the extracted oil (and in the case of cottonseed, the fiber as well) pays part of the cost, these meals are the world's cheapest sources of protein and are likely to remain so. They provide protein at a cost of U.S. $.08 to $.12 per pound compared with U.S. $.61 to $.71 for non-fat dry milk at the current world market price, and U.S. $1 to $2 for most other protein of animal origin."

Of the largely unused sources of protein, soya seems to possess the most immediate possibilities. "More than 60 meatless-meat products now are being fabricated by Worthington Foods, Inc. reports *Food Engineering,* (May, 1969). "They are made from isolated soy protein and other ingredients in a way to closely simulate the originals. . . ."

One of these products is bacon-like slices called "Stripples."

"To produce the Stripple slices," *Food Engineering* explains, "vegetable protein fibers are random-layered to make bacon simulations. Fibers are held

Photo by Bob Conover

In India, leaf protein concentrate has been readily accepted when mixed with pancakes and curry or other spiced dishes. Adding it to the traditional vegetable stews, staple dish in New Guinea, has also proved successful, and in this particular country there has been no difficulty in getting children to eat leaf protein in new-style banana splits.

**BRIAN GARDNER/
"Leaf Protein Extraction,"
World Farming, Dec., 1969**

Inhabitants of Chad and Niger produce a palatable food rich in proteins from a slimy "scum" scooped from the waters of brackish ponds. The scum, really a tangled mass of microscopic algae, is dried in the sun before being used as the basis for a rich soup-like dish known as dihe. The ancient Aztecs also ate a similar algae which grew in Mexican lakes. Now French and Mexican scientists, excited by the food potential, are experimenting with mass production techniques for cultivating the algae. Their research suggests that the annual yield per hectare could be anything from 40 to 45 tons which would produce about 20 tons of quality protein—a yield several hundred times greater than from beef cattle.

**TONY LOFTAS/
"The Troubles of Single-Cell Protein,"
Ceres, Sept.-Oct., 1969**

From Texas A & M comes word of a new process for converting animal blood into a product that looks and tastes like powdered milk. Low in price, the product is 50 per cent protein. Aesthetics aside, the product could be a boon in poor areas of the world.

Inside Industry, Jan. 22, 1970

with an edible binder, and flavor is added. Some layers are colored to simulate lean meat, others are colorless to represent fat. These are formed into a multi-layer slab that is heat-set, then transversely cut into slices. In addition to bacon, meats like ham, pastrami and corned beef may be simulated.

"The ready-to-serve product line is retailed through supermarkets, specialty stores and department stores. Included in the line are simulations of chicken (sliced, diced and fried); beef (diced and sliced); luncheon slices (styled after turkey and smoked and corned beef); and frankfurters and scallops."

Now the reason for going into such detail here is that the Worthington approach may very well be the prototype for the agriculture of the future, which will not be "agriculture" at all, but industry, in much the same way that "natural" agricultural products—wool, cotton, rubber, leather goods, to name a few—have been largely taken over by factory-produced synthetics. Such a view carries with it the happy promise that food would be less costly, that its protein content would be high, and that the pressure of humans on the natural sources of food in the world would be reduced. A side effect might be significant reduction in pollution, since many of the basic ingredients are waste products of other industries.

CELLULOSE PROTEIN: "About 2/3 of the solid material in the average city dump, according to one study, consists of various forms of cellulose (about three pounds per person per day)," says *Technology Review* (February, 1970).

"In nature, cellulose produced by plants is broken down by bacteria and thus re-enters the food cycle. W. Dexter Bellamy of the General Electric Research and Development Center, Schenectady, is studying selected strains of bacteria to see whether the same kind of process can be used, under human control, to convert garbage into protein-rich animal foodstuffs, thus lessening the threat presented by such innovations as the $4 throw-away sleeping bag. . . ."

(Just think of the herds of cattle that could be raised from thrown-away copies of the *New York Times* alone!)

SINGLE CELL PROTEIN: Most of the protein compounds in the world have been produced by microorganisms—principally yeasts and bacteria—and they can grow on virtually anything organic: sucrose, molasses, soybean oil, kerosene, petroleum distillate No. 2, waste paper, surplus and spoiled fruits and vegetables, stalks left over after harvesting cereals or sugar cane, waste products of the lumber industry and methane gas.

"No major differences exist between protein derived from the single cells of yeast or bacteria and the protein of other plants and animals," says Dr. Nevin Scrimshaw. "Sufficient information has accumulated to indicate that single-cell proteins are readily used by animals and man. The advantages of microorganisms as sources of protein are their rapid growth and ability to convert cheap energy sources and nitrogen into high quality protein."

Along these lines Tony Loftas (*Ceres*, Sept.-Oct. 1969), points out that "A bullock weighing ten hundredweight, for example, synthesizes less than one pound of protein in a day whereas the same weight of yeast produces over 50 *tons*.

"The most favoured organisms for producing SCP are the yeasts. For over a decade it has been known that certain yeasts can produce palatable forms of concentrated protein from the sulphite waste liquors of paper mills. However, the substrate which seems to be the most promising at the present time comes not from the paper industry but from the expanding oil industry of the world."

Says James R. Russo (*Food Engineering*, May, 1969), "Standard Oil Co. is producing protein from petroleum on a pilot-scale basing its research facility at Whiting, Indiana. The product is tasteless and looks like tan butter in paste form, or wheat flour in dry form. . . .

"A small manufacturing plant using 1500 barrels of hydrocarbons daily could produce annually as much protein as that contained in a crop of wheat grown on 270,000 acres. And the protein from petroleum would be superior in quality to that from the wheat."

The significance of the protein from petroleum technology is that it reduces a waste problem for petroleum producers, possibly could be a profitable sideline, and many of the protein-short countries of the world have large petroleum sources. Equipment is relatively modest in cost, no long-range distribution would be required, and the single cell protein, properly processed, could be added as a tasteless, odorless compound without requiring a change in established food patterns.

LEAF PROTEIN CONCENTRATES: The green leaves and stalks of grasses, shrubs and trees contain the some proteins as do the plants that are harvested domestically. Since the cuttings are usually a waste product anyway, and the protein extraction process is relatively simple and requires only inexpensive machinery and unskilled labor, it is surprising that more use is not made of this abundant source.

The methods for extraction have been known for 200 years and more efficient extraction-equipment has been developed in recent years. In the tropical and subtropical areas where the protein need is greatest, there is a continuous supply of green leaves that can be harvested all year around. The quality of the leaf protein is nutritionally second only to that of soya, and a side value is that the by-products of leaf protein concentrate are valuable sources of animal and human food.

According to Brian Gardner (*World Farming*, Dec., 1969) "the pulp is believed to have a protein content of 10 to 12 percent and can be processed into stock feed while the waste liquid can be used for cultivating yeasts and other microorganisms. . . ."

Experiments at Rothamsted, England, and Mysore, India, suggest that, "Devoting land to growing successional crops simply for leaf production is justified. More protein can be harvested per acre, per year than by any other method of stock production."

Despite all these advantages, the development of leaf-protein production has been and is—almost minimal. "Extraction equipment," says Pirie, "is in use in India, Ceylon, New Guinea, Nigeria, Sweden and Wisconsin; rather more elaborate equipment was in use in Israel; and leaf protein extraction is either in operation or advocated in the U.S.S.R. and Hungary." ✿

The little pieces of land on which he stands crumbling beneath his feet, his forests dwindling, technological man turns once again to gaze upon his ancient home — the vast and prolific tableland of the sea. Whether the waters of the world can, indeed, make any significant contribution to man's protein needs is an open question. If he uses his technology on water as thoughtlessly as he has used it on land, then there is no hope here. Used with intelligence and love the waters of the world *could* furnish much of the protein man needs. *Could,* we say.

land of bright water

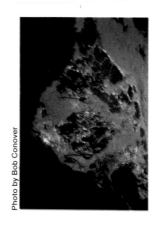

Photo by Bob Conover

If myths were moths, and contained as high a protein content as the latter, there would be no world food shortage. A moth contains protein simply because it is alive. The average myth, as far as our research has extended, contains no protein at all.

But we produce many more myths than moths, so this becomes important in the present context. The particular myth we want to examine here is that man, having loused up that small portion of the earth's land surface that is habitable for him, now thinks of the remaining 7/10 that is water, and figures that seven is bigger than three, and therefore the seas, oceans, rivers and lakes of the world will furnish at least two-and-a-half-times as much protein as the land.

It's the kind of arithmetic that should have been mustered out with the carriage horse; it's the kind of mythologic scenario that could only be written by an aging hack with a worn-out typewriter ribbon in a crummy one room "studio" in an abandoned building at 20th-Century Fox.

In case we dropped someone off along the trail, a myth may be defined as "a symbological narrative or picture representing a cosmic process, or, for the individual, a psychological state." Freud explained myths as a mechanism for wish fulfillment and Jung denoted them the expression of the unconscious dreams of a people.

The moth is "any of the large and varied group of lepidopterous insects. . . . There are 75 families of moths. . . . They have two pairs of wings covered with flattened, dust-like scales." (The last two paragraphs were stolen, or paraphrased, from *The Columbia Encyclopedia,* Third Edition, 1963.)

It is easy to tell a myth from a moth; the myth has only one set of wings, as Icarus discovered.

A great deal of nonsense has been written about the sea as the savior of mankind when he finally has destroyed whatever land he has left. There appear to be at least three things wrong with this:

1. Marine biology is not nearly as advanced a science as we pretend it to be. There has never been the funding that would call forth the most talented young people into the field; talents that, to use a horrible example, were brought to bear on developing nuclear weapons and the space

Every spring, as the warmth of the new
    year seeps down into the ocean, the waters
far below respond to the invisible sun.
    They expand and rise, lifting to the surface,
in untold billions of tons, the salts and
        minerals they bear. Thus fertilized by
food from below and sun from above, the
        floating plants multiply with explosive
violence, the creatures which browse
        upon them flourish accordingly. And so spring
comes to the meadows of the sea.

    ARTHUR C. CLARKE/
    The Deep Range, **1957**

**Planners say by the year 2000 the raising
of cattle and hogs will be practically nonexistent
in Missouri. Instead, farmers in some areas
will raise fish for meat.**

    San Francisco Examiner,
    April 7, 1970

Judging from the fishing industry's behavior toward the sea, one might conclude that if it were to go into the chicken farming business it would plan to eat up all the feed, all the eggs, all the chicks, and all the chickens simultaneously, while burning down the henhouses to keep itself warm.

PAUL and ANNE EHRLICH/
"The Food-from-the-Sea Myth,"
Saturday Review, April, 1970

Man seems to be as ignorant of what he can accomplish by cultivating the sea—aquaculture— as the Masai herdsman roaming the Serengeti Plains is oblivious to the techniques of agricultural science.

DR. HERBERT HARTLEY/
"The Most Exciting Vertebrates,"
Nutrition Today, Sept., 1966

Several companies and institutions are experimenting with dumping garbage at sea. Indications are that it will work, and that we will establish a cycle similar to the farmer who puts nutrients into the land in order to produce a more bountiful crop.

"Feeding the Sea,"
Undercurrents, March, 1969

program. In short, when it comes to understanding the waters and the creatures in them, we appear to know much less than we do about the moon. From last reports, the moon does not appear to be a prolific source of protein.

2. Because it covers most of the planet, water (and the creatures in it) are the largest converters of solar energy on earth. This is done by little creatures called phytoplankton—"tiny green plants that float free in the waters of the oceans." They are the bottom link of the ecological ladder that ends up in tuna and cod and whales. More importantly for humans, they transfer stellar rays and the minerals dissolved in seawater into oxygen and amino acids, without which we wouldn't hardly be around.

Something is happening to the phytoplankton. "Perhaps," says Paul Ehrlich (*Saturday Review*, Apr. 4, 1970), "the most frightening ecological news of 1968 was contained in a short paper entitled "DDT Reduces Photosynthesis by Marine Phytoplankton," which was published in the journal *Science*. The author, ecological chemist Charles F. Wurster, Jr., of the State University of New York, reported that DDT reduced photosynthesis in both experimental cultures and natural accumulations of marine phytoplankton (algae, diatoms, etc.). . . .

" . . . filter-feeding animals may concentrate poisons to levels far higher than those found in the surrounding medium . . . Oysters constantly filter the water they inhabit, and they live in shallow water near the shore, where pollution is heaviest. Consequently, their bodies often contain much higher concentrations of radioactive substances or lethal chemicals than the water in which they live.

"No one knows how long we can continue to pollute the seas with chlorinated hydrocarbon insecticides, polychlorinated biphenyls, and hundreds of thousands of other pollutants without bringing on a world-wide ecological disaster. Subtle changes may already have started a chain reaction in that direction. . . ."

"The greatest threat to mariculture," says S. J. Holt (*Scientific American*, Sept., 1969), "is perhaps the growing pollution of the sea. This is becoming a real problem for fisheries generally, particularly coastal ones, and mariculture could thrive best in just those regions that are most threatened by pollution, namely the ones near large coastal populations and technological centers."

3. We lack at the present time any body of law, any systems of institutions, or any enforcement agencies that will protect the oceans from the destructive practices of man as he has so dramatically demonstrated them on land. Although "the freedom of the seas" doctrine embodies the concept that they are territories held in common by all mankind, the concept has been abrogated mostly by the United States, England, France and Spain. The seas are "free" to whoever happens to have the most powerful navy at the time. When we begin to consider how the bottoms of the seas are to be allocated for commercial exploitation, it is useful to keep this historical experience in mind.

The "Pacem in Maribus" convocation in Malta, sponsored by the Center for the Study of Democratic Institutions, to consider how to establish an international policy to implement the concept that the oceans are "the common heritage of mankind," drew experts from 51 nations.

The convocation appears to have ended in complete agreement: no one really wanted it, if it meant giving up the exploitive rights they already had; they didn't know how to go about it; even if they did know how, they probably wouldn't. The convocation was a success to the extent that it showed that we haven't the slightest idea of what we are doing. This is very hopeful, because human development begins with the statement, "We don't know."

So, those are the three points we wanted to make: that our scientific understanding of the sea and its creatures is woefully deficient; that present practices are polluting the oceans to what may be the point of no return; that we have not so far established international policies for dealing with the complex problems of how the seas are to be used for the maximum benefit of mankind.

We'll go on now to discuss briefly some of the ideas that have been brought forward to increase protein intake from the waters of the world, but we reiterate that none of these make much sense

(Continued on page 146)

Successful fishing depends not so much on the size of fish stocks as on their concentration in space and time. All fishermen use knowledge of such concentrations; they catch fish where they have gathered to reproduce, or where they are on the move in streams or schools. Future fishing methods will surely involve a more active role for the fishermen in causing the fish to congregate. In many part of the world lights and sound are already used to attract fish. We can expect more sophistication in the employment of these and other stimuli. . . .

S. J. HOLT/
"The Food Resources of the Ocean,"
Scientific American, Sept., 1969

Most of the plans for increasing the yield of fishes from the sea disregard the effects of pollution; they are based on the premise that fish stock will be harvested rationally. The history of fisheries so far holds little promise that rationality will prevail. One can, for instance, expect continuation of attempts to harvest simultaneously young and old of the same species, and both the big fishes and the little fishes that big fishes must eat to live. And one can expect pollution to help reduce the size of many or all fish populations.

PAUL and ANNE EHRLICH/
"The Food-from-the-Sea Myth,"
Saturday Review, April 1970

Many years ago it was found that corn was declining in growth in Iowa. After trying all sorts of fertilizers the agronomists concluded that they couldn't change the state of Iowa, so they changed the corn. This is what ichthyologists such as Lauren Donaldson propose to do . . . change the fish.

HERBERT L. HARTLEY/
"The Most Exciting Vertebrates"
Nutrition Today—Sept. 1966

In the future, fish "ranches" might dot the seacoasts of the world. Improved salmon and trout could be raised to migratory size, then released to "pasture" in the open sea until sexual instinct drove them home for "roundup." To simplify marketing, the fish could be irradiated to kill spoiling microbes or perhaps sprayed with a chemical coating that would both retard spoilage from the air and serve as an edible package.

"Here Comes Tomorrow"
By the Staff of *The Wall Street Journal*
Copyright 1966, 1967

In his book "The Deep Range," published in 1957, Arthur C. Clarke suggests a time about 100 years from now when most protein is produced from the sea. He describes the herding of whales through the use of ultrasonic fences along the migratory routes normally taken by the whales, and suggests that killer whales might be caught and trained to act much like sheep dogs—guarding the herds. In addition to their meat, the whales also would produce milk in large quantities, since they produce much more than their calves actually need. Science fiction? Of course. But it doesn't appear nearly as improbable now as it did in 1957.

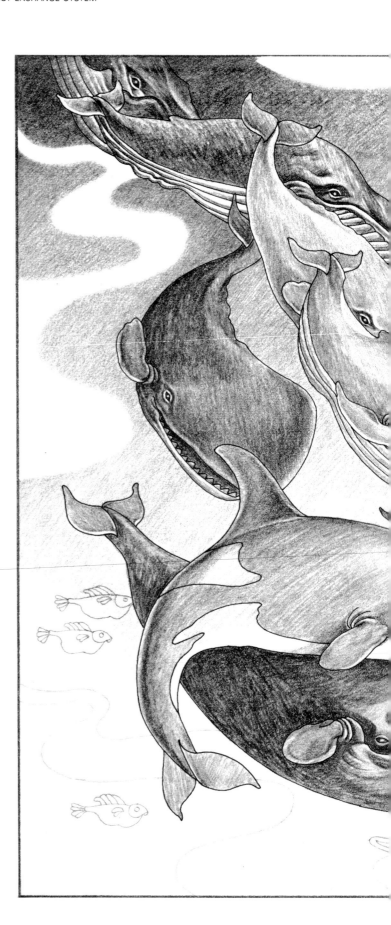

The fish's system selects those minerals for which it has a physiological need and rejects those for which it has no need. The terrestrial animal does not have this advantage. It gets only what the soil has to give him, and in some cases, due to continued heavy cropping, every passing day reduces what the soil has to give.
Biologists have found evidence that many minerals, always available in the sea, can be of enormous value as human nutrients. The next job is to sort out the ones that are of value. We have no idea how to put these minerals together any more than man knows how to make a truly nutritious food from chemicals. But fish can do this. And we do know that the salt-water fish is the only vertebrate that has available to it, in utilizable form, all the minerals on the face of the earth.

DR. ALBERT HARTLEY/
"The Most Exciting Vertebrates,"
Nutrition Today, **Sept., 1966**

It has been proposed many times that the future may produce underwater ranches where herds of fish, turtles and other wandering, but not migratory, marine animals would be bred, raised and fattened for the world food market. In the case of the green turtle (the only sea turtle that is really good to eat) protective ranches may prove to be the only solution to saving them from extinction.

"Turtle Ranches,"
Undercurrents, **March, 1969**

unless marine biology is considerably advanced; unless the senseless pollution of the sea is stopped, and unless there are created international organizations with enforcement powers to guarantee that the oceans are, indeed, the "heritage of mankind."

Since ours is a highly quantitative society, let us play the number game. It won't get us very far, but it is kind of fun.

According to Georg Borgstrom (*The Hungry Planet*, 1967) "if the catch of fish and shellfish (oysters, shrimp and lobster) — everything that China, U.S.S.R., Japan, Europe, the United States and all other nations extract from the sea—were used merely to feed the United States, this country would not receive from this source more protein than is now being consumed in the form of meat—less than half of the protein intake."

"The basis of the food-from-the-sea myth," says Paul Ehrlich, "seems to be theoretical estimates that productivity of fisheries might be increased to many times current yields. However, the most recent analysis by J. H. Ryther of the Woods Hole Oceanographic Institution puts the maximum sustainable fish yield in the vicinity of 100 million metric tons, somewhat less than twice the 1967 harvest of some sixty million metric tons.

"The most careful analysis indicates that the world harvest might be increased to seventy million tons or so by 1980. On a per capita basis, however, an increase of this amount would actually constitute a small *decline*—unless the human population growth rate were to decrease in the next decade."

So, that's one figure.

Here's another. "The present harvest of the oceans is roughly 55 million tons a year, half of which is consumed directly and half converted into fish meal. A well-managed world fishery could yield more than 200 million tons," says S. J. Holt (*Scientific American*, Sept., 1969).

The difference between 50 and 200 is usually considered significant. But the point here is simply that, because we do not know what we are doing, we are playing a game where all the cards are wild. There is a game called "Fairy Chess" where, at the option of the player, any piece on the board can be given the powers of any other piece. Thus a pawn can become a queen. In figuring the potential, sustainable protein resources of the world's waters, we seem to be engaged in a game of "Fairy Chess." Except the option is not ours.

Assuming that we know, within reasonable tolerances, the tonnage of fish caught and used by man throughout the world in a given year (a figure that we really do not know), then it can be said that "in the century from 1850 to 1950, the world catch increased tenfold—an average rate of about 25 per cent per decade. In the next decade (1950-1960) it nearly doubled, and this rapid growth is continuing. . . .

Holt continues: "The first major conference to examine the state of marine fish stocks on a global basis was the United Nations Scientific Conference on the Conservation and Utilization of Resources, held in 1949. . . . The small group of fishery scientists gathered there concluded that the only overfished stocks at that time were those of a few high-priced species in the North Atlantic and North Pacific. . . . They produced a map showing 30 other known major stocks they believed to be underfished.

"The situation was reexamined in 1968. Fishing on half of those 30 stocks is now close to or beyond that required for maximum yield. . . ."

Now back to Ehrlich,". . . examples of over-exploited stocks are East Asian and California sardines; Northwest Pacific salmon; cod in many areas; menhaden; tunas in the Atlantic, Pacific and Indian oceans; flatfish in the Bering Sea; plaice in the North Sea; hake in the North Atlantic; and bottom fish in the West Pacific and East Atlantic oceans. . . ."

Edible fish may very well join the ranks of the buffalo, the passenger pigeon and the condor, i.e., extinct, or virtually so.

There are other ways out. One of these is to use the entire fish (instead of throwing 80 per cent of it away) and extracting from it Fish Protein Concentrates, which have a very high protein content, can be tasteless and odorless, and added to protein deficient foods. So much already has been written about FPC that there is no point in going into details here. The point is that very little of it

Experiments are being conducted in farming oysters attached to off-bottom rafts where the natural bottom is unsuitable for oyster growth. In three-dimensional oyster farming, the shellfish are raised on columns of old shells strung on wires, suspended from rafts, safe from bottom predators. It is probable we will eventually have vast underwater farms producing tons upon tons of oysters annually, and tended by diving oyster specialists.

"Fattening Oysters,"
Undercurrents, 1969

The food chain from algae to fish involves three, four or five steps. Only a food contribution of from 0.001 to 0.1 per cent of the original plant material is eventually available as fish for the diet of human beings. By and large, then, the fish is an inefficient converter of plant to human food. If we wish to use the ocean efficiently as a source of food, we must apparently make unconventional approaches to the harvesting of plant material from it. . . . We might domesticate an ocean-going vegetarian beast—a sea pig.

**HARRISON BROWN, JAMES BONNER
and JOHN WEIR/
The Next Hundred Years, 1963**

is being produced so far and that while a number of mass-production plants have been planned, they are still on the drawing boards. Like statistics, drawing boards are not edible.

There is much, much more that could be said about using the world's waters and its creatures as food..It can be said, and has been said. But it is not being done. We can't eat words, either. ✿

Photo by Bob Conover

chapter 5.

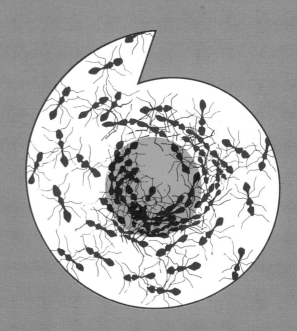

MOBILITY:
From There to Here

5.
The Dance of Life

All life is roads, for all life is movement. Animals began it; then primitive man, then caravans, armies, ships. With them went fabulous wares, rubies and gold for the eyes' delight. Bronze for the helmet, tools for the hand, cedar timbers to build the house—rainbow silks of Samarkand. Ahead of each went the idea. The true roadmaker. MADGE JENISON/*Roads,* 1948

In the early morning hours, it is possible to walk along the beach and, in the inscriptions in the sand, read the night stories of all the little creatures. Here went a snake, a'winding; here a crab, a'crawling, and there a bird a'walking, its tracks ending in eery nothing, as if teleportation were an ordinary part of our lives. Here, in the displaced grains of sand, the patterns and configurations, is a legible record of "mobility."

What we are talking about in "mobility," is observed motion or the record of it. We follow a long, hard trail when we begin to track down what we mean by "motion." It is a trail that leads through the labyrinth of a very few recorded minds. In our limited world of the displaced white European, it appears to begin with Aristotle (in *Physica*) who divided all observed motion into natural and violent. Violent was caused by humans; natural was not.

Something like 1500 years later, we hear Jordanus (in *De ratione ponderis*). "In any motion, whether natural or violent, the velocity obtained is the ratio of the applied force to the resistance which the medium offers."

About 350 years later, Galileo strolled by. He calmly said that "force is something which can change motion; e.g., from rest into motion or from motion into rest." (We kind of doubt he said, "e.g.," but that's the way they put it down, preserved in the amber of encyclopedias.)

The pace picks up, so it is only another hundred years before Newton (in *Philosophiae Naturalis Principia Mathematica*) broke trail by asserting "the three laws of motion."

Ernst Mach wandered along to muse, ". . . It is possible to choose a standard particle, label it as a unit of mass, and determine the mass of every other particle in the universe by allowing it to interact with the standard mass."

So stumbling up the path, his hands full of other people's patent applications, staring into the Prussian glare, comes Einstein, who says, rather diffidently, "Motion is relative to the observer."

Along the way he was helped by other trailblazers in the mathematics of motion: Schroedinger, Heisenberg, Planck. . . .

So that is one trail, not by any stretch of the imagination yet surmounted. In the words of poet Bob Dylan, "Climb that hill, no matter how steep, you still ain't goin' nowhere."

There are other trails. Motion can be defined as the displacement of a figure against a background, or a "surround." Tiger in the bush, scorpion in the sand, adder in the hollow. Move! If you dig rather shallowly, you can pry that one out of contemporary psycho-biology. In the words of the folk song, "the fox went out that night, and he had a long, long way to go, before he reached the town-o." Here we may see a rabbit hopping, because it is hoping; the fox in pursuit, hoping, but not hopping.

It is not a very good trail to follow, because it is circular, and is only observed by a third party, standing outside the two systems, rabbit and fox. The rabbit and the fox, however implicated, are third parties, too. They see each other in relation to a background which, while moving, appears to be static. None of this concerns the rabbit or the fox, their primary question being, "Am I going to have dinner or be one?"

So much for the fox and the rabbit. The small point—the observation of motion—was the function of a third system; in both cases and all around.

We'll try another trail. This is a pretty simple one. Let us say that "x" represents a horizontal in a two-dimensional plane. And that "y" represents a vertical. And that "z" represents depth. Something missing here, so we add "t," for time. Now we can take "xyz," mix liberally with "t," and come up with a model of what is (or has been) going on. We put them on a chart and many businesses and government agencies do this.

And what do we have? What we have is the movement of our eyeballs as we scan a chart from left to right. The "x, y, z, t" bit won't take us very far, either.

Back to the old drawing board. May we make a suggestion? You can't stop us, except to throw this thing into the fireplace or garbage can. But that, too, would be motion, would it not?

So, once more into the breach:

MOTION CAN BE DESCRIBED AS OBSERVED OR EXPERIENCED INTERFERENCE WAVES BETWEEN PLANES OF TIME AGAINST A HOLOGRAPHIC BACKGROUND.

by M. C. Escher, courtesy of Vorpal Galleries, San Francisco.

If "interference waves," "planes of time," and "holographic" turn you off, then forget it.

These far-out concepts have little to do with mobility as we experience it in our daily lives. We move from room to room, we go to work, or the barber or the hairdresser, the laundromat or the bar; to supermarket or school; to the dentist and the doctor; to a friend's house for dinner or cocktails; to visit relatives, mostly aging aunts and decaying grandfathers.

We are nomads, children of the steppes and plains, of hunters and gatherers long since gone, and we express our mobility in many dimensions.

There is economic mobility; you either get richer, or you go broke, and the middle is all for waiting. There is social mobility; you move up or down and the places that used to say, "Sorry, we're all filled up," now say, "This way, Sir."

It can go the other way, too. A place you were long welcome now says, "beat it, buddy," or "I'm so sorry, we already have guests for that night." So, socially, cut them off at the pass and thus reduce mobility. And then there's political mobility —but we already know too much about that.

In the catch-phrases, "Freedom Now!," "Land of the Free," "Free enterprise," we are essentially ringing the changes on mobility. To be "free" is to be able to move without restraint.

We are restless beasts, and we will move, wheels or not. Short of death sentences, our justice system is based on restriction of mobility; prisons, concentration camps, schools, business offices, bureaucracies. Cut the wire or mount the fence or burrow a tunnel under the wall; the human spirit cannot be confined. We'll move some way.

And we greatly value speed. For some reason, we believe that time is money. The shorter the elapsed time between "A" and "B," the more we "make." And so the horse, the camel, the bicycle, automobile, jet. And this, for humans, is "the dance of life," which threatens to become a tarantella, a mad gyration without substance or meaning, as we find still faster ways to go, and thus annihilate experience. And yet it was experience we sought, was it not? Our little worlds are not necessarily enlarged by the number of miles we have traveled.

Now, let's see if we can get the car out of the garage. . . . ✿

move is just a three-letter word--car

"**The delight which comes of rapid movement has never been understood until one occupies a place in a horseless carriage on a smooth road. There is an exhilaration from the swift motion surpassing that of any other form of movement. The Stanley Carriage is capable of a speed from 30 to 42 miles per hour, according to the gear used, and racers are made to exceed even this.**"

1899 ad for Stanley Steamers

Photo by Bob Conover

To think that the private automobile is primarily a form of transportation is to miss the point.

The automobile is the woman in technological man's life; mistress, wife and mother. Take it away and he sulks on a street corner, waiting for a bus that never comes, and crying inside. In urban and suburban areas, the automobile is practically the only place of privacy he has left. The reason the average passenger car carries only 1.5 passengers is that the .5 passenger can't talk back.

For the technological woman, the need for the automobile is much more functional; she needs it to take the kids to school, to do her shopping, to visit friends and relatives. For the most part a car, to her, has little more psychological meaning than her dishwasher or her home laundry-dryer combination. For women are infinitely more practical than men.

For young women, the car may serve the need for freedom and as a gateway to romance; for older women it may serve as a symbol of social and economic status that, because of age, their physical appearance and change of costumes no longer supports. But the car for most women is simply a way to get things done.

In any case, the private vehicle is at least a psychological necessity for technological man and it is not likely to be replaced by any mass transit system now envisaged; not for local, short run travel.

(Once, at a small, nine-cottage motel in Gualala, where the river meets the Pacific in an eternal interplay across a sand dune that is sometimes there and—when the Gualala river is running full and strong—not, there was an "open house" in cottage number one. Some guests, staying in cottage number nine, about fifty yards away, climbed into their new, enormous Lincoln Continental, and *drove* the fifty yards to cottage number one. Transportation was not the point; showing off the new car was.)

You will notice that in the want ads, an old, beat-up car with faulty transmission and tissue-thin tires, is almost always advertised as "good transportation." New cars are not sold on that basis; they are sold as symbols and Detroit designs them that way. They are not only designing transportation but psychological satisfaction as well.

A CAR CALLED HORSE

On the disadvantages of the automobile, by the inventor of the horsemobile, Ignaz Schroppe from Beckum: The automobile needs a relatively smooth and wide thoroughfare; it does not drive over stones, cannot cross fields and forests. Its main flaw lies in the wheels. Man was endowed with legs, not wheels. That is why I invented an automobile with legs. The engine sits inside the body and controls each of the four legs. The motor is started by a crankshaft which is where the horse's tail should be. Exhaust fumes escape via the most likely spot of the construction. The steering wheel controls each pair of legs separately. Collapsible trays on each side of the body may be used by the driver for eating or playing cards.

WELTWOCHE-MAGAZIN, Zurich (From the January, 1903 issue of *Automobil-Welt*)

(In most two-car families, the man drives the big, new car to work, where it sits idle for nine hours, while the wife drives the old clunk—on and off, all day long. To her the clunk is a tool; to the man the car is a symbol in the company parking lot.)

Another factor of considerable importance may be that driving a car is just about the only time most men can exercise some semblance of control in their daily lives. Most of the rest of the time they do what their bosses tell them to do, or their families require of them.

And, for an hour or so each day, being in their own car and driving it themselves, may be the only freedom most men have.

"Having won a freedom, man is unlikely to give it up," says Buckminster Fuller.

There is also the sensation of rapid movement, which appears to be a psychological need for most humans. Why, we do not know.

"Then just what is it that impels people to leave the comfort of home for the uncertainties of the road?" asks Dr. Joseph Smith of the Oxtoby-Smith research firm.

"The answer, psychologists say, lies in the growing discomfort or pain, as they call it, or lack of satisfaction that one gets from sitting home. They don't mean pain in the corporal sense; they mean the reward of what would seem to be a comfortable existence is no longer satisfying. . . . You get out because you've got to get away and you think about the popularly used expressions, 'I've had it up to here. I can't take it anymore. I'm going out of my mind. I've got to cut.' You move from where you are from time to time because those normally gratifying rewards have lost their potency.

"One of the most successful impellents, one that seems to twang just the proper nerve, is the ubiquitous Pan American jingle that . . . invites the tired and jaded 'for once in a lifetime' to 'get into this world.' Turn on your car radio and a happy chorus invites you to:

Leave the train on the track
Take the boss off your back
Leave the gang in a bind
Out of sight, out of mind . . .

                   or

Leave the phone off the hook

Teach the cat how to cook
Be a man, not a mouse
Sell your car, rent your house . . .

        or

Leave the don'ts and the do's
Let a friend fill your shoes
Take a walk with your wife
For once in a lifetime
Get into this world. . . ."

What this amounts to is that the private passenger vehicle is not likely to disappear from the technological man's world before 2000 A.D. But it may change form.

The pressures of population-increase, urban concentration, the sudden, if belated, awakening of technological man to the effects gasoline-burning engines have on his environment—not only smog, but the ubiquitous freeways, roads and turnpikes—lead one to consider that long before the year 2000, the internal combustion engine using gasolines as fuel, may join the dodo, the dinosaur and Watt's steam engine in the limbo of some dimly lighted wing of the Smithsonian.

According to *Fortune* (October, 1970), "Significant progress in cleaning up the internal combustion engine has been achieved, and the auto makers have been pouting about what they feel is a lack of recognition of their efforts. Lynn Townsend, chairman of Chrysler Corporation said, "This accomplishment—at least outside Detroit—may be the best-kept secret of the 1960's." "Still," says *Fortune*, "it's only a beginning."

Henry Ford, II takes a different view (according to "The Environment," by the editors of *Fortune*, Harper and Row, N.Y., 1970). "He freely concedes that the rising production of material goods, including Ford cars, has been purchased at a high cost of environmental pollution. One Ford executive has warned that 'social and political pressures for curtailing automobile use and promoting other forms of transportation will continue to mount.' The Ford Motor Company, therefore, is reacting with the instinct of an entrepreneur, hoping to take advantage of the revolution in public expectations and design systems—such as automated highways—that will better serve the needs of the cities, and, in the words of one official, 'represent an orderly

(Continued on page 158)

el toro solitario

There is a simple method to achieve the right state of mind for driving in Italy. Before you start your car…sit in the driver's seat, hold the steering wheel and think the following: I am the only driver on the road, and mine is the only car…millions of Italian drivers believe it and so can you. An Italian driver's reaction to any

encounter with another vehicle is, first, stunned disbelief then outrage. You don't have a chance unless you can match this faith. It isn't enough to say you are the only driver, or to think it—you got to believe it. Remember, your car is the car; all others are aberrations in the divine scheme.

JACKSON BURGES / "Sex and the Italian Driver"
Holiday, Jan. 1970

Illustration by Masami Miyamoto

The twentieth century has provided the answer
to Mankind's dream in a more effective manner
than either Ilya Rogoff's Bulgarian garlic pearls
or Yugoslav sex tonic. The motor car
has become a fountain of youth. The motor
industry pulls it off with waking dreams
in sheet metal.

HORST VETTEN/
"Motor Car Replaces Sword and Steed as
Attribute of Manliness,"
The German Tribune, **August 20, 1970**

Some people have normal everyday recurring
nightmares like drowning in a tidal wave or
being pursued by apes and sex fiends or wandering
naked through a meeting of the local PTA.
My recurring nightmare is crueler.
I dream I have been sentenced to drive forever
along the Connecticut Turnpike. All exits
have been sealed in concrete and I am doomed
for an uncertain term to feed at the eight
Holiday Houses between Stamford and Madison
till at last I perish of sensory insult.
My dream is only slightly exaggerated.
We are all prisoners of the turnpike, captives
of the limited-oasis thruway with commissary
franchises, held by the most irresistible bidder:
Howard Johnson, Restaurant Associates,
Fred Harvey.
My late Uncle Max always advised: "On the
road, eat only corn flakes." His prudence is
affirmed by specters of *haute* turnpike dining.

GAEL GREENE/
"Indigestion on the Turnpike,"
Life, **August 28, 1970**

transition from Ford's current products'."

And it does appear to be true that some cities—such as New York, Rome, Tokyo, San Francisco, Washington, D.C. either already have banned automobiles from some streets in central city cores, or have legislation pending to do so.

Apparently, all of the car manufacturers are searching for ways to meet the country's changes in transportation needs and the effects on the environment as they can foresee them now.

Says American Motors (in its 1970 Annual Report), "To further reduce emissions from the internal combustion engine, the company is presently concentrating upon development of advanced modifications, including exhaust reactors or afterburners, and catalytic converters...Work on other types of propulsion systems has continued over a period of more than ten years. Investigations have included the rotary engine, electric cars, steam cars and natural gas."

Back to Ford. "A prototype gas turbine engine was installed in a Continental Trailways Silver Eagle bus which began cross-country service late in the year (1970)...The bus supplements work that Ford has been doing with turbine-powered trucks."

In 1906, a Stanley Steamer set a world's record of 127.6 m.p.h. on a Nascar five-mile course. Four years later, Barney Oldfield beat that with 131.7 m.p.h. driving a Benz. After that, the steam car went out of vogue and the combustion engine took over. (The internal combustion engine was invented in Austria in 1864, developed by the Germans in 1886, and then further developed by the Danes, the French and the Italians. The first American copies of these appeared about 1888 or 1889. It was truly an international development.)

Now, because of the introduction of light metals, plastics, electronic controls and improved fuels, it appears that the steam car may be a-steaming down the road again. It has some advantages: pollution free, virtually noiseless, highly efficient, and economical to run. Most of the automobile companies have development programs for steam-driven cars which may result in production models in the next decade.

Some indication of the advances that might be

from *The Drawings of Heinrich Kley*, Borden Publishing Co., Alhambra, California

made in this field is the concept proposed for steam-driven automobiles by William Powell Lear, who invented the first car radio, the first auto pilot for jet aircraft, the eight-track stereo cartridge, and, of course, the Lear businessman's jet airplane.

What he is working on, and has a working model of, is a 22-pound, eight-inch long turbine that has only one moving part and generates 300 horsepower of low pollution energy. The entire steam system could be contained under the hood of an ordinary sedan.

The vapor is produced by mixing a chemical with water. It is nonflammable, nontoxic, noncorrosive, has a very low freezing point (about 80 degrees below zero Fahrenheit) and is a good generator of steam. The chemical is a form of fluorinated hydrocarbon.

The fuel itself is kerosene, which heats the fluid in a small boiler until it is vaporized. The vapor drives a turbine, which moves the wheels of the car. At 100 horsepower, the engine will accelerate a 4,000 pound car from a stand-still to 60 miles per hour in ten seconds, according to Lear.

Whether this actually will be produced remains to be seen, but it seems obvious that the same propulsion system that drives the world's ships, most of the world's trains, and all of its electrical generation, must have some role in the development of the private passenger automobile of the future. If it can be fitted into the design and engineering of the contemporary models, then the transition would be almost painless and could occur in a relatively short time.

For the moment, we reluctantly give up on steam cars as a *politically* possible solution and turn to the electric car. Why not an electric automobile that plugs in at its friendly neighborhood service station to recharge? The same technology that produces the power for industry, light and heat for our homes, space satellites and sea-labs seems somehow not to have produced a small passenger vehicle powered by electricity that can travel ten blocks to a supermarket (and be recharged through parking-meter-like devices while the driver is in the store shopping).

Speaking of the potential for the electric car, Bruce C. Netscherst (in "The Economic Impact of Electrical Vehicles; A Scenerio," *Bulletin of the Atomic Scientists,* May, 1970) says, "In contrast to the positive benefits to the electric utility industry, there would be a major adverse impact on the oil

The dolma, in Turkish cooking, is that delicious concoction of tender young vine leaves stuffed with rice and spice. The *dolmus*, or taxi-stuffed-with-people, is a less familiar Turkish institution although a dolmus is a familiar enough sight in Istanbul: a big, somewhat battered-looking car, picking up and dropping fares at regular stages, and charging each passenger according to the distance traveled.

VERONICA MACLEAN/
"From Turkey by Taxi,"
Vogue, Oct. 1, 1968

A strange and touching scene at Cypress Lawn Monday. A young man killed in a motorcycle accident was buried along with the Harley-Davidson he was riding at the time of the crash. "It was his whole life," sobs his mother.

HERB CAEN/
S.F. *Chronicle*,
Sept. 24, 1970

The advances of technology drove Nevada county horse trainer Larry Filer to drive his 6-year-old Appaloosa by means of a steering wheel, instead of the traditional bit and bridle; the wheel, mounted on the horse's withers, works by a wire ring around the animal's neck, and according to Filer, is more satisfactory to both parties than the old style apparatus.

"Fantasia,"
S.F. *Examiner*,
August 23, 1970

Just about the time the new horseless carriage bucked out of the machine shop, curbside dining entered American social history. It all started when a drugstore soda jerk hustled an order to a customer parked out front.
Drive-in restaurants are geared to people.
Parents can detour a plush potential by feeding children in the seclusion of the family wagon—risking only sticky upholstery. Cops sipping coffee keep tuned in to the precinct radio.
Brink's men lunch on guard. Shoeless hippies, leftover beatniks and lightly clad beach bunnies dig in, away from notices excluding the unshod and "inadequately attired." And many ordinary people, like snails in their shells, simply enjoy eating in the intimacy of their cars.

ELIZABETH ALSTON/
"Wheels & Meals,"
Look, October 15, 1968

industry. Over one-half of the total value of shipments by oil refineries is accounted for by automotive gasoline and diesel-type distillate oil."

Another voice. "The Cooper Development Association's experimental electric vehicle has a range of better than 100 miles, maximum speed of 65 mph., and operating costs of one cent per mile. The batteries can be recharged to 80 percent of rated capacity in 45 minutes." (*Industry Week*, April 27, 1970.)

Another promising concept is the "Urbmobile," recently the subject of a feasibility study by Cornell Laboratory under a Housing and Urban Development (HUD) grant. As described in *Transportation Research Review* (Third/Fourth Quarter, 1968), the Urbmobile is a small, four-passenger car propelled by electricity.

It is one of a family of what is called "dual-mode" vehicles; in this case operated manually and propelled by batteries on city streets and on inter-city, or suburb-city trips, it would get its power from an electrified third rail on tracked guideways.

"On the eight-foot tracked guideway, Urbmobiles could travel almost bumper-to-bumper at a steady 60 mph, with guidance and control fully automatic in this mode."

While on the guideway, the Urbmobile's batteries would be recharged automatically, allowing 40 miles of in-city driving before recharging.

Aside from reducing car-produced smog and virtually eliminating highway accidents, the system could carry, on an 8-foot wide lane, as much traffic as is now carried on *ten* expressway lanes.

To continue, "No modest extension of current technology, the dual-mode system is still fraught with unknowns," says Allan T. Demaree, (*The Environment*, by the editors of *Fortune*, 1969). "Commuters who see the hazards of ordinary short-haul train travel daily increasing are likely to be skeptical about the whole dreamy-sounding proposal.... The fail-safe mechanisms necessary to assure safety at high speeds, bumper-to-bumper, have yet to be developed and proven."

According to Joseph F. Zmuda, ("New Electric Makes Performance Breakthroughs," *Popular Science* February, 1971), "The Voltair...will have a recommended top speed of 90 m.p.h. and the ability to reach 107 m.p.h. at overload for brief bursts. And it will have a range of 300-500 miles! A recharge takes only 20 minutes.

"(It has) Tri-Polar lead-cobalt batteries, series traction motor, solid state control unit, a patented fuel cell which trickle-charge the batteries at a constant rate.

"These achievements came out of many years of experimental work by Robert A. Aronson and his company, Electric Fuel Propulsion, Inc. of Ferndale, Michigan.

"Aronson soon hopes to see plug-in parking meters that permit any electric vehicle to use its slow-charger, or, better yet, multiple fast charges in garages, shopping centers and motels. Courtesy charge points have been set up in 76 such locations from coast to coast."

Says Rick Vogt (in the Contra Costa (California) Times, April 8, 1971), "Private autos may be a thing of the past if a proposal is approved to establish a network of tiny electric autos and a 'dial-a-bus' system in connection with BART (Bay Area Rapid Transit) . . . The unique Public Auto System—PAS . . . would be located along the BART 'corridor.'

"Persons would be able to go down to a corner electric auto stand and pick up an auto which they could drive to the nearest BART station or to run errands in their community."

There are other possibilities. Says Alden P. Armagnac (in "Super Flywheel to Power Zero-Emission Car," Popular Science, Aug., 1970), "The tiny 975-pound car has no engine. No batteries propel it. But it starts from a standstill to 60 mph in just 15 seconds. Silent, exhaust-free, fearless, and designed especially for city driving, it carries two to three people at a maximum speed of more than 70 mph, and cruises at 55 mph.

"A look into a rear compartment solves the mystery of what makes it go—a 222-pound flywheel, 30 inches in diameter, spinning at up to 23,700 rpm in a vacuum can . . . By whirling so fast (2,000 mph at the outer edge), the flywheel stores enough energy to propel the mini-car for two hours at cruising speed—or, 110 miles. Then in a 24-minute 'charging' period, at home or in a wayside garage, electric current revs up the flywheel for another run of equal duration."

When it comes to auto safety, the French have been whipping along in reverse for generations. Pursuing their devil-may-care Gallic image, French drivers have established a record ensuring that one in three of them will be involved in at least one serious accident in his lifetime; compared with their U. S. counterparts, the French chalk up at least three times as many fatalities per kilometer driven. Clearly, it would seem, someone should teach Frenchmen how to drive. But that, it turns out, has been tried; indeed, it may be the problem.

"Schools for Scandale,"
Newsweek, October 20, 1969

The amount of space that automobiles take up just waiting to be used is tremendously wasteful. In our cities, waiting automobiles make it impossible to clean our streets of dirt in the summer and snow and ice in the winter. Perhaps private ownership of automobiles will become a thing of the past in our cities. We may end up with a fleet of mini-autos, self-driven taxis, owned by the city, autos without keys that can be driven by anyone to anywhere he wants to go and then left for the next person who wants to go someplace else. This would eliminate much of the waste of autos just sitting in one place at least 90% of the time.
ERASTUS CORNING, II/
"The Race for (Automobile) Space,"
Bulletin of the Atomic Scientists,
December, 1969

The concept (and it is only that so far) is the brainchild of D. W. Rabenhorst, an aeronautical engineer at Johns Hopkins University's Applied Physics Laboratory in Silver Spring, Maryland.

Thus spake Zarathustra. If we do not establish laboratories which could be whole city-suburban complexes and try experimental systems of vehicles and roadways on them, how are we ever going to know what may work and what might not? Driving an automobile around and around a test oval will give us no answers that are relevant. We need transportation laboratories that duplicate the crazy kid high on pot in his Porsche or Volkswagen; the business exec high on alcohol tooling his Rolls or Mercedes at 70 mph.; the plumber driving his beat-up pick-up, full of tools and valves, trying to find the street and the house number of a housewife whose faucet is leaking; and the little old lady whose bifocals do not fit.

One way or the other, the solution to private transportation may be the application of systems analysis and communication theory (the controlled movement of messages along a network). All of the disciplines necessary already are in existence, but they are not being used.

So, one sort of gives up on the steam and the electric powered vehicles, and pokes around to find what might be done with the mechanical beast we now have available to us.

Perhaps quite a bit. They, the passenger cars, can be built to safeguard the lives of the people who ride in them. The safety requirements are well understood, and increasingly they may be used.

If it is economically difficult to sell safe cars, then perhaps we can design safe highways. Separate lanes for passenger and commercial traffic; separate lanes for autos going in opposite directions; *readable* highway signs posted far enough back to enable the driver to switch lanes without cutting across traffic; these are a few. The fault, Brutus, is not in our drivers, but in our designs.

Instead of our infatuation with the vehicle, we might spend a little more time, energy and money on the development of "systems."

A few that have been suggested: reduction of private ownership of passenger vehicles (as suggested by a FORD TV commercial, April 6, 1971), leading to a more intensive use of the vehicles we already have. This could help alleviate traffic congestion, reduce the acreage of urban parking lots, and probably be a faster and more economical system for people who need to get "from there to here."

We already see this foreshadowed in the car rental system, which works very well. You do not have to ship your car to Hawaii; you simply pick one up at the airport and when you are through using it, you turn it over to someone else who needs it. So, one can envisage a system in which you drive your car to work, leave the keys in the ignition, and someone else can use it while you can't. You would pick up any other car in the lot, under the same conditions, and drive home. It is the same principal as applies to a hotel or motel room. You use it when you need it and turn it over to someone else when you don't. Auto theft would be impossible; how can you steal a car that is readily available to you anyway?

Another solution in urban areas would simply be publicly subsidized taxis. When you get off at your closest freeway, expressway, or rapid transit terminal, a cab takes you to your destination, then returns to its station to pick up other passengers.

You do not pay to go up in an elevator in a high rise building; why should you pay (directly) for the horizontal movement you get there?

Careful examination of zoning ordinances would, for instance, reveal that jobs can be located close enough to workers' residences for them to live comfortably and walk to work. (The complement to "Why Johnny Can't Read," may be, "Can We Teach Daddy to Walk?") Firm answers to both questions hang in the limbo of business and government bureaucracy.

If the distance from home to work is too far for convenient walking, the bicycle might be a solution. The family automobile would be used for longer trips, the bicycle for intraurban commuting. The best of two possible worlds.

There are many people on this planet who sim-

Every year U. S. automakers invest millions of dollars and countless man-hours to produce the thunk that sells. G. M. employs 250 technicians —including graduates of Purdue, Stanford and Michigan State—to work exclusively on doors. Ford, Chrysler and G. M. test and refine their thunks in soundproof chambers that are sealed like bank vaults. Stereo tapes are used to record the effects that subtle design changes have on sound. High-speed movies are made to study vibrations, and oscilloscopes gauge the thunk's duration. The automakers also employ automatic slamming machines, which create sounds ranging from what G. M.'s Hedeen calls the "angry-wife slam" to the "husband-coming-home-late-at-night slam." The former is 50 foot-pounds, and the latter three foot-pounds.

"The Thunking Man's Car,"
Time, October 3, 1969

Underground highways? Most transportation experts don't consider them extravagant at all. Byron A. Bledsoe, principal engineer of the Highway Research Board in Washington, D. C., points out that transportation is basically a utility, like sewage, electricity, and telephone service. "Open sewers have gone underground," he says. "Electric lines and telephone lines are doing so now. In the future, surface roads— especially the ones in downtown areas—may disappear too, leaving the surface for people." The average cost of a surface freeway in an urban area runs about four million dollars a mile. Deep-tunnel mileage costs are now averaging about seven million. But improved technology will make tunneling cheaper, while land costs climb.

FREDRIC C. APPEL/
"The Coming Revolution in Transportation,"
National Geographic, Sept., 1969

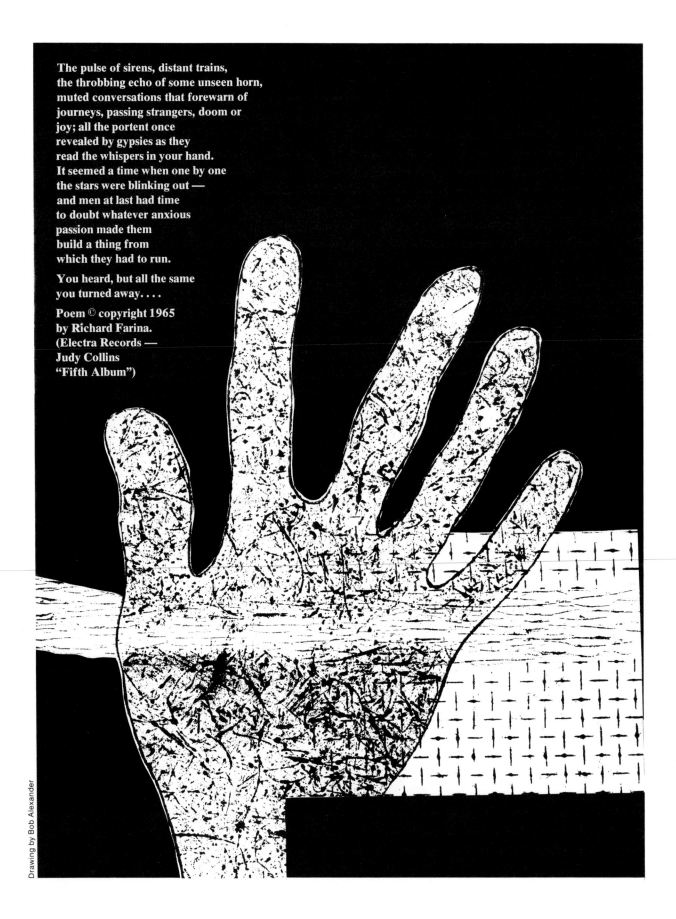

The pulse of sirens, distant trains,
the throbbing echo of some unseen horn,
muted conversations that forewarn of
journeys, passing strangers, doom or
joy; all the portent once
revealed by gypsies as they
read the whispers in your hand.
It seemed a time when one by one
the stars were blinking out —
and men at last had time
to doubt whatever anxious
passion made them
build a thing from
which they had to run.

You heard, but all the same
you turned away. . . .

Poem © copyright 1965
by Richard Farina.
(Electra Records —
Judy Collins
"Fifth Album")

Drawing by Bob Alexander

ply cannot afford an automobile, or who live in countries where automobile production lags far behind demand. This group is probably four-fifths of all the people on this planet. Alternative forms of transportation would seem to be a reasonable, and profitable, suggestion.

There are some advantages to the bicycle. It provides healthy physical exercise for those in sedentary occupations. It is virtually silent. It is smog-free (except in its manufacture). It requires little roadway, and little parking space when it arrives at its destination. In urban settings, it is much faster than private automobiles or public transport by buses.

As Herb Caen, writing in the San Francisco *Chronicle* reported (Jan. 10, 1971) "Still, the tortoise is a winner. A race between a bicycle, a car and a bus through four miles of rush-hour traffic in Chicago produced these results: bike 19 minutes, auto 31, and bus 54."

According to John Hart, writing in *Pacific Sun*, Aug. 26, 1970, some 7.5 million bicycles were sold in the U. S. in 1970 (nearly matching the number of automobiles sold). He goes on to say, "It's not just that more bikes are being sold, but also that the whole sales pattern has changed dramatically. The old basic market, the pre-teens, has given away to older teenagers and adults."

For those too lazy, too old, or who are unable to tool a bicycle, there is always the motorcycle, or its many manifestations.

The motorized tricycles run by "metermaids" and parking control police avoid the difficulties of balance (for the elderly, the ill, or the untrained), take up little room, have plenty of carrying space, and can be parked virtually anywhere. The English have long since had an absolutely silent outboard motor for pleasure boats; why not apply the same system to tricycles? Smog free, sound free, highway and street free, and just make them available at any rapid transit terminal?

There are so many solutions, so few applications, that the mind boggles. But it doesn't have to. Technologically, the solutions are available. The question is why haven't the people who are responsible for running our towns, cities, counties, states and the federal system done so?

Why haven't we insisted that they do? ❖

A bicycle is cheap, creates no smog, causes no snarls, and guarantees its rider improved muscle tone, reduced girth and enormous wind power. And it is being rediscovered by city commuters as an exhilarating and generally trouble-free way to go to and return from anywhere in town. One young doctor flies down California Street each morning at seven, balancing black bag and lunchbox at the ends of his handlebars and easily passing the ongoing traffic.

• • •

Parking a bicycle may not be easy. When I worked in the Federal Building, I used to take my bicycle up to the 13th floor in the freight elevator, walk it down the hall and stash it in my office closet. Once I discovered an egg sandwich, well squashed, in my spokes. Another time a bureaucrat grunted his indignation as we traveled down in the elevator together.

THOMAS & CAROLINE CRAWFORD/
"Biking in San Francisco,"
S. F. Sunday *Examiner & Chronicle*
June 28, 1970

Is the switch from the gasoline engine possible? Look back to 1900 when 4,195 vehicles were manufactured in this country. Of the total, 1,681 were powered by steam, 1,575 by electricity, and only 939 by gasoline engines.

"Electric Cars are Catching On,"
***Industry Week*, April 27, 1970**

The automobile is an extension of the house. Young people used to court in the parlor, then on the front porch, then in the automobile— the porch-on-wheels may be observed at the local drive-in movie "house." Movies are better than ever.

R. BUCKMINSTER FULLER/
***I Seem to Be a Verb*,**
New York, 1970

nomads' land

Frequently called "the 747 of urban transportation,"
the quadruple-deck bus can go a long way toward solving a
city's ecological and financial problems. Capable of
carrying four busloads but taking the road space of only one bus,
it will facilitate traffic considerably. Carbon monoxide fumes
are cut and passengers can enjoy the sights of their city
from an imperial height. With fewer buses needed, fewer
drivers will be needed.

Based on the motorcycle sidecar, so popular in the 30's, the three-wheeled "Bubblecycle" is the ideal vehicle for the family outing. Low on gas, pollution and family friction, it enables the driver to concentrate on his driving while his family enjoys the air-conditioned, soundproof bubble. Thus far production has been halted because of violent protests from members of Women's Liberation.

It should be obvious by now that—in air pollution—direct action is called for and direct action is possible with the pollution fighting helicopter pictured.
By means of an enormous suction vent, all smoke from an offending plant is vacuumed up and then jettisoned back into the building which is responsible for it.

Paths of ivory, trails of amber and jade, roads of gold, streams of tin and silver—these are the pathways of the world. Along them have moved salt and sugar; wheat, rice and corn; cotton, silk and wool; dead animals and live ones; pins, needles, beads and thread; wheelbarrows and shovels; rum and glass, timber and metals and cement; ''a cannon for the courthouse square.'' All carved out their trails, to carry ''something special just for me.''

the
Wells Fargo Wagon
is acomin'

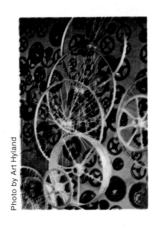

Photo by Art Hyland

The California Zephyr came roaring out of its Oakland, California, terminal, great headlight a'glaring, whistle a'whistling, steam a'steaming, and streaked across California's central valley. It panted up the western ramparts of the Sierra, following the magnificent Feather River below. It slipped down the Eastern escarpment, raced in darkness across the great saline deserts to Salt Lake, then huffed and puffed up the Rockies, to Glenwood Springs, over the grade to Denver, and on to Chicago.

This was (and perhaps will be again) one of the great travel experiences in this country. At one time, there were many similar ones. Those who grew up in the rail age of America remember with fond nostalgia the carnation in its crystal bud vase over the immaculate linen table cloth in the dining car; the gourmet meals served without haste, while the close and exciting landscape rolled past the windows in a kaleidoscope of what was a once-upon-a-time America.

"But the good times are all gone, and I'm bound for moving on," says a line in a popular song. Perhaps our lives have become so hectic that people no longer have time for trains. It would be nice to think that this is not true for everyone and that, sometime before the turn of the century, this enormous pleasure can be enjoyed again.

This is not to castigate the railroads, which unquestionably have highly complex passenger service problems. It is to say that for medium distance intercity transport of people and goods the railroads *could* be the most efficient form of transport, and that much of the change in mobility in the technological countries will be concentrated in this area during the next thirty years.

The technology to operate both freight and passenger trains at speeds of 300 mph or more apparently already exists. The Japanese, the West Europeans, the Scandinavians, and perhaps the Russians may have such systems in operation much sooner than the U.S. Some are already being built.

The new input is the magnetic train. It has no wheels. No wheels at all.

"The secret of the swift, silent ride is simple magnetism," says *Time* (August 24, 1970). To paraphrase—even before World War I, a French inventor, Emile Bachelto, demonstrated the feasibility

Robert Forman Six is president of the nation's tenth largest domestic airline.
He says, "Cities and major carriers throughout the country are building monuments that are concrete wastelands. It's costing a fortune, and we can't afford it. What people really want is fast check-in, better baggage handling."

Robert Six shares his customer's disgust with the miserably long hike between airport ticket counter and debarkation point. Big-bellied, three-engine jets are past the drawing-board stage, and Six sees passengers waiting in the plane "instead of crowded terminals full of sticky gum wrappers, empty pop bottles and other debris." In these super-fancy jets, Six says, the passengers will be able to smoke, read, have a drink or go to the john on the plane before takeoff. "Does a passenger really give a damn for long airport tunnels lined with mosaics on the wall like in Albuquerque? It's the greatest waste of money I ever saw. There are little, individual square mosaics—millions of them in color— that some architect wanted and the mayor liked."

AL ROTHENBERG/
"Mr. Six and Number 10,
Look, **October 17, 1969**

This exciting new generation of vehicles— more versatile hydrofoils, air-cushion boats and trains, automated cars, V/Stol aircraft, jumbo jets, supersonic transports—can revolutionize our transportation system.
Will they?
I hear the cautioning words of former Transportation Sec. Boyd: "Don't forget, innovations will have to be superimposed on a system which already exists . . . a system being built to last a long, long time."

FREDRIC C. APPEL/
"The Coming Revolution in Transportation,"
National Geographic, **Sept. 1969**

of lifting railroad cars slightly off the track and pro-pelling them forward with strong electro-magnetic forces. But the technology of the day was not suf-ficient to get it off the ground.

The Japanese expect to have such a super-speed magnetic train in operation by 1980, between Tokyo and Osaka, easily eclipsing the world's fast-est train, the Tokaido express.

Continues *Time's* article: "In a similar design proposed by Stanford Research Institute . . . the magnetic train rides on a concrete pathway about twelve feet wide. Ordinary rails have been re-placed by two L-shaped aluminum guide strips. As the train's speed increases, the magnets on the underside of the cars act like the moving armatures of an electrical generator, causing currents to flow in the aluminum strips. These currents, in turn, build magnetic fields of their own.

"Just as like poles of ordinary horseshoe magnets repel each other, so do the train's super-conduc-tive magnets repel their magnetic mirror images in the aluminum strips. In this way the train can be

lifted as much as a foot off the ground.

"Nicknamed 'Maglev' (for magnetic levitation) by the Stanford engineers, the train could use any number of propulsion systems; propellors, jet en-gines, or even rocket motors. But both Japanese and American designers now seem to favor linear induction motors . . .

"The California researchers have already deco-rated their office walls with a poster that reads, 'MAGLEV, NOT WAR.'"

Says *Cryogenics and Industrial Gases* (October, 1969), in the article "Magnetically Suspended Trains," — "In general, the costs for the train are much less than for a comparable jet airliner . . . If the demand for such transportation is large, it should be considerably cheaper than air travel."

These magnetic trains can carry people in their own automobiles, containerized freight, trucks and highway vans at speeds of 250 to 300 mph. "In the year 2000, a high-speed rail train will run between Hamburg and Munich every four minutes . . . In time there will be direct service from Frankfurt to

from *The Drawings of Heinrich Kley,* Borden Publishing Co., Alhambra, California

Paris and from Munich to Rome and Vienna."

In the U.S., to break into this happy and hopeful scenario, lawyers are arguing before the I.C.C. that more passenger trains have to be cut off because "they are losing money."

Well, it kind of depends on what accounting system is being used, and how it is applied. But one can imagine that intercity passenger trains, running on time, serving meals at reasonable cost, and with stewardess service, might well attract enough paying customers to make the operation profitable, not only because many people cannot or do not want to fly, but because there is *little* a man can do in his office that he cannot do on a train.

Why U.S. trains do not offer low fares on empty freight cars, equipped with portable chemical toilets, with pickup meals available at major stops, for the young-at-heart, low-in-purse, back-pack, sleeping-bag set is not clear. It would provide revenue, it would provide transportation, it would be safer than hitchhiking. If insurance is a problem, let their ticket be a waiver for liability; or have you ever read the waiver on any *airline* ticket you just bought?

And why not use the empty flat cars to move automobiles, or containerized household goods, at low cost for people who have been transferred? In rail operations, it's the empties that cost money and reduce profits. Why are they empty?

A generation of Americans grew up "riding the rods," because they couldn't afford a ticket. The new generation can, if it doesn't cost too much.

Nevertheless, the time may easily come before the end of the century when people get as good service from the railroads as do livestock, or military goods, or almost any commodity. The clock is rapidly approaching twelve, and the pumpkin may turn into a coach again.

Tired now of trains? Let's try mass transit in urban areas and buses. When they are good (as in Montreal, Toronto, Paris or Leningrad) they are very, very good. And when they are bad they are horrid.

Take on the buses first. In urban areas, one is haunted by the late night bus, windows all aglow, no passengers, driver huddled over steering wheel, worming its way to some final, empty stop before it heads back to the car barn.

Most bus lines run at a deficit because their schedules no longer seem to fit the needs of rapidly shifting population patterns.

General Motors, according to *Product Engineering* (Jan. 1, 1970) is evaluating a cab that follows a guideway supported by air cushions and propelled by linear motors. Each cab would carry two to four passengers from the place of boarding to destination . . . After the passengers indicate their destination on a control panel, a computer and peripheral controls would stop, start, and space the cabs.

"To move groups of people from civic centers, airports, and railroad station downtown," continues *Product Engineering*, "GM is considering a series of small capsules for two to four people that would be compatible with the guideway in the central business district. They could use existing highways (ten capsules to a flatbed truck) or existing rail rights-of-way (twenty capsules to a car)."

A somewhat less exotic, but eminently practical interim solution might be to use "mini-buses," carrying six to eight passengers, to pick up travelers along sparsely-used routes and deliver them to major bus or mass transit stops. Passengers would just call a central computer and the pickups would show up as lights along the route printed on the instrument panel in the mini-bus. The difference in capital investment for rolling stock would be between about $3,800 for the mini and $25,000 for the big buses.

When there are not a sufficient number of passenger pickups flashing on his route schedule, the mini-bus driver could sit there drinking ersatz coffee from a paper cup and reading *Zap* or *Playboy;* thus raising the educational level of this country by several notches.

A less sophisticated system appears to be working quite well in Redwood City, California. Says Phil Garlington, Jr. in an article, "Redwood City Lauds Its Mini-Muni," (Sept. 27, 1970): "If Dagwood Bumstead lived in Redwood City he probably would never have to gulp his coffee and knock over the postman at the door as he rushes for his streetcar. (Streetcars in Redwood City? Never mind, the point is still well made.)

"That's because the buses in Redwood City will stop in front of a passenger's house or any place

**For those Americans who by desire or
necessity ride trains, all that's left of a once
full-fleshed national rail network is a bare-
bones skeleton.**
**Hardest hit have been thousands of small towns
across the country which didn't have air
service to fall back on when they lost their
passenger trains—towns like Dry Prong, La.;
Horse Cave, Ky.; Oaktown, Ind.; Broken Bow,
Neb.; and Green River, Wyo.**

**JOHN S. LANG/
"Death Rattle for U.S. Trains,"
S.F. *Examiner,*
May 31, 1970**

**In Amsterdam, mail boxes are located on the
backs of streetcars; as all streetcars must pass
a post office anyway, this is an efficient method
for posting mail.**

**JACK PAAR/
TV Special,
October 5, 1970**

along the route if flagged down by a frantic commuter. The buses also play stereo music, are air-conditioned and run on time."

So, it can be done. And, true, the system runs in the red. What transportation system doesn't, once you deduct government subsidies for roads, rail rights-of-way, and airports?

Onward and downward. There is an urban mass-transit system on the drawing boards called the "gravity vacuum tube," or GVT, for short, which operates within an underground tube that curves gently down from one ground station to the next.

In the GVT system, the train is propelled by gravity and the passengers are barely aware of the acceleration (says *Product Engineering*). "Tube vehicles are potentially the fastest of all ground transportation units." This is partially because the tube is evacuated of air and therefore there is no air friction. What the passengers are supposed to be breathing does not seem to be explained. But then, it is a breathtaking trip.

One doesn't really have to go that far. Says Wolf von Eckard, (in "The World's Happiest Subway," *Times-Post* service, Nov. 16, 1969)—"The first line of Mexico City's new subway . . . was completed in two years. It speeds people in noiseless, cheerful comfort some seven miles under the traffic-clogged center of the city.

"Riding along with the first commuters . . . was an experience that has become all too rare these days—an experience in public happiness.

"It was a surprisingly quiet happiness, particularly for noisily exuberant Mexico. A happiness hushed by pride."

One hears Herb Alpert's "Tijuana Brass" exuberantly in the background and wonders why we cannot do as well.

Digging ourselves out from underground tubes and subways, getting, most blessedly, off the freeways and rails, let us, like Icarus, fly. And, like Icarus, have our wings melt away in the sun of bureaucracy, inadequate safety standards, overcrowded air corridors, indifferent maintenance, airports that apparently have been designed by people who have never been on, or even tried to get on, an aircraft in the kind of terminals they design.

The airlines used to be a delightful way to go, but now have become a dreary negation of experience. At 31,000 feet and 600 mph., the only experience is a grade "B" movie flickering on the screen, and plastic stewardesses serving plastic food in plastic dishes.

The design of the aircraft is superb, as is their safety record. Their crews are well trained and courteous. But the airlines themselves suffer from a terminal ailment.

Yes, terminal. For the most part, most airlines have not as yet figured out a smooth transition from air transport to ground transport. The solution of this problem undoubtedly will occur in the next thirty years, if only because it has to.

Is there any reason why ground transport should not take passengers directly to the aircraft waiting on the ramp? Or why non-ticketed passengers should not pay their fare to the stewardesses, as they did on the "shuttle" between New York and Washington? Is there any reason why, if ter-

minals are necessary for customs or other reasons, moving underground sidewalks should not take passengers to an underground elevator that lifts them hydraulically to the plane? Is there any reason why aircraft should not use "people-pods" which are loaded, passengers, baggage and all, trucked to the airframe, lifted into place, bolted on and up, up and away? The technology exists.

Why duplicate flights by competing airlines leaving at nearly the same time from one city to another should travel one-third full, when the bookings for passengers could be consolidated and each plane fly with a full (and profitable) load, is not easily understood, either. It would appear to be in the interest of each scheduled airline to pool passengers going to the same place at the same time, and thus reduce air traffic, maintenance, and operating overhead. There are something like 10,000 empty seats *each day* on commercial airlines from Chicago to New York. Why?

One technological solution, delayed far too long, is the development of vertical take-off and landing aircraft that can pick passengers up at the jet terminal and deposit them atop buildings in downtown areas within minutes. The elaborate and costly systems either being used, or proposed, of taxicabs, airport buses, rapid transit or monorails would be almost entirely unnecessary. When helicopters can be built at lower cost, they also can help solve terminal-to-downtown problems in cities that provide landing facilities for them.

Forrest Wilson, writing in an editorial in *Progressive Architecture* (September, 1969) says "the (terminal) problem is not insoluble. A similar Gordian knot was hacked to pieces by one beetle-browed John L. Lewis, president of the United Mine Workers, over thirty years ago when he conceived the idea of 'portal to portal' pay . . . Perhaps this simple underground concept is the answer to overhead transportation. If airlines were held responsible for a portal to portal time package in which passengers were transported from here to there, the problem might prove to be quite simple."

Again, what is needed, apparently, is the application of general systems theory to interlocking systems of transportation.

"No one," says *Challenge* (published by the Missiles & Space Division of the General Electric Company, Winter, 1968), is proposing that jets should be jettisoned, airports abandoned, cars barred from the streets, and concrete poured no more. To function properly, our complex urban society needs a comprehensive transportation system in which each mode of transportation is used to its best advantage, and all of them mesh without friction or loss of time. The comprehensive system should be designed to move *people,* not just vehicles, and should make that mobility pleasant and enjoyable, avoiding displacement, spoiled scenery, noise, bad air. Such a system . . . will take national and rational transportation planning. It will take research and development. It will take continued technological advances. Without technology, we might as well get out and walk.

Or swim. The situation of the merchant marine in this country is almost too ridiculous to describe. In December, 1970, two-thirds of all the passenger flagships in the American merchant marine passed each other under the Golden Gate. The other third was already at a dock in the bay.

One wonders why, if operating luxury liners is, for a number of reasons, no longer profitable, they aren't turned over for low-fare use by young people who would cook and serve their own meals and make up their own cabins. Only a skeleton crew of seamen would be required. Under such circumstances the ships could run full, perhaps make money, and provide a useful service.

Things are much better with freighters, tankers and ore carriers. They get larger and larger, with higher pay-loads and smaller crews. Containerization and barge-to-shore operations that do not require deep water channels nor expensive piers, and improved navigational aids all help. The day may easily come before the end of the century when freighters, at least, will operate entirely by instructions from satellites, and will carry a crew of only three highly trained electronics engineers.

The nice thing about freighters is that if something goes wrong, you can always cling to a hatch cover, or a floating part of the deck cargo, or, in extremity, wrap your arms around the bosun's neck: he is big and fat and will float indefinitely.

Assuming there are still such things as bosuns.

"Where did you go for your vacation?" asked the tall man waiting for an elevator in the Smithsonian Institute.
"Cayman Islands," replied the second.
"Where on earth are the Cayman Islands?" the first inquired.
"I've no idea," said the second. "We flew."

R. BUCKMINSTER FULLER/
***I Seem to Be a Verb,* 1970**

Someday, perhaps in your lifetime, it could be this . . .
You ride toward the city at 90 miles an hour, glancing through the morning newspaper while your electrically powered car follows its programmed route on the automated "guideway." You leave your car at the city's edge—a park-like city without streets—and enter one of the small plastic "people capsules" waiting nearby. Inside, you dial your destination on a sequence of numbered buttons. Then you settle back to finish reading your paper.
Smoothly, silently, your capsule accelerates to 80 miles an hour. Guided by a distant master computer, it slips down into the network of tunnels under the city—or into tubes suspended above it—and takes precisely the fastest route to your destination.
Far-fetched? Not at all. Every element of that fantastic people-moving system is already within range of our scientists' skills.

FREDRIC C. APPEL/
"The Coming Revolution in Transportation,"
***National Geographic,* Sept. 1969**

L'apres-midi D'un Faune

If all the vehicles we have discussed so far were to disappear in some unique catastrophe in the next ten seconds, it would make little difference to mobility on this planet. Continents drift, currents shift, winds blow, snakes slither, hawks glide, the little fish flash in silver schools of motion. In most of the inhabited world, most people still walk to act out their daily roles. We know very little about the morning of life, except that it was where mobility began; we like to think we know a little more about the afternoon. In that mossy glade, with the late sun illuminating the dance of a creature half beast, half god, we dimly see, as in an X-ray, the mobility that is his heritage. We should be thankful we can not see his evening as clearly.

We are involved in studies of the use of laser beams for tunneling, sharing the cost of experiments on an air-gulping vehicle that, in theory, can move in tunnels at high speeds with relatively low power consumption. Such tube vehicle systems could provide all-weather operation, increase safety, decrease air pollution, and conserve surface right-of-way.

ALAN S. BOYD/
"Slow Motion,"
Business Today, Spring, 1969

The history of concern for safety and survival on public roadways spans thousands of years. In Bible times when Assyria was ruled by King Sennacherib, charioteers who disobeyed traffic regulations were promptly executed and hung on stakes in front of their homes. No solution. But courteous pleas from those who desire to see traffic accidents reduced do not seem to provide the whole answer, either.

MAX CHRISTENSEN/
"Reverence for Life Calls for
Safe Driving,"
S. F. *Examiner,* July 11, 1970

Sponsoring companies, pointing the ATV (All Terrain Vehicles) at the snowmobile market, push frequent rallies complete with competitive timed events not only for poppa but mamma and all the little baby bears as well. With the buggies going for a mere $1,500, and speeds as high as 35 to 45 mph, a whole clan can climb into shiny nylon racing suits and bright helmets and roar off around the track. It could well be that families that race together, stay together.

WILLIAM J. McKEAN/
"And Now Here Comes the ATV,"
Look, July 14, 1970

As the blind army ants marching to their deaths in endless circles in our introduction show, mobility on earth, in some form or another, will continue for as long as there is life.

Mechanical devices to move people, animals and things from there to here and vice versa are relatively recent innovations in the evolutionary scheme of things. Yet, even before the invention of the first wheel, whole groups of peoples had migrated from one continent to another, and the continents themselves are thought to have broken apart and to have been propelled by silent forces to resting places on different parts of the planet. Spiders, caught up in high altitude wind currents, came tumbling down oceans away from their original nesting places. Arctic terns flew ten-thousand-mile circuits on their annual late-summer migrations from the northern colonies to the seas near Antarctica. Species of South American lizards drifted across the Pacific on natural rafts to end up on the Galapagos Islands. Salmon returned from the sea to their fresh water spawning grounds, traveling thousands of miles and overcoming countless obstacles along the way.

Before we go much further, we should describe the sort of mobility we're really talking about here. By its very definition, the basic process we call "life" necessitates mobility. Movement may be easily discernable, as with a horse galloping, a kitten climbing, a baby crawling. It may be a little more subtle, when we realize the single vine of ivy we planted last year now covers the entire gate, when the snail in the aquarium is "suddenly" at the other end. Or, motion may be so slight that we can't see it at all with the naked eye—an amoeba changing shape to encircle a food particle, a cell nucleus undergoing mitosis on the road to reproducing itself. However obvious, however subtle, life *is* movement.

Apart from the life processes that demand involuntary motor acts—respiration, digestion, circulation—there are also voluntary actions that physically move mammals and insects, fishes and birds, reptiles and people from one spot on earth to another. Whatever their motivations (the search for food, escape from a predator, the quest for a mate) these creatures have learned to control their

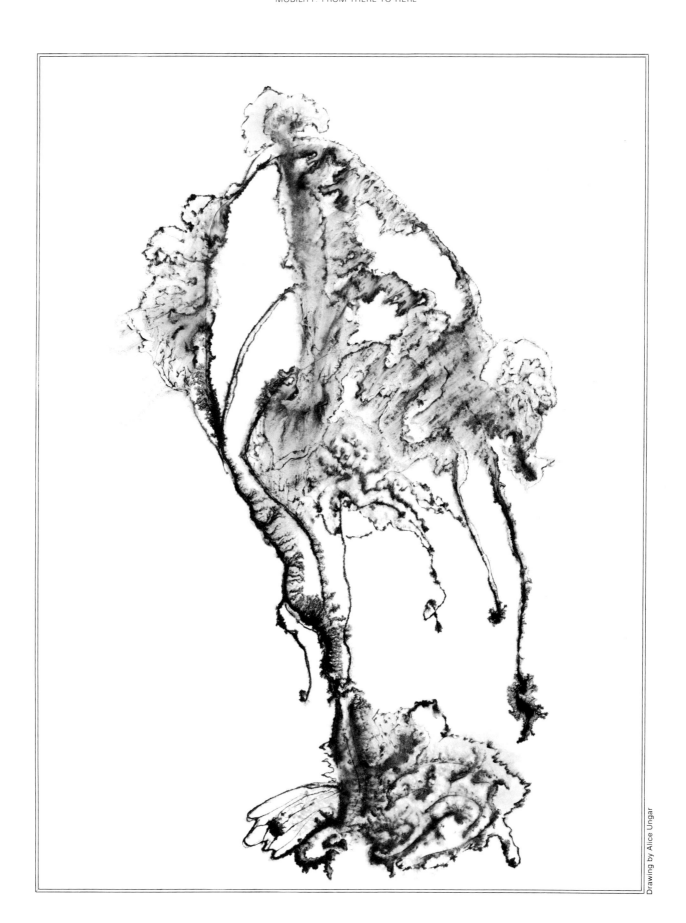

Drawing by Alice Ungar

bodies by alternately contracting opposing sets of muscles and to achieve mobility. Hence, the snake slithers in serpentine, concertina or side-winding movements, the dolphin churns the water as he moves with his school, the kangaroo jumps over the Australian bush, the honey bee darts from blossom to blossom.

Then man arrived on the planet and teamed up with the animals to move himself and his goods.

Alone, man could carry only about 90 pounds for no more than 20 miles a day. By piling his load on the back of a mule or an ox, he found he could triple the weight he moved. The next step was to build a land sledge, pile about 3,000 pounds on it, hitch up a team of oxen, and let them drag it.

Then, in about 3000 B.C., an anonymous Sumerian invented the wheel and upset everything. We've already examined the results of his "contribution" — the eventual mechanization of most of society. This made possible a new combination (man, beast and wheel), which in turn was responsible for the settling of new frontiers and the movement of even more goods over even greater distances. And it's all gone on from there.

Or has it? In spite of all our technological "achievements," this same combination of man, beast and wheel is still the vital one in most of the "underdeveloped" world. Oxen pull carts in S. E. Asia, and mules help Spanish farmers bring in grain from the fields.

And in what appears to be an appropriate statement on "just how far we've come," in one of the most far-reaching scientific experiments now going on, man is relying on an animal rather than another man or a machine for some elementary mobility. In the Sea Lab experiments, where research divers are living on the ocean floor for weeks at a time in a specially designed module, highly-trained dolphins are being used as messengers to carry tools and samples back and forth between the divers and a supply ship topsides. They're faster than machines, and don't have to undergo decompression as divers would.

So take away the jets and the trucks and the cars and the buses. We'll still be a mobile planet with the most versatile of all transportation systems... life.✿

Roger!
I read you loud and clear.
Roger? Roger? Roger?

Illustration by Masami Miyamoto

I can't hear you.

Hal...

Is this trip necessary? Many business and vacation trips melt away under the hard rays of this World War II question. In the "electronic village" McLuhan has described, a large part of business and vacation travel may not be economically supportable nor psychologically necessary by the end of the century.

One is reminded of the story about the Washington, D.C. executive who drove from his suburban home in Alexandria; a trip of eight miles taking forty minutes (under the traffic conditions), in order to make a telephone call from his office. Why didn't he make the call from his home telephone?

Or, if he *had* to use his car, why not use his car phone and cruise along the lovely roads that run beside the Potomac and Shenandoah? According to *The German Tribune* (in "Convenient Car Phones Catch On," Dec., 1970), "Within the foreseeable future car phones will be as much part and parcel of a motor car as a TV set is of the living room . . . Compactly built, car telephones are small in size. In the new Mercedes the phone even fits into the ashtray slot."

We don't exactly recommend the driver on the freeway listening to the radio, shaving with his electric razor, perhaps playing his guitar, and making telephone calls tooling along at 70 mph. But maybe that's the way it's going to be. At least for awhile.

We'll talk about after awhile. To answer the question we asked to begin with, let's listen to Jack Mullins of American Airlines (in *Saturday Review*, Jan., 1970). "All sorts of technical advances are being developed that may prove to be sensible surrogates for business trips. We think that television telephones may well affect us. It's a great concern. We look upon it as a bigger threat to our travel than Metroliners or high-speed highways.

". . . You dial a Touch-Tone phone, and the customer on the other end comes into view. Picturephone subscribers can have their sets linked to a computer and transmit inventory charts, stock market reports, production schedules and sales charts on a screen.

"Xerox's Telecopier enables a businessman to dial a client or associate thousands of miles away and, as they talk, it transmits reports or sketches in

a matter of minutes directly through the telephone lines . . . RCA has developed a similar device, called Interpolated Voice Data, which can transmit copy and voice simultaneously to overseas offices."

Don't take these developments lightly. They are here. They are technologically feasible. Everything that is accomplished, now, by bringing people together in huge office building, and—on their way—clogging the highways and filling the parking lots, can now be done simply by dialing or pushing a button.

Says Dr. John Pierce, executive director of research at Bell Laboratories, Murray Hill, N.J., "I believe many workers of the future won't commute to work. They will *communicate* to work. Their homes will be connected to their offices via electronic communications. It's entirely within the realm of existing technology."

Nor is one talking solely about office-types. A foreman in a manufacturing plant, sitting at home and scanning the operation on his stereo-tv, could be equally effective as the prototype now, walking down the line. An engineer, confronted with a breakdown, can scan the offending apparatus and suggest what needs to be done, even though he is sitting on the patio, a thousand miles from the plant site. True, there will still have to be some people in the factories; but it is doubtful that there need to be anywhere near as many as are now there. The result *could* be to reduce the pressure on the highway systems, return urban parking areas to tax producing properties, hopefully reduce smog and pollution, and make the worker much more productive because he or she would not waste hours every working day trying to get to someplace where they perform the same functions they could easily do at home.

To the extent that vacation travel represents new environmental inputs, and thus refreshes the psyche, it is quite possible that full color, stereo, three dimensional television in the home, subscribed to as the telephone now is, would be a reasonable substitute for many families. Such systems probably will be commercially available within another five years. This doesn't mean that no one will ever go anyplace except to the refrigerator for another beer. It does mean that recreational experiences (such as round-the-world trips, a stay in Majorca or the Bahamas) may be made available as electronic experience to families who cannot afford such trips. It is true one cannot catch a trout sitting in the living room; but it appears equally true that he cannot catch one even if he goes bodily to the lake or stream.

Looking much further ahead, but still quite possibly within our time-span of thirty years, we may see the electronic transmission of matter. For many items, trucks, vans, freight trains and ships would simply be unnecessary. Human beings might be transmitted the same way. There appears to be no theoretical reason why these things cannot be done, and at least as far as material objects are concerned, the technology already has been worked out on a laboratory scale.

Meanwhile, there are other ways of mobility, too. Robert Graves in "A Journey to Paradise," (*Holiday*, August, 1962) gives us a graceful way out on the mobility theme, one we may pursue further later on.

"Of all the priests and Sunday school teachers who taught me about Paradise when I was a child, none claimed to have been there. I never dreamed myself that I would one day enter the Garden of Delights, confirm their account . . . and return to tell the tale. No: I am not talking in metaphors, nor am I a mystic. Paradise is where I went.

"The point of departure was New York City . . . Four friends had gathered in an apartment overlooking the East River, prepared to set out with me under the guidance of our host. The Greeks had a word for his function, namely 'mystagogue' . . . At 7:30 he prepared us for a journey . . . at eight, he began turning out the lights . . . while we settled down in easy chairs and waited the revelation.

". . . We remembered the mystagogue's warning: 'You are going where God dwells, and will be granted all knowledge . . .'

"I knew from a study of Celtic and Middle Eastern religion that the road to Paradise often begins under the sea or from a lake bottom, so the greenish water now lapping about me came as no surprise. I entered a marble grotto, passing a pile of massive sunken statuary, and found myself in a high-roofed tunnel lit by brilliantly colored lamps. The sea lay behind.

the end of the road

Maybe you must deny people the mobility they now have, suggests Laurel van der Wal Roennau, Rand Corporation's coordinator for transportation research. (She rides a bicycle to work.)
Use telecommunications to reduce the need for travel. When there is a megalopolis from San Francisco to San Diego, we can no longer pursue the auto as a means of transportation and more freeways as the answer.
We will have to change the industrial way of life, change the style. Not the quality. Maybe it means staggering work weeks, or reducing the need for commuting.
Instead of having people commute to offices in center city, have the work come to their homes by videophone. A kind of cottage industry.
My job, your job, could be done at home in space subsidized by the company. . . .
California Living, Jan. 25, 1970

"This was perfect schizophrenia. My corporeal self reclined in a chair, fully conscious, exchanging occasional confidences with friends; but another 'I' had entered the tunnel. Could it be the same tunnel through which, four thousand years before, the epic hero Gilgamesh made his approach to the Babylonian Paradise of the goddess Siduri?

"My spirit followed after into the clear blue air, gazing down on cornfields, fields of poppies and the spires of a heavenly city.

"At last the music ended. The visions were fading now. My corporeal self sighed, stretched luxuriously and looked around. Most of the company had left the room. Only one remained. I asked him: 'So the journey seems to be over?'

" 'Ah, but close your eyes, and you can get back at once,' he said."

There are many ways to get from there to here. ✿

shall we dance?

from *The Drawings of Heinrich Kley*, Borden Publishing Co., Alhambra, California

chapter 6.

TELECOMMUNICATIONS:
One World-Mind

Illustration by Masami Miyamoto

6.

to whom it may concern

"Dear Pen Pal: I am fine, how are you? The wether hear is good, but I have not herd from you in sometime…"

There comes a time in the course of human events when it becomes self-evident we have armour in our chinks, but the voice cannot get through. Somehow, there is always a commercial on, and our voices crying in the technological wilderness are gone with the wind. Something there is that does not like a wall. Let's join hands and see if we can find another world.

Now is the nature of our discontent made vainglorious by this wall of words and all the clouds that obscure our lives have from the deepest subconscious risen.

As in Poe's "The Telltale Heart," our love for each other beats rhythmically against the obdurate brick of words. But there may be a way out. Follow us, anyone?

In the way we are using the term here, "telecommunications" is intended to mean a shared awareness between two or more organisms. The "tele" comes tumbling down the millenia from the Greek, a sort of verbal fallout and it simply means, "at a distance." In recent years, the word has been applied mostly to describe mechanical and electronic phenomena, but don't let that fool you; all communications between—and within—any species are at a distance, including the one that most immediately leaps to your mind. Even between colonies of molecules there is a measurable distance. There always seems to be a synaptic gap.

"Shared awareness?" You have to reach for that one. Still, some sort of event seems to be experienced and some sort of transaction appears to take place. Some process occurs, some parts of it are shared. We feel that "something" changed hands, or bodies, or minds. But with the limitations of our current knowledge, we do not seem to be able to say, nor even to label, exactly what was exchanged.

The readily accessible sources are not much help. Just try some on for size:

The *Encyclopedia Britannica* says: "Information is interpreted in its broadest sense to include the messages occurring in any of the standard communication mediums, such as telegraphy, radio or television..."

Let's try another:

According to the *American Heritage Dictionary,* "Information is knowledge derived from study, experience or instruction; knowledge of a specific event or situation; new; word; a nonaccidental signal used as input to a computer or communications system."

They left a man on third base in the top of the ninth inning with the score tied; don't we all? Let's go to bat just one more time:

George A. Miller, in *Language and Communication* says, "Information is the occurrence of one out of a set of alternative stimuli. A descriptive stimulus is a stimulus that is arbitrary, symbolically associated with some thing (or state, or event, or property) and that enables the stimulated organisms to discriminate this thing from other things..."

Swimming up from these Olympian depths, we'll try, too. May we suggest that what is exchanged in the communicative transaction may be matching, or at least similar, wave patterns between two or more systems? The patterns (as we describe them) may be electro-magnetic or (as we experience them) psycho-neural. Some kind of transaction takes place; something is exchanged. Perhaps what are exchanged are wave patterns. The crest and the trough, the frequency, the duration, all appear to suggest a form or mode of communication—whether it be between galaxies and astronomers, or sea urchins clustering on the shoals of some ancient, outworn sea. H. G. Wells described it magnificently in the last part of *The Time Machine,* so we're only playing catch-up here.

If the *process* of the message may be an exchange or matching of wave patterns, we still haven't really described the nature of the message. A tough one to take on, but, fortunately, (for ourselves) we do not walk this path alone. We have friends. Here's one:

In *The World as a Communications Network,* Lawrence K. Frank says, "The world, as Norbert Wiener once remarked, may be viewed as a myriad of 'To Whom it May Concern' messages. The significance of this statement becomes apparent when we recognize that everything that exists and happens in the world, every object and event, every plant and animal organism, almost continuously emits its characteristic identifying signal. Thus, the world resounds with these many diverse messages, the cosmic noise, generated by the energy transformation from each existent and event.

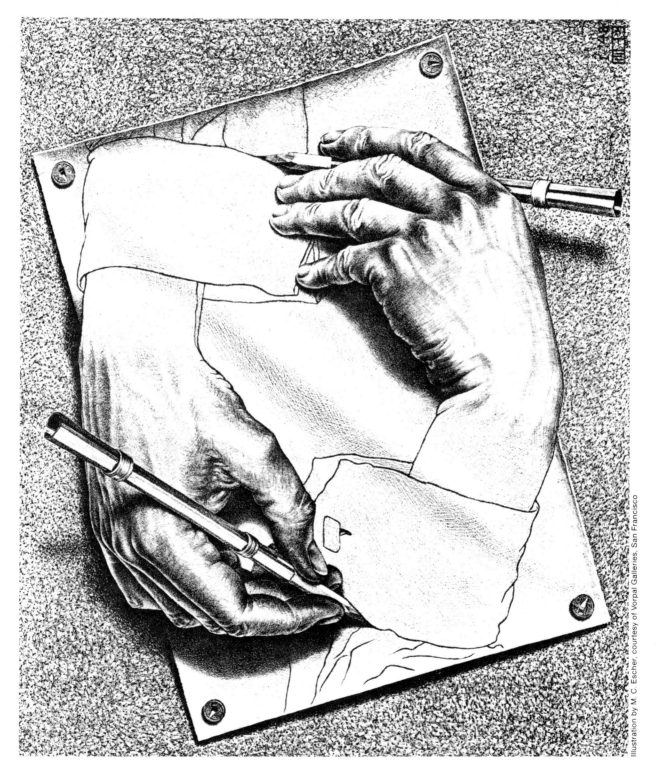

And here, beyond the ape, beyond all expectations (whatever the preceding species had in mind) — the hands. Here, the world of human begins. It has been said that, "The left hand does not know what the right hand is doing." Could they be mirror images of each other? And thus, between them, may they not create a "third world," which may be the province of our explorations of the future?

ALL HANDS ON DECK!

We know that when any group with a particular set of values is cut off from communication with others, or cuts itself off, it tends to become more dogmatic, sterile and unproductive in its thinking.

ROBERT THEOBALD/
"Communication to Build the Future Environment,"
Main Currents in Modern Thought,
March-April, 1970

The limits of our language mean the limits of our world. A new world is the beginning of a new language. A new language is the seed of a new world.

"Pre-Experiencing Alternative Futures,"
Technology III, **Dec. 12, 1969**

According to Norbert Wiener:
"Society can only be understood through a study of the messages and communication facilities which belong to it."

GENE YOUNGBLOOD/
Expanded Cinema, **1970**

. . . to communicate with someone is to effect some form of change in their store of experiences. This change may affect their level of perception, their way of seeing things, their information bank and even their pattern of behavior.

FRANCOIS ALLAIRE/
Canadian Industries Limited *Oval,*
Spring, 1970

Nobody yet knows the languages inherent in the new technological culture; we are all technological idiots in terms of the new situations. Our most impressive words and thoughts betray us by referring to the previously existent, not to the present.

MARSHALL McLUHAN/
Counter-Blast, **1969**

"While every thing and event contributes to this cosmic noise, each emits its identifying message and also a highly selective receptivity for only a selection of these multiple messages, while indifferent or insensitive to others.

"Through evolution, each organism has developed a concern for those messages which are essential to its living functions and survival as a species, while ignoring what is not biologically relevant nor useful. Accordingly, in any geographical area, many different species; bacteria in the soil, worms, insects, fish, reptiles, birds, amphibians, and the array of mammals, carry on their life careers, selectively receiving and responding to the signals that are of concern to each species, while unaware of the many other messages that are being concurrently transmitted."

What Frank has said may be a significant contribution to a theory of communication. Most of these theories have been concerned with what is transmitted and not very much with the selective process that picks out the essential message from the background "noise." The selection defines the message and completes the "loop." Thus, full circle. The selectivity was the prime ingredient; without it, nothing appears to happen. Think about it.

And now we have pulsars and quasars, and other strange beasts that roam the communicative universe. Helium, apparently, was a message from our little sun, but daddy wasn't listening, for several million years. The same thing might be said of X-rays, cosmic rays, radiation and various nuclear and magnetic forces. They—whoever "they" are—had been broadcasting all the time, but the message was not received by humans until someone chose to "hear" it. Then everyone heard.

One wonders what other messages are being broadcast that we do not choose to hear now. Only recently have we heard the song of the whales, the chatter of the dolphin, the chirping of shrimp, and beetles following the ant trails in the night. There may be an infinite number of such messages.

It may very well be that the message is the medium. Happy medium.

You take it from here. ❖

voice
of the
dolphin

¿Habla Usted Dolphinese?

Sprechen Sie Dolphinese?

Parlez-vous Dolphinese?

Bbl говорите по-Dolphinese

Dolphinese ה־יכול אתה לדבר

貴方 Dolphinese 話せますか

Ομιλείτε Dolphinese

Hey, man, you talk Dolphinese?

DOLPHINESE SPOKEN HERE

There are several advantages to making investigations of possible communication with a species other than man. There are advantages to picking a creature whose brain is equal to the size of ours so that one may one day realize communication at the same complex abstract levels at which one operates. There are advantages to choosing an entirely different body form and entirely different modes of communication, to delineate by contrast the modes and means that are interhuman.

* * *

As we sharpen up our man-to-dolphin communications, so do we sharpen up our human-to-human communications. As our basic understanding is expanded by an attempt to communicate with another species, so our understanding of our own communication problems is highlighted and better understood.

* * *

Margaret Howe's report in 5th week of living with dolphin Peter:
"At the moment Peter is at this point: he can listen, he can hush up. He responds with a good 95% humanoid, only occasional dolphinese comments on the side. He can somewhat imitate the word 'ball' and 'hello.' These are not too clear . . . but are there. He is obviously working on 'L' and 'M'. . . probably from 'hello,' 'ball,' and 'Margaret.' "

JOHN C. LILLY/
The Mind of the Dolphin, 1967

In his supreme arrogance, technological man has not bothered to try to "talk" with the other species with whom he shares this planet. True, "Kitty, kitty, kitty," will flush out a bevy of cats and "Here, Rover" may conjure up enough dogs to chase the cats who stalk the birds and eat the mice. But few humans—in a technological society—have seriously talked to a cat or a dog. They are "dumb" animals. Presumably they are "dumb" because they don't speak English too good. Perhaps they don't speak Russian or Chinese too good, either. But then, neither do we.

Quite recently, some serious attempts have been made to establish nonverbal communications with some other species. This effort has largely been made possible through technological advances. We can listen, record, play back at different speeds, both audio and visual, use instant replay, stop-action and other techniques, scan the array and begin to understand, just a little—the highly complex and effective communication systems that go on outside our own reasonably simple, usually ineffective, verbal one.

No one, apparently, has made a serious study of communications between plants, but someday there may very well be one.

So, a good place to start might be with the ant, one of the planet's most successful species in terms of numbers, longevity and social organization. It has long been known that chemical trails left by exploring ants serve as guides for the workers who follow the paths to secure the food. Chemical secretions also appear to constitute a part of the complex communication within the ant colonies. In addition, there seem to be tactile languages of considerable sophistication.

Ever study a column of ants, to and from the nest and see how quickly they exchange information by antennae (or whatever) contact? Maybe we could learn something about human vehicular traffic systems by studying columns of ants. Chemical highways and electronic antenna controls are human possibilities. Never saw an ant in a head-on collision with another. Have you?

It should be technologically possible for humans to isolate, define and synthesize the ant chemicals and then work out a chemical language with ants.

Why try? Well, they've been around a lot longer than we have, and it might be interesting to find out what they have to say. But instead, we have "exterminators," who try to eliminate ants instead of learning from them.

One of the most provocative recently published studies of communication by ants is the article by Bert Holldobler (in "Communication Between Ants and Their Guests," *Scientific American,* March, 1971). It is a long article, so we'll quote only a little, and try to paraphrase a bit.

The thesis is that certain species of beetles live in ant nests, sometimes eat the ant larvae, but are nevertheless apparently welcome there.

"Ants," says Holldobler, "as highly social animals, possess a complex system of internal communication that enables the colony to carry out its collaborative activities, food gathering, care of the young and defense against enemies. The fact that the ants do not treat their alien guests (the beetles) as strangers suggests that the guests must have broken the ants' code; that is, attained the ability to 'speak' the ants' language, which involves a diversity of visual, mechanical and chemical clues."

What appears to us to be exciting about this is that if little, dumb old beetles can "break the code," perhaps man, in all his technological might, might be able to do so, too. In other words, there's hope.

One more paraphrase and quote on the ants and then we're bound for movin' on to higher (higher?) species. The paraphrase: some species of beetles have summer and winter "homes" with different species of ants. A sort of jet set; like wintering in the Bahamas or Hawaii and summering in Canada or Europe.

The quote: Holldobler again, "Before leaving the *Formica* nest at the beginning of fall, the *Atemeles* beetle obtains a supply of food for its migration by begging from its *Formica* hosts. For this it employs a technique of tactile stimulation. The beetle first drums rapidly on an ant to attract attention. It then induces the ant to regurgitate food by touching the ant's mouth part with its maxillae and forelegs."

So, now, climb the ladder, up or down, wrong by wrong. Trying to get to dolphin country.

If we were placed underwater and looked at one another by means of sonar, (like dolphins do) what would each of us look like to the other? Sound waves in water penetrate a body without much external reflections or absorptions. Skin, muscle, and fat are essentially transparent to the sound waves coming through the water. The internal reflections are from air-containing cavities and from bones. Thus we see a fuzzy outline of the whole body plus the bone and teeth fairly clearly delineated; the most sharply delineated objects are any gas-containing cavities. We have a good view of portions of the gut tract, the air sinuses, the head, the mouth cavity, the larynx, the trachea, the bronchi, the bronchioles, the lungs and any air trapped in or around the body and the clothing. You can imagine again the conventional person's unease at being able to see inside another person's stomach and lungs.

Thus, living dolphin-wise, we should have little need for external facial expression. We would try to express similar things probably with our air sacs on our head. The truth of our stomachs would be immediately available to everyone else. In other words, anyone could tell when we were either sick or angry by the bubbles of air moving in our stomachs. The true state of our emotions would be read with ease.

For some persons this might lead to disadvantageous situations in, say, a bargaining transaction. I can imagine in a game of poker for high stakes this might be very inhibiting.

JOHN C. LILLY/
The Mind of the Dolphin, 1967

They are the largest mammals in the world. Like porpoises, they are apparently of extraordinary intelligence. They emit sounds—clicks, hisses, and eerie high-pitched wails that seem like infants crying, or violins throbbing, or distant flutes keening, or bass viols thrumming. The sounds repeat and repeat. Are they conscious rhythm? Conscious verse? Conscious communication?

DAVID PERLMAN/
"Tuned-In to a Singing Humpback Whale,"
San Francisco *Examiner,* Dec. 13, 1970

We have a rich heritage of animals talking together and to humans, from Aesop's Fables through Bre'r Rabbit to Snoopy. Most of it is preserved in comic strips and animated film. Strangely enough, the animals all speak English; as if they didn't have a language of their own.

We were going to do something about the bees, also eminent survivalists, with their hive dance, their navigation by polarized light, and all that; but nearly everyone knows that story, and it only serves to reinforce our little thesis here: that we can learn a lot from our fellow, nonhuman companions on this planet. And Lord knows we need to learn something about communication before it is too late to have anything—or anyone—to communicate with.

We could go on to the grey squirrels, the deer, the beaver, antelope, bears, apes and find highly complex forms of communication (we left out the birds and the fish but they belong in there, too). Semanticists may argue that there is a difference between "signs" and "symbols" and that the sudden silence of a squirrel's talk, (signaling danger), the flash of white fur, the slap of a beaver's tail, the call of the wolf to its brood are "signs" and that the cave paintings of ancient man are "symbols." And this (for reasons completely obscure) constitutes one of the "differences" between men and animals. Fortunately, the problem appears to be that of the semanticists; not ours. We can go on believing that animals have a lot to say, if we'd ever stop to listen. And what they have to say may determine whether we survive as a species or not.

If wave patterns are exchanged between all living organisms, some transactions occur in space and time. The *form* is not important; the selection and exchange of wave patterns may be.

What about the dolphins? Don't we ever get to the dolphins? (A still, small voice asks, echoing Dylan Thomas' "A Child's Christmas in Wales.")

No more stopping along the trail; we go marching to Cetacea.

It is a grand and glorious world—that of the Cetaceans. For those who do not know them well, the Cetaceans are mammals that fled the land for the sea many millions of years ago. Perhaps to escape predators, maybe because of a change in climate. Only they know. Or the reason may be simply, as any skin diver can tell you, that living in water is more fun than living in air (particularly the kind we have now). The sea otters would probably say the same thing (as in *Ring of Bright Water*).

We'll only talk to two Cetaceans here—the whale and the dolphin. We'll have to talk fast, because they may not be around very much longer. We also will have to pass politely by the seals and sea lions, crouching there in their ecologic niches; the dugong and manatee, on their lonesome Australasian beaches, although they may have something to tell us, too. No one seems to have tried to find out.

Let's pick up a whale and play with it for awhile. The whale is kind of big, and kind of extinct, and his kind may not pass this way again, but despite Captain Ahab, he has always been kind to men. In our little interlude let us at least try to find out what he has learned in his millions of years of survival.

Using contemporary hydrophonic techniques, Dr. Roger Payne, of the New York Zoological Society, has recorded the language of the humpbacked whale. These may have been the sad songs the sirens sang, and what Ulysses heard (without hydrophones) until they strapped him to the mast. As recorded by Dr. Payne, it is a rich musical language, something like the modulations and intonations of the Cantonese. Given word enough and time we may be able to "read" it. The score is richer even than Mozart, more profound than Beethoven, more exciting than Stravinsky. One would think Bernstein was conducting the Young Whales Philharmonic. As a matter of plain old, cold fact, Dr. Payne's recording led to a 12-minute composition for the New York Philharmonic entitled "And God Created Great Whales." They had been singing all these years, but only lonely sailors in the night, over the creaking of the hull and windsong in the rigging, heard their chorus as they passed.

"The sperm whales have brains six times the size of ours," says John C. Lilly (in *The Mind of the Dolphin*). "Before they are annihilated by man, I would like to exchange ideas with a sperm whale. I am not sure that they would be interested in communicating with me because my brain obviously is much more limited than theirs'.

"If a sperm whale wants to see-hear-feel any past experience, his huge computer can reprogram it and run it off again. His computer gives him a re-living as if with a 3-dimensional-sound-color-taste-emotion-re-experiencing motion picture . . .

(Continued on page 12)

THE RAINBOW THAT WASHED AWAY

✿My Siamese Cat (whose name is Mouse!) and I, glad to find the sun shining and the sky blue, (or almost blue!) decided to go for a walk. We were hailed by two old friends of ours, Fox and Coyote Old-Man. It was one of those wonderful spring days—warm sunshine and fluffy white clouds. ✿Fox exclaimed, "Look at the Canyon behind you!" We looked deep into the Canyon and saw an amazing sight: four concentric Rainbows. ✿Fox said, "Look at the top of that Rainbow! The colors are running off!" And that is just what they were doing! ✿The rain was washing the rainbow colors down the side of the Bow. The Oak trees and the Redwoods were splattered with pink and yellow. Deer and Pig and Porcupine were green and orange and bright blue respectively. Yellow Frog was sitting on a purple rock. Pink Hawk landed on a red branch.

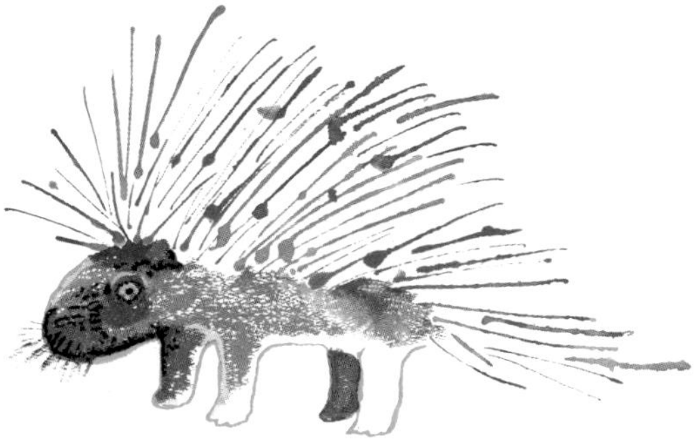

No two drops of rain were the same color. Mouse had all sorts of colors mixed in his fur. Coyote Old-Man was dripping in Technicolor! Fox had become an elegant plum color with a few bright polkadots here and there.

Coyote Old-Man ran off through the brush. He returned, accompanied by the Foreman of the Rainbow Keepers, who explained about the care and maintenance of the Rainbows. When it is raining, the Rainbow Keepers bring them out and place them into the proper positions. When the storm is gone, they carefully dry them off, mend them if necessary, and touch up the paint jobs before putting them away.

"Well," the Foreman went on, "it seems the Purchasing Agent made a terrible mistake. He thought he was ordering more Rainbow paint, but instead he ordered FINGER PAINT, which, as you know, WASHES RIGHT OFF!!"

Story by Bob Nash, Illustrations by John Larrecq

If and when we encounter intelligent
extraterrestrial communicating life forms from
other places in this universe, we will need
results from communication research to apply
there and then. It is man that we have to examine
more carefully and objectively to avoid possibly
planet-wide fatal errors during those possible
future encounters. Some of the vast sums going
into the space program should be invested
in the communication program as a life insurance
for the future of man.

JOHN C. LILLY/
The Mind of the Dolphin, 1967

Some years ago in England, an energetic
scientist could be seen morning after morning
hiking down an oak-lined trail to a blind
hidden deep in the forest. Wedging into the small
enclosure, Dr. Jan Taylor, of the British
Ministry of Agriculture, would settle himself
on a stool with notebook and binoculars. Presently,
out of leaf nests and hollows of trees, gray
squirrels emerged. They scrambled down trunks,
flicked their tails and chased each other gaily
through the leaves as gray squirrels do. Taylor
was trying to learn why squirrels strip bark from
trees—but gradually he was discerning something
else, something startling that has been observed
by almost everyone but seldom comprehended.
The squirrels were not playing; they were
communicating with those tail flicks
and chases.

JEAN GEORGE/
"Surprising Signals in the Wild,"
Readers Digest, June, 1969

He can imagine changing it to do a better job next time he encounters such an experience. He can set up the model of the way he would like to run it next time, reprogram his computer, run it off, and see how well it works."

This would be anthropomorphism at its highest ebb, but this man seems to know whales better than anyone else, and the prospects are exciting. Perhaps instead of building more and more complicated computers, men should just "program" a whale. It could make a whale of a difference.

Dolphins, anyone? We're there.

Within the recorded history of man, the dolphin has been a constant companion. Friezes from early temples show men riding dolphins, and any seaman can tell you what a delight they are, easily outrunning the ship, cutting in and out in front of the bow. In the South Pacific during World War II, sailors frequently interpreted their glowing phosphorescent wakes at night as torpedoes, so everybody was up all night manning battle stations. But the dolphins were just having fun. The men weren't. And there's the difference.

"In earliest times, man believed dolphins once were men," say Eleanore Devine and Martha Clark (in *The Dolphin Smile*, 1967). In one of his hymns, Homer describes how Tyrsenian pirates, threatened by Zeus for kidnapping his son Dionysus, jumped into the sea and were changed at once into dolphins. It is said, too, that Pharoah's forces pursuing the Israelites into the Red Sea were turned into dolphins and doomed to wander the seas until the end of time. Here, in folklore is the first clue to the kinship men have always felt for dolphins and dolphins for men.

Some 1200 years later, Brunetto Latini (who was Dante's master) said, "The dolphin is a great sea fish that follows the voices of man and is the swiftest thing in the sea, for he skips clear over it as if he were flying; but he does not like to go alone; very many go together, and through them sailors perceive the storm that is to come, when they see the dolphin fleeting amid the sea and tumbling as he flees, as if the thunderbolt were driving him."

And then, the master's voice in our own time. Said Ernest Hemingway (in *The Old Man and the Sea*), "During the night two porpoises came around the boat and he could hear them rolling and blowing. He could tell the difference between the blowing noise the male made and the sighing blow of the female.

"They are good," he said. "They play and make jokes and love one another. They are our brothers like the flying fish."

In a few isolated instances, we are now beginning to listen to what the earth's nonhuman creatures have to tell us and teach us. One example: in 1966, after a nearly disastrous collision between a plane and a herring gull at the Newark, N.J., airport the Port of New York Authority called in a bird signal expert to work on the problem. John Kadlec had already been experimenting with the use of taped bird distress calls to prevent such accidents. He brought to the airport tapes of the distress calls of herring and blackheaded gulls, mounted a loudspeaker on an automobile, placed a tape-player in the trunk and drove around scaring off the gulls. In the time since then, it has been apparent that the gulls have changed their flight patterns, frightened away by their own calls of alarm. The Newark airport has been virtually free of them ever since.

Men have also listened to our friends, the dolphins, and have developed the "Sonic Dolphin." This is an acoustical generator that produces pulses very similar to those produced by dolphins in echo location and recognition when darkness or muddy water prevents use of vision. The *Sondol,* as it's called, has been tested by human subjects, and appears to have great potential as an aid to the blind person in sensing his environment and to the scuba diver for perception in muddy waters. It seems that anyone with normal hearing will be able to use the *Sondol,* with practice, to find his way around in total visual darkness.

As Lilly has suggested, "even though we are several millions of years behind the dolphins, we may be able to catch up. By the use of machines we have finally caught up with some of the birds' flight in air. Why shouldn't we similarly catch up with the dolphins' life and thinking underwater?"

Looking forward, perhaps they are the only hope we have. If the dolphins cannot tell us, perhaps no one can. ✿

Fish with a weak electrical current have been found to possess receivers for electric fields. They are able to distinguish between underwater objects of varying electrical efficiency.
On closer examination of their anatomy it can be seen that the receivers are cup-shaped formations on the skin's basal membrane. They also receive the fish's own electric signals and are able to comprehend their surroundings from them. For example, the fish knows exactly whether a rod stroked along his body is made of conductive metal or a nonconductive plastic.

ERNST H. HAUX/
"Scientists at Dusseldorf discuss Aspects of Animal Language,"
The German Tribune, March 31, 1970

We assume that our familiar senses give us a complete picture of our environment, but nothing could be further from the truth. We are stone-deaf and color-blind in a universe of impressions beyond the range of our senses. The world of a dog is a world of scent; that of a dolphin, a symphony of ultrasonic pulses as meaningful as sight. To the bee, on a cloudy day, the diffuse sunlight carries a direction sign utterly beyond our powers of discrimination, for it can detect the plane of vibration of the light waves. The rattlesnake strikes in total darkness toward the infrared glow of its living prey— as our guided missiles have learned to do only in the last few years. There are blind fish in muddy rivers who probe their opaque universe with electric fields, the natural prototype of radar; and all fish have a curious organ, the lateral line, running along their bodies to detect vibrations and pressure changes in the water around them.
Could we interpret such sense impressions, even if they were fed into our brains? Undoubtedly yes, but only after a great deal of training. We have to learn to use all our *own* senses . . .

ARTHUR C. CLARKE/
Profiles of the Future, 1967

"We all, in one way or another, send our little messages out to the world. We say, 'help me, I'm lonely. Take me, I'm available. Leave me alone, I'm depressed.' And rarely do we send our messages consciously. We act out our state of being with nonverbal body language. We lift one eyebrow for disbelief. We rub our noses for puzzlement. We clasp our arms to isolate ourselves or to protect ourselves. We shrug our shoulders for indifference, wink one eye for intimacy, tap our fingers for impatience, slap our forehead for forgetfulness."

JULIUS FAST / *Body Language*, 1970

every little movement...

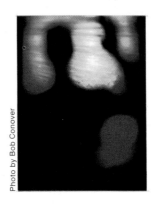

Photo by Bob Conover

The sleek black cat follows us from one room to another. She stays close by, taking care not to put her paws in the line of our next step. When we pause for a moment, she begins her version of what seems to be the universal "cat dance"—rubbing her head and back against our ankles, sinuously curling in and out of our legs, dragging her tail across our shoe tops.

She continues her dance until we reach down and scoop her up, wondering, as we do, how this nine-week-old kitten knows so well how to use the dance to communicate with us. Is it instinct, as honey bees appear to be born with knowledge of the wiggle dance that enables them to direct other bees to secret caches of honey? Is it learned behavior, from seeing her mother perform the same ritual? Or is it trial and error, reinforcing her knowledge of which act causes which results?

No matter. We reach down and gather her up against our chest. She relaxes completely, closes her eyes, and prepares to catch a quick nap. At that instant of relaxation, we *know* that she trusts us, that being in our arms is what she wanted, and that she's totally happy.

We reach up with our free hand to stroke her soft fur. With that one touch, we *know* that she eats well (because her ebony coat glistens with health), that she spends a great deal of her private time each day grooming herself, and that she's a house cat.

The same stroke also carries messages from us to sleepy cat. She senses from our touch that we love her, that we'll comfort her, and that we'll protect her at all costs from the huge Tom that lives on the next apartment balcony.

All these messages exchanged between us without a word...or meow. Nonverbal communication between *different* species goes on constantly. It's a sort of "body language." The snake's coiled body tells the mouse it's about to strike; the flight of seagulls inland warns city dwellers of an approaching storm; when the pointer hunting dog becomes suddenly rigid, crooks a paw and points his tail, his master knows he's located the prey; a circling buzzard advertises the presence of raw meat to all predators in the area.

With abundant examples of interspecie nonverbal communications, it should come as little surprise that intraspecie nonverbal communication (i.e., between human beings) is even more common. Once we learn to recognize and read messages transmitted via body movement rather than over vocal cords, we find the level of message transmission may be more honest and complete. Stooped shoulders and heavily lidded eyes can belie a speaker's cheerful words. Darting eyes and quick shifts of weight betray a listener's impatience. A rigid, straight back might signify an inflexible attitude toward the subject being discussed.

There seems to be a veritable "alphabet" of body movements, which, when strung together and acted out, do, in fact, "speak louder than words." One group of scientists, studying body language and its meaning calls the study "kinesics"—an examination of the behavioral patterns involved in nonverbal communication, within given cultures and on a universal scale.

The "Kinesticians" (that's our name, not their's) have determined that there are some body movements and reactions that appear to be cross-cultural, and most probably inherited. Studies in New Guinea, Brazil, Japan, Borneo and the U. S. found that in each of these cultures facial expressions conveying sadness, fear, hate and amusement were virtually the same, and pictures of "foreigners" portraying these emotions were readily identified by people in each culture for what they were. It seems that no matter where or when one lives, his face reddens in anger; he blushes in embarrassment; he is drenched in a cold sweat of fear; his pupils dilate with pleasure. "But look you, Cassius, the angry spot doth glow on Caesar's brow." Each a visual physical display, and each instantly deciphered by the alert "receiver" of the message.

There are some nonverbal movements which are learned (rather than instinctual) and which also allow man to communicate with others no matter what their spoken language. Dancing and lovemaking convey emotion as no words are capable of doing. Mathematical formulae and musical scores communicate the ideas of Einstein to a Swiss physicist and to a Rumanian microbiologist; the genius of Beethoven to a Russian violinist and to the New York Philharmonic.

The way you move . . . is saying something.
It's an unspoken method of communication . . .
a form of expression. Along with the way you
look . . . sound . . . smell . . . something in the way
you move sets you apart in that very personal
zone of space you occupy. It's part of your
aura . . . an aspect of your being that has
the power to attract or repel, depress or elate
everyone you meet.

"Bodyspeak," *Vogue,*
Sept. 1, 1970

Psychologist Albert Mehrabian has done
extensive lab measurements on what happens
when one person talks to another. He finds
that only 7% of a message's effect is carried
by words, while 93% of the total impact reaches
the "listener" through nonverbal means—facial
expression, vocal intonation. Feelings are
communicated mainly by nonverbal behavior.

LAYNE A. LONGFELLOW/
"Body Talk/The Game of Feeling
and Expression,"
Psychology Today, Oct., 1970

. . . Early communications were probably nonverbal, using . . . messages such as chants,
dances, change in gait or stance, postures,
including bowing and kneeling and other forms
of obeisance, gestures of arms and hands, facial
expressions, and varied tones of voice . . .
These were used in the early rituals and cere-
monies, the choral dances and dramatic per-
formances by which people attempted to
communicate, to propitiate and to invoke favors
or protection and, at the same time, to
exhibit their group solidarity.

LAWRENCE K. FRANK/
"The World as a Communication Network"

And there are hundreds of nonverbal clues and gestures peculiar to each culture. Hawaiian hula dancers tell stories with their hands (and not with their hips, as enthusiastic male admirers would have you believe!). Mime troops act out complicated social commentaries, understood in every detail by audiences acquainted with Mime gestures. Charades is a favorite party game, once "standard" gestures are learned by new players.

An American woman talking to her psychiatrist shakes her head from side to side while telling him that she loves her husband. The simple little head movement may be interpreted by the doctor to contradict what her lips are saying—and he sometimes feels the physical negation of her comment is the more honest of the two messages she is transmitting. In India, the same side to side head motion would reinforce her declaration of love. In that culture, horizontal head shakes mean "yes."

Another "learned" move that communicates emotion is man's treatment of space. Each person establishes his own "territory," an area of space surrounding him wherever he goes and which must not be intruded upon. The interesting thing is that the size of the space varies from culture to culture.

One group of body movements helps preserve our spatial territories. "Masking" actions are motions designed to cover up true feelings and to project an image of ourselves that we think is the acceptable one for public places. Women learn to sit in their short skirts in a special way that masks their sexuality. We adopt facial expressions that mask our discomfort—we smile charmingly at boring cocktail parties; we sit wide-eyed and alert during dull classroom discussions, counting the minutes until we can escape; we look properly solemn during our uncle's funeral and mentally count the money we might inherit. With practice, masking movements can be read and understood as easily as the more obvious crossed arms, pouting smile, or pinched forehead that tell a man whether or not he might approach an attractive woman with any luck at all.

It seems to be true; "Every little movement has a meaning all its own." Once learned, understood, and transferred, there's no more honest level of communication. ✤

Photo by Michael Jakub

crystal set

The walls of the room were pulsating liquid crystal. The input was from optical fibers and lasers, all from a computer in Des Moines. The host asked his guests, "What will you have?" One said, "The Bahamas." Another said, "Hongkong." And one other said, "Paris—in the spring." The host (perhaps MacBeth awaiting the ghost of Banquo) said, "We'll have them all. We'll start with Paris." He leaned forward and pushed a button. And, lo, they were there.

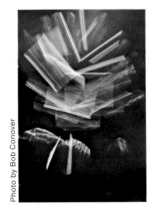

Photo by Bob Conover

The research notes for this section, typed on 4 x 6 cards, are stacked in neat piles on a table. Each stack has a title card on top, identifying the subject covered in the cards below.

Let's scan the array and see if against this background, a figure emerges; for the discernment of a figure is the difference between message and noise.

The first thing that comes across is that there are fourteen stacks of cards under the loose title "Electronic," and only one stack under the title "Print." To one raised on printed matter, the message of the pattern is loud and clear. Books, magazines and newspapers, as we know them, are, as McLuhan has said, dead.

Another scan, at a different interference angle, produces another figure. Most of the subject titles on top of the stacks of cards are almost entirely new to the English language. They are composed of acronyms, capital letter abbreviations, and unusual associations of older words. They all represent fields of technology that did not exist prior to World War II; some of them entered the public domain only within the last few years. Below, in no particular order, are the subject titles:

Kinaesthetics	Holography
PBC-TV	Magnetic Tape Cassettes
Pay-TV; CATV	Microfiche
EVR	Plasma Crystals
Laser; Sonar	Computer Graphics
Unifor Facsimile	Voice Recognition
Quadrasound	Synaesthetic Cinema

Here, it appears, may be the shape of things to come. Indeed, already here. Communication is the basis on which all segments of a society—business, industry, education, government, religion — are founded. For nearly all of their time on earth, humans have communicated by spoken or written words. That day is almost gone.

The "new" language is excited phosphors on an oscilloscope or TV screen; turned-on molecules of silver chloride on film; on-off magnetized molecules; displays of various sensory stimuli; coherent light beams; the pulsing of electrons in crystal lattices; the beat of unseen electromagnetic waves.

Someday, perhaps well before the year 2000, the description of "illiteracy" may be "the ability to read words." The Chinese, though they invented printing, have known this for more than 2,000 years. "A poster is worth ten thousand tracts." Artists, musicians, dancers and other practitioners of the lively art in all cultures have known this, too. The only humans who didn't were writers.

(Not that words on a page are not "pictures." Take a look at this page. The one right in front of you. It is a pattern made up of molecules of black against a background of white. The only way it differs from a photograph or painting is the degree of resolution. The degree of resolution is a projection of yourself. There simply is more "information" in a photograph than there is in printed words because the degree of resolution is at a finer level and, therefore, transmits more messages within the field of observation.)

The verbal world will rapidly disappear as a means of any but highly personal communication (as in "Pillow Talk") in a relatively short time. Even that will disappear with the development of telepathy (which will be discussed in the next section). The electronic nonverbal revolution might well be a sort of "half-way house," a transition, between verbalism and extra-sensory perception in all its modes.

All of the electronic and electromagnetic communications systems listed earlier already exist, although at different stages of development. The rather obvious task of the next three decades is to create a grand orchestration of those systems (and others still to be discovered) into an intermedia synthesis. It will be done because these systemic waves are mutually reinforcing. They may crest before the turn of the century into a wave of the magnitude of a cave painting, the invention of spoken language, and later of written and printed communication, sweeping all that we know before it and creating a world we can only dimly imagine now.

Let's play a game and see (out of the infinite number of possible syntheses of varying degrees of probability) whether we can put a pattern of systems together. It will not be easy, but if one thinks of words as ideographs, and ideographs as cave paintings at a time when verbal language was but a grunt, then it may be possible.

It might be best, in a compartmentalized world, briefly to describe some of the systems available now. Then, as in a jigsaw puzzle, we can attempt to assemble the parts into some sort of pattern of things to come, as we may experience it in our lifetime.

We may begin very simply with an "either/or" experiential distinction between particles and waves. The distinction appears to be a verbal one and what is experienced quite possibly may be the same phenomenon observed with different interference waves in the scanning process. What *does* seem to matter is that humans can, technologically (and perhaps psychically) control the motion of particles and waves in time and space (to use four old-fashioned words now out of vogue). The continuum is maneuverable.

Once we begin to discern the systems of particles/waves, as we observe them in "nature," (possibly only a projection of our psychoneural arrays), then it becomes possible to control them technologically. We can construct simulated systems, or build "models" of natural processes which we can then manipulate to create an environment or "surround" that appears to meet our needs at the time.

It should be observed that these developments were seldom the result of "tinkering" in the laboratory or workshop but were the projections of intuitive minds — Newton, Planck, Heisenberg, Bohr, Fermi and others. What is important is that the intuition was projected into the hands—quite literally—of the tinkerers who translated them into "things" or "processes" that humans could use. And that is perhaps the highest form of communication we now have.

So, now we have all these new systems and processes and we will describe a few of them here. If we've left some out, it's simply a combination of being kind of dumb and short of space.

Where to start? Hard choice.

Say films, as we now know them. Photons striking molecules of silver chloride suspended in a film laminate, react in such a way as to give the human eye the impression of varying shades of darkness within the field being observed . . . Once it was found this process could be manipu-

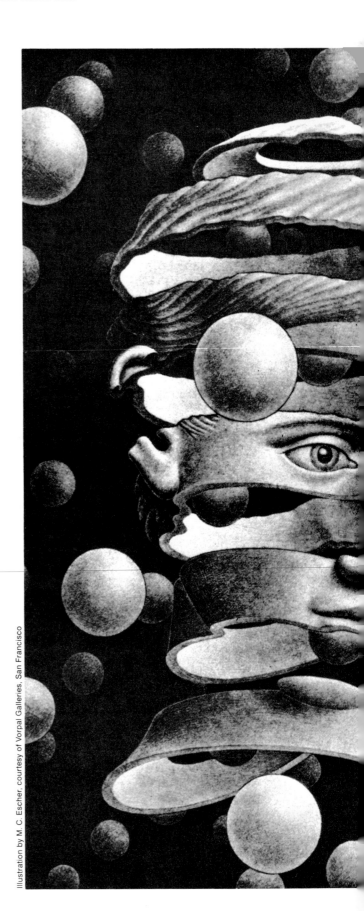

Illustration by M. C. Escher, courtesy of Vorpal Galleries, San Francisco

lated, we got Charlie Chaplin, and W. C. Fields, and Marilyn Monroe and—you name them. The recorded film, itself, was composed of frozen slices of time which, through sequential patterning, gave the illusion of motion and through repetition, reinforced images, which ultimately became the visual symbols on which our mythology is based.

KINAESTHETICS/SYNAESTHETIC CINEMA

These big words are just a way of saying that movies are better than ever. They are not necessarily better in content, but the technology is there.

Says Youngblood, who insinuates ubiquitously through these pages, "When we say expanded cinema we actually mean expanded consciousness . . . Expanded cinema isn't a movie at all; like life, it's a process of becoming, man's ongoing historical drive to manifest his consciousness outside of his mind, in front of his eyes . . . This is especially true in the case of the intermedia network of cinema and television, which now functions as nothing less than the nervous system of mankind."

*Michael S. Laughlin (***Easy Rider***) says, "Films are to communicate, to say something. Our generation has gone beyond mere entertainment. We are too well educated, too intelligent to be just entertained. We want to be moved emotionally, intellectually and sensually." ("New Kind of Movie Shakes Hollywood,"* **Business Week**, *Jan. 3, 1970.)*

Robert Kaufman, a screen writer, put it this way: "We are approaching today a kind of film journalism. We want to record, reflect, discuss the most immediate problems facing our culture. Our audiences insist that we make our reflections honestly and unflinchingly. The kids can see a copout a mile away."

And in seconds.

Youngblood flows again, ". . . through synaesthetic cinema man attempts to express a total phenomenon—his own consciousness.

"Synaesthetic cinema is the only aesthetic language suited to a post-industrial, post-literate, man-made environment with its multi-dimensional simulsensory network of information sources. It's the only aesthetic tool that even approaches the reality continuum of conscious existence in the nonuniform, nonlinear, nonconnected electronic atmosphere of the Paleocybernetic Age . . ."

So, now we have at least two voices crying in the cybernetic wilderness—McLuhan and Youngblood, or vice versa.

Youngblood ("Yes, sir! Here and countable." Okeh, sound off!) "It is quite clear that human communication is trending toward these possibilities. If the visual subsystems exist today, it's folly to assume that the computing hardware will not exist tomorrow. The notation of 'reality' will be utterly and finally obscured . . . We're entering a mythic age of electronic realities that exists only on the metaphysical plane."

Youngblood? Where are you? "Not here, sir. On leave for another reality." They call it "R & R!"

There is not only a new generation of technological film-producing devices, but also a whole new generation of young film makers who are trying (and often succeeding) to make film a communication medium instead of an entertainment box office medium.

As Peter Fonda has said (in "The New Communicators," TV Special, April 14, 1970), "The new communicators are everywhere—in grammar schools, high schools, colleges, film institutes, and in what is often referred to as the underground.

"These new film makers are making personal statements about themselves and about the world around them. And in most cases, they're doing it with very little money and with very little equipment.

"But what they lack in money, they make up with ingenuity."

Said Francois Truffaut about his recent film, **L'Enfant Sauvage**, *"I simply wanted to make a film in praise of communication between people—in praise of the unspoken language. It is my answer to all those films about noncommunication that keep filling our cinemas."*

A replay of the Hallelujah Chorus would be most appropriate here.

V.T.R.—*The Acronym stands for* **V***ideo* **T***ape* **R***ecording. It simply means that images (and sound) can be impregnated on a reel of magnetic tape, and then played back through a home television set. This is the audiovisual counterpart of paperback books. It may very well completely destroy television as we know it now. Commercial TV, CATV and Pay-TV may join the nickelodeon and the player piano in some honky-tonk joint where a girl with a painted face gives an ersatz smile, and makes change of dubious value.*

A number of highly placed manufacturers are working on Video Recording systems— EVR—CBS, Sony, Motorola, Westinghouse, Phillips (in England) and Nordemande (in

Germany), and perhaps many others. Although most of the systems are based on the same concept (i.e., the VTR is a briefcase sized-unit with wires that clamp onto the antenna terminals of standard TV sets), they are not yet "compatible" so that cartridges from one manufacturer will not fit some other manufacturer's system, but no doubt something will be worked out.

Meanwhile, it does appear that VTR systems will be mass-produced and marketed worldwide shortly. The systems are in sound and color and the image can be stopped, replayed for discussion or review as needed. It also can be erased, at your friendly neighborhood VTR shop, and something else put on it. As someone has said, "it's like a returnable milk bottle." TV conversion costs are low, and the cartridges ultimately will cost no more than LP records do today.

Because of the initial high cost, VTR systems will probably be used mostly by business and government; for providing sight-and-sound reports, recording personnel interviews, for training programs, and to present a new product, service, or political candidate. As the price drops, VTR's will move into the educational systems (perhaps making teachers and instructors unnecessary) and then into private homes.

The recording of books, periodicals, plays, opera, ballet and sports already existing will create an enormous industry. The introduction of new material, specially designed for VTR, will be even more enormous.

In the comfort and privacy of one's own home, through VTR, one may enjoy the visual and audial panorama of the world, selecting his own experience as one does in a book from a library shelf.

It will be a different world—and very, very soon.

LASER—Light Amplification (by) Stimulated Emission (of) Radiation. This is the acronym used for "coherent light;" i.e., it does not scatter from the source. Or, as the **American Heritage Dictionary** defines it, "Any of several devices that convert incident electromagnetic frequencies to one or more discrete frequencies of highly amplified and coherent visible radiation." Got it?

Next to nuclear power, the laser is probably the most significant technological "breakthrough" of our century. Its capacity for information carrying is enormous, compared to any sytems now in use.

"One of these days," says **The German Tribune**, Nov. 7, 1970, "the entire flow of

I call it the Paleocybernetic Age: an image of a hairy, buckskinned, barefooted atomic physicist with a brain full of mescaline and logarithms, working out the heuristics of computer-generated holograms or krypton laser interferometry. It's the dawn of man: for the first time in history we'll soon be free enough to discover who we are.

GENE YOUNGBLOOD/
Expanded Cinema, 1970

Bumper-sticker:
"All the world is watching the United States, and all the United States is watching television."

The man who views the world through his newspaper can think about it, bit by bit at a time. The child who grows up with television, to which he devotes more hours than to school, feels that the world surrounds him.

It was the funeral of President Kennedy that most strongly proved the power of television to invest an occasion with the character of corporate participation. It involves an entire population in a ritual process. (By comparison, press, movies, and radio are mere packaging devices for consumers.) In television, images are projected at you. You are the screen, The images wrap around you. You are the vanishing point.

HERBERT BRUCKER/
"Can Printed News Save a Free Society?,"
Saturday Review, Oct. 10, 1970

information of a large office block may pass spontaneously through a single thread of glass fiber thinner than a human hair.

"The carrier will be a laser ray capable of transporting telephone calls, teleprinter messages, data and TV programs, yet will follow every turn made by the 0.05 cable. (The message) is trapped in the core of the glass fiber by the laws of refraction."

Up until recently, laser was considered a "line of sight" phenomenon, which greatly limited its use for everyday terrestrial communication. (Real good for satellite and interplanetary communication, though). Now this new development, by AEG-Telefunken and expected to be operational within a few years, changes the whole ball game.

The consequences of this advance are almost incomprehensible to us now. It's like the invention of the wheel.

One stumbles from laser to holography.

HOLOGRAPHY — (from the Greek **holos** — whole, entire). It may be defined as "the technique of producing images by wavefront reconstruction, especially by using lasers to record on a photographic plate the diffraction pattern from which a three-dimensional image can be projected." (Or, at least that's the way it is described in "Seeing by Radio Waves . . . the Promise of Radio Frequency Holography", **Mitre Matrix**, March-April, 1969.)

"A **hologram**, whether produced by light or radio waves – is basically an elaborate record of the pattern of interference created by the intersection of two beams of radiated energy." (Interlude: what happens if three—or more—beams intersect?) Back to **Mitre Matrix**. "The entire picture is contained on a sheet an eighth-of-an-inch thick . . . and every part of a holographic picture is always in focus, no matter how far the subject was from the film."

The extraordinary thing about a hologram is that the entire picture can be reproduced from any part of the film, and, when projected (by laser) it is fully three-dimensional.

According to Richard Kahlenberg and Chloe Aaron ("The Cartridges are Coming," **Cinema Journal**, Spring, 1970), " 'Selectavision,' " RCA's answer to EVR, is a holographic, rather than a photographic, system. Original images, in color, are converted into embossed holograms from which a master can be made that presses the copies onto vinyl—a material as cheap as paper and similar to the plastic used to wrap meat in supermarkets. Playback requires that the beam from a low-powered

laser pass through the vinyl strip into a simple TV camera. The playback mechanism, the laser and the TV camera are all housed in the player (about the size of the CBS EVR machine) which is wired to the antenna terminals of a standard color or black-and-white TV set."

The prospects are almost beyond our ken. ("Dear Ken: How are you? I am fine.")

Home entertainment in full glorious sound, color and available dimensions is certainly going to change things around the old home scatter. The moppets will never leave the living room floor, mama will never get any meals fixed, and daddy won't go to work at all. They'll be caught and transfixed in the amber of an electronic experience; trapped in the waves.

"Eventually," says John Tebbel ("TV and the Arts," **Saturday Review**, April 26, 1969), "an entire library may be carried on a holographic crystal the size of a matchbox, or a thick volume on one no bigger than an aspirin."

Through the use of laser it should be possible to transmit "matter," in the sense that 3-D information can be sent from one place and assembled at another from the molecules available there. Patent applications for this have been filed in a number of countries, and the process has been demonstrated on a laboratory scale in Europe. Not, alas in the U. S. Intersecting laser beams, inside a plastic block, recreate the transmitted object. It may mean, not too long from now, that furniture need not be manufactured in Grand Rapids but only be transmitted from there. The computers will take over, send the instructions by laser through optical fibers (or bounce them off a communications satellite) and the physical object recreated wherever there is a market for it. "Dial-a-chair," or any other physical object may become the new life style. Most of the technology is already here.

PLASMA/LIQUID CRYSTALS—There's a new boy on the communication block; he may change the whole neighborhood.

Technicians call it liquid crystal; a fluid that behaves as a liquid in almost every way, yet has a molecular structure similar to a crystal. There are several kinds of liquid crystals, and some of them have the ability to receive, store (and when scanned) transmit photoelectric images.

The image can be implanted in the liquid crystal by a direct current and erased by an alternating current. Meantime, the image can be stored as long as needed.

According to Hughes Aircraft Company,

"When energized, crystal images appear almost instantaneously and they can be short-lived or long-lived; they can be stored indefinitely or stored temporarily or left to decay (become transparent) normally, or they can be erased immediately, only to be recalled at a later time.

"The liquid crystal itself is about a thousandth-of-an-inch thick and is sandwiched between two glass plates, held there by capillary action . . . The substance is clear until photoactivation is used to initiate sufficient current in it to produce the light-scattering phenomena, or mode, which agitates the molecules and causes certain sections to become opaque. By controlling the shape and size of the areas in agitation, the opaque areas can be formed as desired." (**Vectors**, Summer, 1970.)

How can they be used? Well, obviously, for information storage and retrieval in the scientific and business worlds, where they may outperform most electronic computers. For home use?

"The plasma crystal panel," (says Youngblood), "makes possible billboard or wall-sized TV sets that could be viewed in bright sunlight. The Japanese firms of Mitsubishi and Matsushita (Panasonic) seem to be leaders in the field, each having produced workable models."

The communication future is as clear as a crystal.

COMPUTER GRAPHICS — *These are visual arrays or displays produced by computers from programmed instructions. This may well be one of the most exciting art-forms of the future, and artists will abandon canvas and easel in order to sit before an electronic console, projecting their dreams, much as a musician or composer works out his music by manipulating a piano keyboard.*

*"In 1963," (says San VanDerBeek, "New Talent—the Computer," **Art in America**, Jan.-Feb., 1970), "computers began to develop possibilities for making graphics. An electric microfilm was introduced; it can plot points and draw lines a million times faster than a human draftsman. This machine and the electronic computer which controls it thus make feasible various kinds of graphic movies which heretofore would have been prohibitively intricate, time-consuming and expensive.*

"The machine can compose complicated pictures or series of pictures from a large number of basic elements; it can draw ten thousand to one hundred thousand points, lines or characters per second . . .

CHART OF THE PAST

1800-1850	Camera / Babbage calculator / Telegraph
1850-1900	Telephone / Phonograph / Office machines
1900-1910	Vacuum tube
1910-1920	Radio
1930-1940	TV
1940-1950	Radar / Tape recorders / Electronic computers / Cybernetics
1950-1960	Transistor / Maser / Laser
1960-1970	Communication satellite

CHART OF THE FUTURE

1970	Translating machines
1980	Personal radio
1990	Artificial intelligence
2000	Global library
2010	Telesensory devices
2020	Logical languages / Robots
2030	Contact with extra-terrestrials
2050	Memory playback
2060	Mechanical educator / Coding of artifacts
2080	Machine intelligence exceeds man's
2090	World brain

ARTHUR C. CLARKE/
Profiles of the Future, 1967

"Making holograms is like making records," explains Emmett Leith of Michigan. "Sound waves are encoded as hills and valleys on the disc, just as an image is encoded as dark and light lines on a hologram. These hills and valleys distort the movement of a phonograph needle and the result is sound. The interference lines on a hologram distort lightwaves and the product is an image."

"A World in Three Dimensions,"
News Front, Aug., 1968

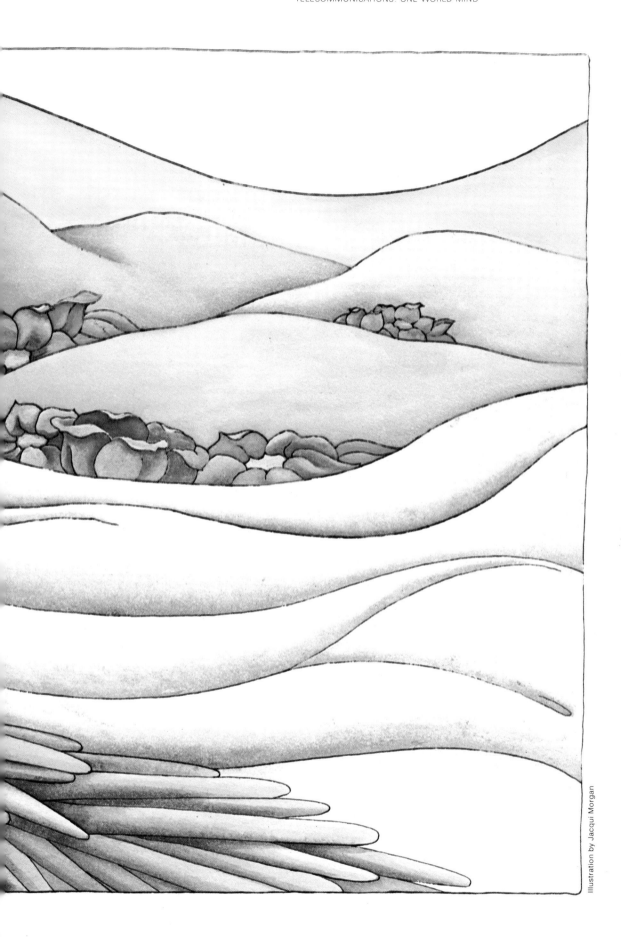

Illustration by Jacqui Morgan

"The image revolution that movies represented has now been overhauled by the television revolution, and is approaching the next visual stage—to computer graphics to computer controls of environment to a new cybernetic 'movie art.' "

What is exciting here is that computers, which usually have been used to run off payrolls or to construct simulation models of future expectancies, have now emerged as a new medium for the visual arts.

Youngblood says, "The computer amplifies man's intelligence in about the same ratio that the telescope extends his vision. The man/computer symbiosis is developed to the point where the machine instructs its user and indicates possibilities for even closer interaction. One needn't read the manual but may consult the machine directly with the order, 'I want to do something; instruct me.' It is not even necessary to be in the presence of the computer to do this. One can carry out one's work thousands of miles away, linked to the computer through remote viewing and operating consoles."

John Whitney, Jr., who has worked on computer graphics for thirty years and produced the magnificent film **Permutations**, which is now widely used on television, has this to say: "We don't know how to integrate realist and nonobjective images yet. But I think our computerized optical printer will help show the way. The use of the realist image is just a basis, a starting point. Working with optical scanning you transform the images, and this seems to be a key to bringing nonobjective and realist imagery together. And why bring them together? Because it may lead to new insights and new experience."

Back to Youngblood. "The computer does not make man obsolete. It makes him failsafe. The computer does not replace man. It liberates him from specialization. The transition from a culture that considers leisure a 'problem' to a culture that demands leisure as a prerequisite of civilized behavior is a metamorphosis of the first magnitude. And it has begun. The computer is the arbiter of a radical evolution; it changes the meaning of life. It makes us children. We must learn how to live all over again."

Due to a natural disinclination to work and a shortage of space, we cannot go into a description of microfiche, voice profiling, Unifor facsimile, CATV, nor a number of other electronic techniques that are already here.

Now we turn, in all too short a compass (ever seen a short compass? Probably imported by some Lilliputian Columbus) to electrostatic printing and the outlook for the printed media.

ELECTROSTATIC PRINTING — The printed word is not dead; he's just pinned to the floor by 300 years of tradition. But he'll get up and go to his corner, and come out fighting against radio and television. And in a very few years. Dr. Herbert Krugman, a General Electric scientist has said, "Print is something you **do**, television represents something done **to** you."

"Now we learn—rather flatteringly I think," says Dick Nolan (**San Francisco Examiner**, Nov. 1, 1970), "that when you read this you are awake, but if I were to sing you the same song on color television, gorgeous as I am, you would be essentially asleep.

"Print clearly involves use of the headbone and brain, the exercise of which is necessary if the culture is to survive. Television, dreamily and drearily flashing its message, turns the brain to cabbage."

The printed word is a participative ideograph. In order for it to have any meaning at all, the reader must make some sort of personal effort to communicate with it. Television and film are, on the contrary, explicit; short of moving the eyeballs they require virtually nothing of the observer. The same appears to be true of radio. Keeping one's ears unplugged is about all that is required. And keeping a closed mind.

So, print media may be around for a long time to come. But the expensive, archaic, utterly inefficient method by which print is now produced will end.

Speaking of typesetting by electronic beam, Gerard O. Walter ("Typesetting," **Scientific American**, May, 1969) says, "In the days of setting type by hand, highly skilled compositors achieved remarkable speeds as high as one character per second; mechanical typesetters built since the turn of the century cast about five characters per second. Nowadays photographic typesetting machines that select the characters mechanically are capable of setting as many as 500 characters per second. In contrast, the new electronic method can produce up to 10,000 characters per second... Electronic typesetting will undoubtedly foster a considerable increase in the demand for and volume of printed material, since it reduces the cost of printing and speeds up the output... news can become available *in print almost as quickly as the bulletins on radio or television."*

Along the same line, Lawrence Lessing ("The Printed Word Goes Electronic," **Fortune***, Sept., 1969) says, "Around the year 1450, Johann Gutenberg spent about five years casting and composing the movable type for his historic Bible, and three years printing some two hundred copies of it . . . Today, through use of a radically new kind of computerized machine, the entire Bible can be set in type and composed into pages electronically in 77 minutes flat.*

". . . researchers are working on various methods of introducing roll film into the cathode-ray tube for direct exposure by its electron beam to get top speeds up to 60,000 characters or more per second . . . Before words and pictures can be carried by electronic impulses straight through from computer to printed page, some entirely different printing system must be adopted, a system compatible with the electronic generation of type and images. The likeliest prospect, most investigators agree, is some form of electrostatic printing . . . a process in which dry or fluidized pigment particles . . . place an image on paper, not by impact or pressure but by electrical attraction."

While it is quite possible that mass printed periodicals as we now know them will disappear, electronic printing systems may make possible the proliferation of many smaller circulation periodicals aimed at specific audiences, thus greatly broadening the spectrum of choice in printed material.

Recipe for the communications future:

1 cup	LASER
2 cups	VTR
1 tbsp.	HOLOGRAPHY
½ cup	Liquid Crystals
2 tsps.	Microfiche
⅓ cup	Electrostatic Printing

Mix liberally with computers, COMSAT, advances in communication theory and systems analysis, to taste. Put in a nuclear oven until done. Result: Global Mind. But make sure it doesn't come out half-baked.

Eye, there's the rub. For in that sleep, what dreams may come? For the same mortals who control mass media today, may very well control them tomorrow, and tomorrow, and will creep in their petty pace from day to day.

Oh, what fuels these mortals be!✸

We may soon be reading newspapers and magazines made of plastic, notes *Canadian Business.* Japanese scientists have come up with a film, pressed from polystyrene, which is only one-tenth as thick as regular paper and will not tear when run through the printing process.

"For Light Reading,"
EXEC-U-SCOPE, **Sept., 1970**

If its proponents are right, as many as 30-million homes—half the households in the U. S.—will be wired for cable TV within five years. With 1,000 times the capacity of a telephone wire, and at least four times the effective capacity of standard television transmission, cable's capability to carry messages is awesome.

"Cable TV Leaps into the Big Time,"
Business Week, **Nov. 22, 1969**

In another generation, most of the homes in America will have an electronic communication center connected to a national control for both entertainment and news. If you want live television, you press one button; if you want a fresh daily newspaper printed right in your home, you will press another. The video cartridge, or cassette, will transform television by the mid-1970's, and for that matter phonographs and records, as we know them, may disappear because in this home electronic center anybody can bring to heel virtually anything he wants at any hour of the night or day in the line of amusement or information, by sight, sound, or both—and in color at that.

RICHARD L. TOBIN/
"Publishing by Cathode Ray Tube,"
Saturday Review, **Oct. 10, 1970**

give a PSI

There seems to be something going on inside us that we do not understand. Some sort of cosmic, transcendental forces flow through us, as if we were a telephone line. Call these forces God, or ESP, or PSI—the labels do not matter. But we do not make use of these forces, although every preceding culture of which we know has done so. We shiver, lonely in the cold wind of a technological culture, standing on the runway with a dollar in our hand, while all the time the warmth is within mind's reach. But may the mind not be a way to breach the wall? Think what delights may be on the other side! Come along?

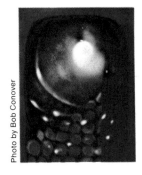

Photo by Bob Conover

May we suggest that the electronic "revolution" we have described in the preceding section is only a "half-way house" between where we have been and where it appears we are going? Somewhere beyond drugs and solid state physics there must be at least one other way.

In our rationalist and quantitative society, we consider ourselves as colonies of events which we have chosen to label molecules and cells. There may be at least one other dimension in which we live, but which we have not, so far, bothered to explore.

Could it be the powers of the human mind? After all, atoms, molecules and cells are but constructs—perhaps projections—of the mind. Could this projection not extend further?

This brings us to the field of parapsychology, a discipline that only recently has been "accepted" by the National Academy of Science as legitimate.

The field that is tilled here is usually labeled ESP (for Extra Sensory Perception) or PSI (for Parapsychology). In either case, the phenomenon might be defined as an exchange of wave patterns between two or more neural systems, without the use of "normal" channels. Such channels usually are defined as voice (sound patterns), sight (light patterns), touch (molecular vibrations), taste and smell (chemical arrays). ESP appears, as we experience it, to occur outside of these five modes. Yet it is hard to find a human who has not had this type of experience. So far as we know everyone dreams, yet the dream experience does not appear to be the product of any of the five "normal" modes. Certainly dogs and cats appear to have "paranormal" experiences; they not only dream but can see a ghost walking across the room, invisible to humans in the same place at the same time.

ESP also seems to function outside of space and time, as they are now defined (although both traditional definitions are breaking down).

The human documentation of ESP appears to be at least as sound as the evidence, say, for the existence of the atom, or the nature of stars and planets, or the biologic "cell" or virtually any system we now call "scientific." Science is "to know," and PSI is, in that respect, as much a "PSIence" as

Professor Piccardi has made certain experiments in chemical reactions under exactly similar conditions of time, heat, outside temperature, etc., and has discovered to his surprise that these reactions varied according to the date and place at which they were made.

From this he deduced not only that they were influenced by the relative positions of the earth and the celestial bodies, but that the position of the earth must have an influence on our health, our temperament, our thoughts, and our actions, not only individually but collectively.

DOUGLAS HUNT/
Exploring the Occult, **1964**

A popular plot in science fiction concerns astronauts on a planet where beings share their consciousness. Science fiction has a way of coming true; our planet is coming close to shared consciousness through communications.

"Communication Systems will Shape Your Future,"
Industry Week, **May 4, 1970**

Currently, the wired cities of America are being laid out by the same kind of rugged individualist and venture capital that in another age built our railroads, then permitted them to lapse into extinction. For the most part, the charters and regulations for the wired city are being drafted by the same mentality that plotted the interstate highway system at the sacrifice of a series of rapid transit systems.

FRED W. FRIENDLY/
"Asleep at the Switch of the Wired City?"
Saturday Review, **Oct. 10, 1970**

It is worth remembering that even in the period of the Renaissance many universities required students to have a degree in astrology before they were admitted to the study of medicine.

DOUGLAS HUNT/
Exploring the Occult, **1964**

. . . despite all these strange qualities, our dreams are real to us while we are dreaming; as real as any experience we have in our waking life. There is no "as if" in the dream. The dream is a present, real experience, so much, indeed, that it suggests two questions: What is reality? How do we know that what we dream is unreal and what we experience in our waking life is real? A Chinese poet has expressed this aptly: "I dreamt last night that I was a butterfly and now I don't know whether I am a man who dreamt he was a butterfly, or perhaps a butterfly who dreams now that he is a man."

ERICH FROMM/
The Forgotten Language, **1951**

"You took the very words out of my mouth." When you say this it is often an example of telepathy. Sometimes, of course, you have unintentionally "led" the person you are talking to, as a clever counsel "leads" a witness; but often you will be aware of a sudden sharing of ideas with the mind to which you have been sending your thoughts over a bridge of words. Indeed one research worker suggests that we are always in telepathic communication with one another when we are conversing.

DOUGLAS HUNT/
Exploring the Occult, **1964**

chemistry, physics, biology, geology, mathematics or astronomy, or any other you might care to name.

Now it seems that most ESP experiences are not repeatable under laboratory conditions. But then, neither are birth nor death, which are usually accepted as "real" phenomena. (Unless one is schooled in the Oriental philosophies, in which case they are not only repeatable, but, as experienced, identical phenomena.)

One might suggest a "science of the absurd" to match "the theater of the absurd," in which the validity of an experiment would be that it cannot be repeated. But if science is to "know" then that would be a science, too, would it not?

In the way that we now use the words "rational," "logical," "scientific," "reality," they are projections of minds that, at their very best, are primitive; hung-up on the Grecian Platonic and Aristotelian syndromes.

There seems to be a whole spectrum or array of experience available to us. It is fluid and continuous. That we select one band of the continuum and say "now *that* is real," is the kind of nonsense that is taught in our schools. "But that's what we learned in school today; that's what we learned in school."

It might help if we tried to define some of the modes of PSI. In doing so, we run the risk of doing the same donkey-tail labeling we have done for the "sciences." Parapsychology—like most disciplines—is broken down into little compartments, each with its own label, although it must be obvious to anyone that the phenomena, as experienced, appear to be the same. So, on to the donkey tails.

TELEPATHY — an exchange of awareness, or shared images, between two or more neural systems, without the apparent use of "normal" channels.

CLAIRVOYANCE — an exchange of wave patterns that transcends "space and time" as usually defined, and most often applies to "past" experience.

PRECOGNITION — the ability (or the exercise of it) to use the power of the mind to perceive in detail a "future" event or events. (This appears to be the same as clairvoyance, except that it has a different vector. The angle of interference is simply turned 180°.) Any good card player knows this.

TELEKINESIS — the ability (or exercise of it) to use the power of the mind to influence the observed behavior of material objects in space and time. (Any good dice player knows this.)

TELEPORTATION—the transmission of a human body, including its personality, from one "place" to another, without using mechanical or electronic means. The projection may be an array; i.e., one "person" in more than one "place" at a given "time." The Asiatics, East Indians, Mexicans, Africans, South Americans and Australian aborigines appear to have had this ability. Only the Western technological human seems to have lost it. Perhaps this was because no money was involved. How could you charge for automobiles, trains, airplanes and ships if anyone could be anywhere at any time that he or she willed it?

REINCARNATION — the "same" personality reappears within an observed time span. As individuals, we do this every morning after a night's sleep. That this appears to occur over time spans of decades, centuries or millenia should come as no great surprise. Yet, somehow having defined birth and death, our scientific bureaucracy says it cannot be.

Any leaf that falls to the ground, becomes humus, and is fed back through the tree system to become a leaf of the same shape and size, knows all about reincarnation. So, we might point out, does any ripple in a stream. So, in fact, does everything in nature, except the uptight humans who believe there is a beginning and ending to "things."

This is not to say that conventional science is totally wrong; it is to say that it sometimes is. The scientific lens with its bifocals takes in too short a time span to measure the phenomena it purports to describe. The "eternal verities" are, it seems, neither eternal nor verities.

Which kind of leaves the door open for parapsychology, does it not?

How about ASTROLOGY? If one believes in a holographic world, then the motion of the planets would appear to influence organisms on this

... now the great highway of the ether will be thrown open to the whole world, and all men will become neighbors—whether they like it or not. Any form of censorship, political or otherwise, would be impossible; to jam signals coming down from the heavens is almost as difficult as blocking the light of the stars. The Russians could do nothing to stop their people from seeing the American way of life; on the other hand, Madison Avenue agencies and censorship committees might be equally distressed— though for different reasons—at a nationwide switch to uninhibited telecasts from Montmartre. Such freedom of communication will have an ultimately overwhelming effect on the cultural, political, and moral climate of our planet. It holds danger as well as promise.
ARTHUR C. CLARKE/
Profiles of the Future, 1967

Better than 99% of modern technology occurs in the realm of physical phenomena that are *sub* or *ultra* to the range of human visibility. We can see the telephone wires but not the conversations taking place ... Yet world society has throughout its millions of years on earth made its judgments on visible, tangible, sensorially demonstrable criteria.
BUCKMINSTER FULLER

According to John McHale, "The Plastic Parthenon":
"World communications ... diffuse and interpenetrate local culture tradition providing commonly-shared cultural experience in a manner unparalleled in human history. Within this global network the related media share and transmit man's symbolic needs and their expression on a world scale. Besides the enlargement of the physical world, these media virtually extend our psychical environment, providing a constant stream of moving, fleeting images of the world for our daily appraisal.
They provide *psychic mobility* for the greater mass of our citizens. Through these devices we can telescope time, move through history, and span the world in a great variety of unprecedented ways."
GENE YOUNGBLOOD/
Expanded Cinema, 1970

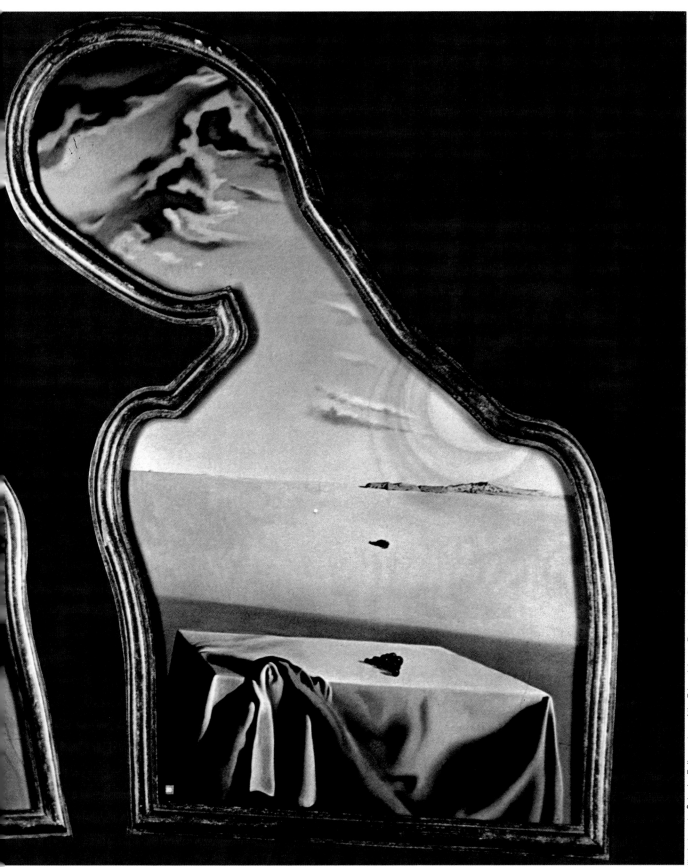

Symbolic language is a language in which inner experiences, feelings and thoughts are expressed as if they were sensory experiences, events in the outer world. It is a language which has a different logic from the conventional one we speak in the daytime, a logic in which not time and space are the ruling categories but intensity and association. It is the one universal language the human race has ever developed, the same for all cultures and throughout history.
Yet this language has been forgotten by modern man. Not when he is asleep, but when he is awake.

• • •

Most of our dreams have one characteristic in common: they do not follow the laws of logic that govern our waking thought. The categories of space and time are neglected. People who are dead, we see alive; events which we watch in the present, occurred many years ago. We dream of two events as occurring simultaneously when in reality they could not possibly occur at the same time. We pay just as little attention to the laws of space. It is simple for us to move to a distant place in an instant, to be in two places at once, to fuse two persons into one, or to have one person suddenly be changed into another.

ERICH FROMM/
The Forgotten Language, 1951

. . . occultism . . . It is simply the study of what is hidden. It in no way implies a belief in the supernatural. It means no more than a search for those laws of nature which our scientists have not, as yet, discovered. It is a study of those quite indubitable phenomena which present-day science cannot explain.

DOUGLAS HUNT/
Exploring the Occult, 1964

planet like any other force. To paraphrase, "One cannot pluck a petal without shaking a star."

Whatever universe we live in, we make up, and our communication consists of telling each other the way we feel about it at the moment. In a little time, we may begin to do this without words on paper, or radio, or television. Simply mind to mind. Until another, now unimaginable one comes along, this may be our communication system. Some people already are doing it. Some have for thousands of years.

It is an end devoutly to be wished.

This is a strange field we wander now, and it is dark. We grope. The ghosts of all our yesterdays roam about, luminescent in the gloom of all our tomorrows. We don't even know what it is we have lost in this technological graveyard. But something, somehow important to us. Some force, apparently, that we cannot identify.

Are these electromagnetic waves? The Russians, who appear to be somewhat further along this trail than we are, say not. In an elegant experiment in an iron cage shielded with lead, which is supposed to screen out all of the electromagnetic wave patterns, the telepathic subjects appear to have functioned as well as they would have in an "ordinary" room.

So, it would seem, some other force is involved in ESP or PSI communications. "Where do we go from here boys; where do we go from here?"

We'll skip the Jersey City pier, and go on to a better place to rest. Let's assume that the brain (of any organism) transmits waves. They have been categorized in the taxonomy of parapsychology as "Alpha, Beta and Delta." Whatever happened to Kappa we don't know; she may be hitchhiking to some rendezvous with life—who knows?

Now, these brain waves do not appear to be very strong; they only seem to carry a few feet. But, then, we do not know how good the instruments that measure them are, either. ESP or PSI phenomena appear to span thousands of miles and many centuries. We do not, as yet, have the instrumentation to measure this type of phenomena.

Now, we'll briefly dip into the Alpha wave pool, if only because that is where most of the work, so far, has been done.

According to Dr. Lester Fehme, professor of psychology at the State University of New York in Stony Brook, Long Island, "Alpha waves are one of four known brain waves. They are generated, billions of them, by the tiny electrical pulses that surge through the brain as it does its chores. High production of alpha waves is often associated with the objective state of peak mental and physical performance . . ."

Barnard Law Collier, writing in *Saturday Review* (April 10, 1971) in an article called "Brain Power: The Case for Bio-Feedback Training," says, "Projects in hospitals and research laboratories around the world are convincingly demonstrating that it may be possible to learn personal mastery over the functions of our visceral organs — the heart, liver, kidneys, intestines, glands and blood vessels — in the same specific way we learn to manipulate our fingers to play Chopin or our legs to kick a field goal . . . These studies indicate that man may possess the ability to will himself into whatever state of consciousness seems most appropriate to his environment, to accomplishing a task at hand, or to some special pursuit.

"Dr. Neal E. Miller, a professor of physiological psychology at Rockefeller University of New York . . . has traced back to Plato the dogma that the organs controlled by the autonomic nervous system function at a kind of cavemanish level, learning only in Pavlovian fashion to react to such stimuli as sour lemons and growling bears . . .

"We are now able to regard the activities of our internal organs as behavior in the same sense that the movements of our hands and fingers are behavior. This is the basic stem of it all, but just where this will lead, we can't be sure yet."

Dr. Martin Orme, director of experimental psychiatry at the University of Pennsylvania Medical School in Philadelphia, is studying the alpha wave phenomenon with an eye toward finding out what exactly an alpha state does to or for an individual . . . "It's not enough to know you can contemplate your navel. You then have to ask, 'What happens?' "

This is a kind of interesting game—the rationalist against the nonrationalist, trying to make both each. It won't work. There is no way we know of to make an either-or society work. That there is another way, we do not doubt. The only question is, will we find it in the time we have left? This may be the question of our next thirty years. Somewhere between the navel and the mind . . . someplace in there. Somewhere . . . somewhere.

We could, of course, explore the middle planes. But we don't seem to have many Lewis and Clarks around anymore. We go by book and candles; both prefabricated; both absurd. Do we ever wake up?

No way, man, no way.

One of the questions that rather naturally arises — in the confrontation between rationalist and nonrationalist — in the field of ESP and PSI, is the validity of the statistical approach.

Certain ESP/PSI phenomena are scored against "normal" statistics, and may be considered higher or lower, as the case might be, in relation to the norm. Once one looks into it, it is kind of difficult to find out how the "norm" was established. So, scoring "hits" or "misses" against a "norm" does not appear to do very much down the vales of ESP/PSI.

What is "normal"? Can you define it? Can anyone? If any deviation is "aberrant," then perhaps all of us are. This is the rich lode the psychiatrist works. Certainly there must be a better way.

We need to find it soon. ❈

POSTSCRIPT. That a "light body" of some kind actually exists seems no longer open to doubt. I read in the German Press that Russian scientists had succeeded in photographing such a body emanating not only from men and animals, but also from plants. In the case of the last-named, the rays constituting the "body" were seen to disappear as the plant died.

DOUGLAS HUNT/
Exploring the Occult, 1964

Whatever world you experience may be only your reflection in a crystal ball. What else did you expect?

BIBLIOGRAPHY

We don't really like "bibliographies." They're so arbitrary. It's easy to keep track of the books we consulted in preparing this series —they're all massed on our shelves collecting dust. It's not so easy to keep the hundreds of magazine and newspaper clippings that we relied on even more than the books. [They were more current, and often so interesting that we couldn't resist passing them along to colleagues studying the present and the future. Those that weren't rerouted fell victim to a giant clean-up campaign when the paper pollution around here became more than we could bear.] And it's even more difficult to list the conversations with experts in their fields, the lectures, seminars, and conferences that all contributed to our understanding of each topic and had to have had considerable influence on our mental "sets" before beginning to write.

So, all things considered, here's a partial bibliography, at best. A quick glance through the pages of each chapter, with special attention to the marginalia items, gives a much more accurate picture of the range of people and publications who were instrumental in contributing, knowingly or otherwise, to DIMENSIONS OF CHANGE.

ECOLOGY: The Man-Made Planet

Because this chapter set the tone and the mood for the entire series, sources consulted for it were used throughout the study and provided a general background upon which the more specific chapters were based.

CHARTER, S.P.R., *Man on Earth*, Angel Island Publications, Inc., Sausalito, CA, 1962.

COLE, Lamont, C., "The Ecosphere," *Scientific American*, April, 1958.

de CHARDIN, Teilhard, *The Phenomenon of Man*, Harper & Row, New York, 1959.

EISELEY, Loren, *The Unexpected Universe*, Harcourt Brace Jovanovich, Inc., New York, 1969.

EWALD, William R., ed., *Environment and Change*, American Institute of Planners, Indiana University Press, Bloomington, Indiana, 1968.

FULLER, R. Buckminster, *Operating Manual for Spaceship Earth*, Southern Illinois University Press, Carbondale, Ill., 1969.

GOLDBERG, Maxwell, ed., *Needles, Burrs & Bibliographies*, Center for Continuing Liberal Education, Pennsylvania State University, University Park, PA, 1969.

KOESTLER, Arthur, *The Ghost in the Machine*, The Macmillan Company, New York, 1967.

KUHNS, William, *Environmental Man*, Harper & Row., New York, 1969.

MARINE, Gene, *America the Raped*, Simon & Schuster, New York, 1969.

McLUHAN, Marshall, *The Gutenberg Galaxy*, University of Toronto Press, Toronto, Canada, 1962.

ODUM, Dr. Eugene, *Ecology*, Holt, Reinhart and Winston, Inc., New York, 1963.

THOMAS, William, ed., *Man's Role in Changing the Face of the Earth*, University of Chicago Press, Chicago, Ill., 1956.

von BERTALANFFY, Ludwig, *General Systems Theory*, George Braziller, Inc., New York, 1968.

WHYTE, W. H., *The Last Landscape*, Doubleday & Company, Inc., New York, 1968.

From Sea to Shining Sea, The President's Council on Recreation and Natural Beauty, U.S. Government Printing Office, Washington, D.C., 1968.

SHELTER: The Cave Re-Examined

CONRADS, Ulrich and Hans G. Sperlich, *The Architecture of Fantasy*, Frederick A. Praeger, New York, 1962.

EHRLICH, Dr. Paul R., *The Population Bomb*, Ballantine Books, New York, 1968.

Ekistics, the Future of Human Settlements, Doxiadis-System Development Corporation, Washington, D.C., 1969.

FEUERSTEIN, Gunther, *New Directions in German Architecture*, George Braziller, New York, 1968.

FULLER, Buckminster, *Ideas and Integrities*, Prentice-Hall, Inc., Englewood Cliffs, New Jersey, 1963.

.... and John McHale, *World Design Science Decade, 1965-1975*, World Resources Inventory, Carbondale, Illinois, 1963.

JACOBS, Jane, *The Death and Life of Great American Cities*, Random House, Inc., New York, 1961.

Le RICOLAIS, Robert, "The Trihex," *Progressive Architecture*, February, 1968.

SUMICHRAST, Michael, National Association of Homebuilders, speeches, various dates.

ENERGY: Transactions in Time

CURTIS, Richard and HOGAN, Elizabeth, *Perils of the Peaceful Atom*, Doubleday & Co., Inc., Garden City, New York, 1969.

DE BELL, Garrett, ed., *The Environmental Handbook*, Ballantine Books, New York, 1970.

DEREN, Mary and GABEL, Medard, eds., *World*

Game Report, The New York Studio School of Painting and Sculpture in association with *Good News,* 1969.

EHRLICH, Paul R. and Anne H., *Population Resources Environment, Issues in Human Ecology,* W. H. Freeman and Co., San Francisco, CA, 1970.

FALLER, James E. and WAMPLE, Joseph E., "The Lunar Laser Reflector," *Scientific American,* March, 1970.

FISCHMAN, Leonard L., FISHER, Joseph L. and LANDSBERG, Hans H., *Resources in America's Future,* Resources for the Future, Inc., Johns Hopkins Press, Baltimore, Md., 1963.

FULLER, R. Buckminster, *Nine Chains to the Moon,* Southern Illinois University Press, Carbondale, Ill., 1938, 1963.

GUSTAFSON, Philip F., "Nuclear Power and Thermal Pollution: Zion, Illinois," *Bulletin of the Atomic Scientists,* March, 1970.

LESSING, Lawrence, "Power from the Earth's Own Heat," *Fortune,* June, 1969.

McHALE, John, *The Future of the Future,* George Braziller, New York, 1969.

McHALE, John, *"Phase II (1967) Document G,"* *World Design Science Decade 1965-1975,* 1967.

SCHURR, Sam H. and NETSCHERT, Bruce C., *Energy in the American Economy, 1850—1975, Its History and Prospects,* Resources for the Future, Inc., Johns Hopkins Press, Baltimore, Md., 1960.

SPORN, Philip, *Energy: Its Production, Conversion and Use in the Service of Man,* Pergamon Press, The Macmillan Company, New York, 1963.

WILSON, Mitchell, "Energy," *Life,* Time Incorporated, New York, 1963.

"Can We Meet the Expanding Need for Energy," *Nation's Business,* Nov., 1969.

FOOD: An Energy Exchange System

BERG, Alan, "The Role of Nutrition in National Development," *Technology Review,* Feb., 1970.

BROWN, Lester R., "The Optimistic Outlook for World Food Production," *The Futurist,* Vol. III, No. 4, August, 1969.

................, *Seeds of Change,* New York-Washington: Praeger Publishers, 1970.

de ROOS, Robert, "Hunger, the World's Terrible Aphrodisiac," *This World,* Sunday, July 5, 1970.

DUNLAP, Lloyd W., Jr., "Basic Needs," *Chemical & Engineering News,* March 11, 1968.

ENLOE, Cortez F., Jr., "The Malnutrition of Affluence," *Today's Health,* Vol. 47, No. 11, Nov., 1969.

EHRLICH, Paul R. and Anne H., "The Food-from-the Sea Myth," *Saturday Review, April 4, 1970.*

GARDNER, Brian, "Leaf Protein Extraction," *World Farming,* Vol. 11, No. 12, Dec., 1969.

GIBBONS, Euell, *Stalking the Wild Asparagus,* David McKay Co., Inc., New York, 1962.

HOLT, S. J., "The Food Resources of the Ocean," *Scientific American,* Vol. 221, No. 3, Sept., 1969.

LACHANCE, Paul A., "The 'New' Proteins," *Food Technology,* Vol. 24, No. 3, March, 1970.

LOFTAS, Tony, "The Troubles of Single-Cell Protein," *Ceres,* Vol. 2, No. 5, Sept.-Oct., 1969.

MANN, George V., "Nutrition Education — U.S.A.," *Food and Nutrition News,* Vol. 41, No. 2, Nov., 1969.

MAYER, Jean and HARRIS, T. George, "Affluence: the Fifth Horseman of the Apocalypse," *Psychology Today,* 1969.

McHALE, John, "Phase II (1967), Document 6. The Ecological Context: Energy and Materials," *World Design Science Decade 1965-1975,* World Resources Inventory, Southern Illinois University, Carbondale, Illinois.

MILLIKAN, Max F., "Population, Food Supply and Economic Development," *Technology Review,* Feb., 1970.

MUNRO, Hamish N., "Nutrition and Human Evolution," *Technology Review,* Vol. 72, No. 6, April, 1970.

NADER, Ralph, "The Chemical Feast," May 25, 1970.

PARPIA, H. A. B., "Waste and the Protein Gap — They Can Both Be Reduced," *Ceres,* Vol. 2, No. 5, Sept.-Oct., 1969.

PIRIE, N. W., "Leaf Protein Research in the International Biological Program," *Agricultural Science Review,* Vol. 5, No. 4, Fourth Quarter, Cooperative State Research Service, 1967.

. . . ., "Implementing the Possibilities," *Science Journal,* May, 1968.

. . . ., "Orthodox and Unorthodox Methods of Meeting World Food Needs," *Scientific American,* Vol. 216, No. 2, Feb., 1967.

. . . ., "The Present Position of Research on the Use of Leaf Protein as a Human Food," *Plant Foods for Human Nutrition,* Vol. 1, No. 4, Nov., 1969.

RORTY, James and NORMAN, N. Philip, *Tomorrow's Food (The Coming Revolution in Nutrition),* Prentice-Hall, New York, 1947.

SCRIMSHAW, Dr. Nevin S., "Infant Malnutrition and Adult Learning," *Saturday Review,* March 16, 1968.

. . . . .̇. . . . ., "The Potentials for Increasing World Protein Supplies," *Technology Review,* Feb., 1970.

SEBRELL, Dr. William H., Jr., "Fortification of Foods with Synthetic Nutrients," *Technology Review,* Feb., 1970.

SHELTON, Maureen, "Game Ranching: an Ecologically Sensible Use of Range Lands," *The Environmental Handbook,* (Garrett de Bell, ed.,), Ballantine Books, New York, 1970.

TEAL, John J., Jr., "Domesticating the Wild and Wooly Musk Ox," *National Geographic,* Vol. 137, No. 6, June, 1970.

WATTS, Alan, "Murder in the Kitchen," *Does It Matter?,* Pantheon Books, New York, 1968, 1969, 1970.

MOBILITY: From There to Here

APPEL, Fredric C., "The Coming Revolution in Transportation," *National Geographic,* Sept., 1969.

BURGESS, Jackson, "Sex and the Italian Driver," *Holiday,* Vol. 47, No. 1, 1970.

CORNING, Erastus, II, "The Race for (Automobile) Space," *Bulletin of the Atomic Scientists,* Dec., 1969.

CRAWFORD, Thomas and Caroline, "Biking in San Francisco," San Francisco Sunday *Examiner & Chronicle,* June 28, 1970.

EMCH, Tom, "A Woman in a Think Tank is Planning Your Travel Tomorrows," "California Living," San Francisco Sunday *Examiner & Chronicle,* Week of Jan. 25, 1970.

GREENE, Gael, "Indigestion on the Turnpike," *Life,* August 28, 1970.

JOHNSON, Dale W., "Urban Transportation . . . Highways," *Consulting Engineer,* March, 1969.

KUSSEROW, H. W., "Work Begins on Steam Bus Engine," San Francisco *Examiner,* July 9, 1970.

LANG, John S., "Death Rattle for U. S. Trains," San Francisco *Examiner,* May 31, 1970.

LOWENHAR, Herman, "Toward Aviation Growth: the Airport Hangup," *Space/Aeronautics,* May, 1969.

McKEAN, William J., "And Now Here Comes The ATV," *Look,* July 14, 1970.

MONICELLI, Mino, "Auto Revolution in Russia," (from *L'Expresso*), San Francisco *Chronicle,* June 1, 1970.

NETSCHERT, Bruce C., "The Economic Impact of Electric Vehicles: A Scenario," *Bulletin of the Atomic Scientists,* May, 1970.

POWELL, James R. and DANBY, Gordon R., "Magnetically Suspended Trains: The Application of Superconductors to High Speed Transport," *Cryogenics and Industrial Gases,* October, 1969.

ROTHENBERG, Al, "Mr. Six and Number 10," *Look,* October 17, 1969.

SHLOSS, Leon, "Transportation Modes Must Be Integrated," *Government Executive,* May, 1970.

STOESSEL, Robert F., "Transport in the 70's: Revolution Ahead," *Business Management,* Nov., 1969.

TOYNBEE, Arnold J., "The Coming of the Worldwide City," *Think,* July-August, 1968.

von ECKARDT, Wolf, "The World's Happiest Subway," San Francisco *Chronicle,* Nov. 16, 1969.

WOHL, Martin, "Urban Transport We Could Really Use," *Technology Review,* Vol. 72, No. 8.

"Can Technology Untangle the Transportation

Snarl and Get the Country Moving Again?," *Challenge,* Winter, 1968.

"Electric Power and the Vehicles of the Future," *The German Tribune,* May 19, 1970.

"High Speed Rail from Hamburg to Munich," *The German Tribune,* No. 421, May 7, 1970.

"Electric Cars are Catching On," *Industry Week,* April 27, 1970.

"Swinging Designs Cast Shadow of Air-Minded Cars of Future," *Product Engineering,* May 5, 1969.

"The Thunking Man's Car," *Time,* October 3, 1969.

"The Adaptable Urbmobile," *Transportation Research Review, Third/Fourth* Quarter, 1968.

"Computer Predicts Car Motions, 'Draws' Cartoons," *Transportation Research Review,* Third/Fourth Quarter, 1968.

TELECOMMUNICATIONS:
One-World Mind

ALPERT, Hollis, "The Cassette Man Cometh," *Saturday Review,* Jan. 30, 1971.

ASIMOV, Isaac, "The Fourth Revolution," *Saturday Review,* Oct. 24, 1970.

BROCKWAY, Robert E., "EVR: New Training Tool," *A-V Communications,* April, 1970.

BROWN, Beth, *The Truth About Mental Telepathy,* Simon & Schuster, Inc., New York, 1970.

BUCK, Jerry, "Everybody Wants to Join the Cassette Revolution," San Francisco Sunday *Examiner and Chronicle,* Dec. 20, 1970.

CAREY, James W. and QUIRK, John J., "The Mythos of the Electronic Revolution," *The American Scholar,* Spring, 1970.

CLARKE, Arthur C., *Profiles of the Future,* Bantam, (paperback), 1967, Harper & Row, New York, 1963.

CORDTZ, Dan, "The Coming Shake-Up in Telecommunications," *Fortune,* April, 1970.

FAST, Julius, *Body Language,* M. Evans & Co., Inc., New York, 1970.

FRIENDLY, Fred W., "Asleep at the Switch of the Wired City," *Saturday Review,* Oct. 10, 1970.

FROMM, Erich, *The Forgotten Language,* Grove Press, Inc., New York, 1951.

GEORGE, Jean, "Surprising Signals in the Wild," *Reader's Digest,* June, 1969.

GOULD, Jack, "The Coming War over the Little Black Boxes," San Francisco Sunday *Examiner and Chronicle,* June 7, 1970.

HAUX, Ernst H., "Scientists at Dusseldorf Discuss Aspects of Animal Language," *The German Tribune* No. 416-31, March, 1970.

HUNT, Douglas, *Exploring the Occult,* Ballantine Books (paperback), New York, 1964.

JOHNSON, Nicholas, "What Do We Do About Television," *Saturday Review,* July 11, 1970.

KAHLENBERG, Richard and AARON, Chloe, "The Cartridges Are Coming," *Cinema Journal,* Vol. IX, No. 2, Spring, 1970.

KARPEL, Craig, "The Last Great Show on Earth," *Esquire,* August, 1970.

LESSING, Lawrence, "The Printed Word Goes Electronic," *Fortune,* Sept., 1969.

LILLY, John Cunningham, *The Mind of the Dolphin* (paperback), Avon Books, Doubleday, New York, 1967.

LONGFELLOW, Layne A., "Body Talk/The Game of Feeling and Expression," *Psychology Today,* Oct., 1970.

McELHENY, Victor K., "Seeing Each Other More, Enjoying It Less?," *Technology Review,* May, 1970.

McLUHAN, Marshall, *Counter-Blast,* Harcourt Brace Jovanovich, Inc., New York, 1969.

MENDELSON, Lee, "The New Communicators," Script for TV Special, April 14, 1970.

PERLMAN, David, "ESP Comes of Age," San Francisco *Chronicle,* Dec. 28, 1970.

............, "Tuned-In to a Singing Humpback Whale," "This World," San Francisco Sunday *Examiner and Chronicle,* Dec. 20, 1970.

SARNOFF, Robert W., "Toward a Global Common Market of Communications," an address, Paris, France, Feb. 12, 1970.

SCHMEIDLER, Gertrude R., "Studying Individual PSI Experiences," a paper presented at the Winter Review Meeting of the Institute for Parapsychology, January 3, 1970.

SCHWITZGEBEL, Robert L., "Behavior Instrumentation and Social Technology," *American Psychologist,* 1970.

SMITH, W. John, "Messages of Vertebrate Communication," *Science,* July 11, 1969.

TEBBEL, John, "TV and the Arts," *Saturday Review,* April 26, 1969.

TOBIN, Richard L., "Publishing by Cathode Ray Tube," *Saturday Review,* Oct. 10, 1970.

TOMKINSON, Craig, "Patented Facsimile System says 'Good-Bye' to Presses," *Editor & Publisher,* Jan. 10, 1970.

ULLMAN, Montague and KRIPPNER, Stanley, "ESP in the Night," *Psychology Today,* June, 1970.

WALTER, Gerard O., "Typesetting," Scientific *American,* May, 1969.

WATTS, Alan, "Do You Smell?," *Alan Watts Journal,* Vol. 1, No. 12, Oct., 1970.

YOUNGBLOOD, Gene, *Expanded Cinema,* E. P. Dutton & Co., Inc., New York, 1970.

"A Video Cartridge Bows to Muffled Applause," *Business Week,* Nov. 14, 1970.

"Cable TV Leaps into the Big Time," *Business Week,* Nov. 22, 1969.

"Holographic Player Turns Home TV Set into Theater," *Electrical/Electronic Power & Control,* Nov. 3, 1969.

"Laser Intercomputer Link Coming," *Industrial Research,* April, 1970.

"Communication Systems Will Shape Your Future," *Industry Week,* May 4, 1970.

"Seeing by Radio Waves . . . the Promise of Radio-Frequency Holography," *Mitre Matrix,* Vol. 2, No. 2, March/April, 1969.

"Communications in the '70's," *News Front,* Sept., 1969.

"Holography Now Sets Type, May Move on to Computer Memories," *Product Engineering,* Nov. 3, 1969.

"As We SEE It," *TV Guide,* July 18, 1970.

"Liquid Crystals," *Vectors,* Vol. XII, Summer, 1970.

"Bodyspeak," *Vogue,* Sept. 1, 1970.

INDEX